CW00933257

KOREAN ENTERPRISE

KOREAN ENTERPRISE

The Quest for Globalization

Gerardo R. Ungson
Richard M. Steers
Seung-Ho Park

Harvard Business School Press
Boston, Massachusetts

Library of Congress Cataloging-in-Publication Data
Ungson, Gerardo R.
    Korean enterprise : the quest for globalization / Gerardo R.
Ungson, Richard M. Steers, Seung-ho Park.
        p.   cm.
    Includes index.
    ISBN 0-87584-630-0 (alk. paper)
    1. Industrial policy—Korea (South) 2. Industrial management—
Korea (State)   3. Competition, International.   I. Steers, Richard
M.   II. Park, Seung-ho, 1961-   III. Title.
HD3616.K853U54   1997
338.95195—dc20   96-41599
                                                                CIP

The paper used in this publication meets the requirements of the American National
Standard for Permanence of Paper for Printed Library Materials Z39.49-1984.

Contents

Preface

From its mythical beginnings, Korea has repeatedly faced challenges of seismic proportions. According to legend, Hwanung, son of the divine creator Hwanin, descended to earth, where he married a bear turned woman and had a son named Tan'gun. Tan'gun welded the various primitive tribes into a single unified kingdom, which he then ruled from 2333 B.C. to 1122 B.C. In 1122 B.C., Kija, a descendent of the mythical Shang royal line in China, invaded Korea and made himself ruler, whereupon Tan'gun resumed his spirit form and returned to the heavens. In many ways, this ancient legend foretells the challenges and tribulations Koreans would face through the ages. Throughout its history, Korea has repeatedly emerged from obscurity to build renaissance civilizations, only to see them destroyed and its people subjugated by foreign invaders. Early recorded Korean history is filled with such examples, from the warring three kingdoms period (57 B.C.–A.D. 668) to the Silla dynasty (668–936) to the subsequent Koryo (936–1392) and Yi (1392–1910) dynasties. Indeed, Korea's superhuman determination to succeed today likely resulted from these repeated invasions and setbacks and by foreign attempts to subjugate a people unwilling to be suppressed.

In 1592, in response to a Japanese invasion by Hideyoshi Toyotomi, Admiral Yi Sun-sin exhibited unyielding determination, daring strategy, and innovative Korean technology in the form of ironclad ships to defeat successive attacks. These ironclad vessels, known as "turtle ships" because of their unique shape, predate similar Western technology by almost three hundred years. Even so, the Koreans eventually lost to Japan, as they had to China earlier and as they would to Japan again later. Later still, their homeland would be torn apart by a bloody civil war precipitated by external powers and leading to independence for only the southern half of Korea in 1953. A Korean nation was formed, but it was hardly whole and it lived under the constant threat of invasion by its northern brothers.

Nation building in the South commenced in earnest in the 1960s. Under the tight control of successive military regimes, South Korea rapidly rebuilt its infrastructure and turned its attention to industrial development. Family-based firms, using government loans, foreign technology, a low-cost, disciplined, and educated workforce, and protected local markets, grew at almost unbelievable rates to become some of the world's largest conglomerates (called *chaebols* in Korean). By the mid-1980s, economic observers in the United States, Europe, and Japan began taking note of Korea's significant entrepreneurial success. Companies like Samsung, Hyundai, Daewoo, and Lucky-Goldstar (later LG) were becoming familiar corporate imprints around the world. By the mid-1990s, however, such admiration was accompanied by fear and apprehension. Perhaps Korea would become too powerful, threatening the technological preeminence of Japan and the West. Indeed, Korea had become an economic and technological power to be reckoned with.

While the road to prosperity has been long and arduous, Koreans have repeatedly responded to adversity with discipline, determination, and a trait not widely recognized by outside observers: a strong sense of entrepreneurship. Korea has long been a land of cultural development and technological innovation. During the Silla dynasty, Buddhism flourished, as did the arts and architecture. The world's oldest known astrological observatory was built in 647 in Kyongju, Silla's ancient capital. Objective civil service examinations based on Confucian principles were introduced as a condition of government employment in 958 during the Koryo dynasty. Movable-type printing was first used in Korea in 1234, two centuries before it was "invented" in Germany by Johann Gutenberg. In the fifteenth century, under the leadership of the legendary King Sejong (1418–1450), Korea again outpaced Europe in the development of science and technology, education, and medicine. Astronomical and water clocks were developed, as were rain gauges and scientific weather forecasting, two centuries before their introduction in Europe. A new alphabet, *hangul*, was developed that allowed for easy recording of the complex Korean language; Koreans had previously attempted to crudely represent Korean sound patterns using alien Chinese characters. Indeed, the technological prowess we see today in Korean advances in electronics, semiconductors, LCD displays, shipbuilding, and steel making have deep and enduring roots.

Business researchers were late in recognizing Korea's rise to economic power. Indeed, the first scholarly books on Korean enterprise appeared only in 1989. Leading this effort was Alice Amsden's *Asia's New Giant: South Korea and Late Industrialization*, perhaps the most influential book of its time, which described the emergence of the Korean institutions that facilitated the country's development as a late industrializer. At the same time, Kae H. Chung and Hak Chong Lee published *Korean Managerial Dynamics*, an in-depth look at the management structures of Korean *chaebols*. Also in 1989, Richard M. Steers, Yoo Keun Shin, and Gerardo R. Ungson published *The Chaebol: Korea's New Industrial Might*, a look at the economic, strategic, and managerial foundations of Korean enterprise. In 1992, Choong Soon Kim published an insightful ethnographic study on the inner workings of a typical Korean firm, entitled *The Culture of Korean Industry: An Ethnography of Poongsan Corporation*. In 1994, Chan Sup Chang and Nahn Joo Chang provided a rich source of data on the economic and political foundations of Korean enterprise in their book *The Korean Management System: Cultural, Political, and Economic Foundations*. This same year, journalist Mark Clifford's book, *Troubled Tiger: Businessmen, Bureaucrats, and Generals in South Korea*, examined the turbulent history of Korea's major firms from their origins until the beginning of the current decade. These collected works form an emerging library detailing Korea's rise to prominence as an economic power.

Subsequent to the publication of these books, however, beginning in the early 1990s, significant changes began casting a dark shadow over South Korea's competitive landscape. For the first time in its economic history, exports began to waver. Economic growth fell below the double-digit levels that characterized the previous two decades. Buoyed by the early success of Korea, other Asian countries (notably Taiwan, Hong Kong, and Singapore) began aggressively pursuing trade and investment strategies that rivaled Korea in product quality and manufacturing excellence. Further competition emerged from Thailand, Malaysia, the Philippines, Indonesia, Vietnam, and China—many of which had significantly lower labor costs than did Korea. Indeed, a growing belief emerged that these new Asian economies would replace Korea as the low-cost leader in key industries. Meanwhile, foreign powers began pressing their claims that Korea open its traditionally closed markets. Japanese and American firms became increasingly reluctant to share emergent technologies in the knowledge that, once shared, Korean firms might become formidable competitors. With reduced access to advanced technologies, increased labor costs and competition at home, and a government less able or willing to provide assistance and support, many Korean firms recognized that they were facing a crisis that could threaten their long-term viability, if not their very existence. Something had to change if Korean companies were to regain their momentum and evolve into world-class competitors by the dawn of the twenty-first century.

The challenges facing Korean firms today—and the ways in which they are attempting to meet these challenges—constitute the subject of this book. Indeed, with the exception of chapter 2, we say little about the growth and development of Korea's chaebols. Earlier books have covered this topic in detail. Instead, our focus is on what has happened during the past several years as Korean firms ready themselves for the challenges of the next century. We begin our book with a look at the government of Kim Young Sam, who was elected president in 1992. Since taking office in early 1993, President Kim has initiated a series of economic reforms—generally referred to as the New Economy—aimed at transforming the Korean economy from a group of large-scale Korean firms doing business internationally to a group of truly global firms headquartered in Korea. The difference is significant. Indeed, globalization, or *segyehwa* in Korean, has become the hallmark of President Kim's entire administration. Through the *segyehwa* movement, Kim's government aims to advance Korea's economic interests through increased deregulation of enterprises, enhanced market liberalization, reduced reliance on government as an economic partner, greater support for small and medium-sized firms, and a more equitable partnership between management and labor. *Segyehwa* is meant to be a social as well as an economic revolution, capable of creating a more competitive economic force for Korea's future through changes in education, government, and business practice. According to President Kim, the purpose of *segyehwa* is not to copy foreign models but to "raise Korean standards in all these areas to the level of the world's advanced economies."

In order to achieve its goal, however, we argue that Korea and its firms must successfully overcome seven challenges standing between them and greater economic prosperity. They must develop and implement a new industrial policy that supports the national economic goals of the country. They must restructure the major conglomerates so they are more competitive in global markets. They must provide tangible support, not just rhetoric, for small and medium-sized firms as entrepreneurial engines of growth. They must move from a country of international players to a country of global players. They must acquire or develop appropriate technologies and form strategic alliances to prosper in the new world order. They must develop new management structures capable of organizing, coordinating, and administering their rapidly changing firms in turbulent environments.

And they must continue to develop their human capital so it represents a strategic asset in global competition. The extent to which Korea and its firms can successfully meet these seven challenges, we believe, will determine in large measure whether Korea becomes a true economic powerhouse of the twenty-first century or just another Asian "tiger" trying to move up the developmental ladder.

As with most efforts of this magnitude, this book could not have been completed without the help and support of many colleagues, friends, and associates on both sides of the Pacific. On the corporate side, many organizations provided valuable assistance during our interviews, including Hyundai, LG, Samsung, Daewoo, Sunkyong, Ssangyong, KIA, Hanwha, Doowon, Kumho, Bank of Korea, Korea Development Bank, Industrial Bank of Korea, KorAm Bank, Shinhan Bank, Hanyang Securities, Shinheung Securities, Postrade, and the Korean Ministry of Trade and Industry. Research of this nature and scope could not be conducted without the generous support and cooperation of such organizations, and for this we are deeply appreciative.

Within these organizations, we are also appreciative of the time and valuable assistance given by the following executives and managers: Ahn Kil-Hyo, An Sung-Chol, Cha Duk-Keun, Chang Byung-Ju, Chey Jong-Hyon, Choi Jung-Ha, Chung Mong Yoon, Paul Chung, Han Hyo, Jim Hartman, Hong Kye-Hwa, Hong Sung-Won, Hwang Young-Jae, Kang Shin-Chul, Kim Duck-Hwan, Kim Jun Ho, Kim Young-In, Kwak Heung-Song, Lee Byungnam, Lee Chong-Suk, Lee Daechang, Lee Hong Hyung, Lee Hong-Kyu, Lee Joon-Jae, Lee Kang-Jin, Lee Suk-Chun, Lee Young-Sang, Nam Yong, Noh Jeong-Ik, Park Je Hyuk, Park Jushik, Park Ungsuh, Rhee Hak-Rae, Rhew Ki-Won, Ryu Jea-Wan, Ryu Young-Hwan, Seo Jeoung-Guk, Shin Dae-Soon, Shin Dal-Sun, Shin Joong-Ouk, Shin Yoo Keun, Shyn Dong-Soo, and Youk Dong-Joon. We are also deeply indebted to Hong Keum Pyo, Kim Kyeong-Sik, and Rhee Hak-Rae, who greatly facilitated our visits to Korea.

We would also like to express our appreciation to several of our academic colleagues in both Korea and the United States who have provided valuable input throughout our continuing studies of Korean enterprise. These include Alice Amsden, Cho Dong-Sung, Martin Hart-Landsberg, Hwang Eui-Gak, Juhn Sung-Il, Kim Jooup, Kim Linsu, Sang Lee, Nam Sanghoon, Park Oh Soo, Rhee Song Nae, Shim Won-Shul, Shin Yoo Keun, Suh Induk, and Yoon Suck Chul. We also wish to acknowledge B. J. Chun, Sam Cho, and Chris Sheahan for their research assistance; Pam Hoyle for her secretarial assistance; and Elizabeth Lyon for her editorial assistance.

Special acknowledgment is due to the Charles H. Lundquist College of

Business at the University of Oregon, the School of Management at the University of Texas at Dallas, and the Oregon Joint Professional School of Business (a consortium of Oregon business schools) for their generous financial support of our research. We are also indebted to the Korea Foundation, the Federation of Korean Industries, Korean National Statistics Office, and KUSEC for their continued support of archival materials that make research projects such as this possible. We wish to acknowledge a special debt of gratitude to the editors and staff at the Harvard Business School Press, including Carol Franco, Nicholas Philipson, Barbara Roth, David Smagalla, and India Koopman, without whose help this project would not have been possible.

Finally, we wish to express our appreciation to our families for their patience, support, and love throughout this project. These include Suki Ungson and Melissa and Carlo Riego; Sheila and Kathleen Steers; and Ja Young, Alexandra, and Amelia Park. This book is dedicated to them in recognition of their significant contribution to the completion of this work.

Gerardo R. Ungson
Richard M. Steers
Seung-Ho Park

CHAPTER ONE

The New Competitive Landscape

In December 1985, *Business Week* sounded the alarm. Splashed across its front cover was the warning, "The Koreans Are Coming."[1] At the time, America's image of Korea was based largely on reruns of *M*A*S*H*. Few Westerners had ever thought of Korea as a potential industrial power, let alone a global competitor. The prevailing fear in the 1980s was that Korea would flood the American market with cheap cars and inferior-quality TVs and VCRs, much as the Japanese had done following World War II. Only one decade later, in July 1995, *Business Week* again graced its cover with news on Korea. This time, however, the headline read, "Korea Headed for High Tech's Top Tier."[2] In one short decade, Korea had gone from a mass producer of second-rate goods to an industry leader in such high-tech products as DRAM memory chips and liquid-crystal-display (LCD) panels. Korea had reached the top of the technology ladder in record time, an accomplishment few had thought possible a decade earlier.

To see how far Korea has come in a relatively short period of time, consider the following statistics:

- South Korea currently ranks fourteenth in the world as a trading nation and is a world leader in shipbuilding, steel production, consumer electronics, computer chips, and personal computers.[3]

- In 1995, Korea produced 2.7 million automobiles and exported more than 1 million of them, making it the fifth largest car-exporting nation in the world.[4]

- South Korea is currently America's eighth largest trading partner. In 1995, Korean firms exported $22 billion worth of goods to the United States, while U.S. firms exported more than $30 billion in goods and services to Korea. Korea is currently the sixth largest market for overall American exports and the fourth largest market for American agricultural exports.[5]

- Per capita income in Korea rose from $100 per year in 1960 to approximately $10,000 in 1995. It is estimated that per capita income will reach $42,000 by 2010.[6]

- In 1995, Korean firms invested more than $2 billion in building their U.S. operations. By the year 2000, Korean firms will have spent more than $20 billion to establish overseas production bases.[7] American firms currently have more than $3 billion in direct investment in Korea.[8]

- Total GNP for South Korea is expected to rise from $377 billion in 1995 to more than $2 trillion in 2010.[9]

By any measure, Korea represents an economic success story. Its rise from the ashes of war and occupation in the 1950s to the pinnacle of economic success across a wide spectrum of advanced products and services today is considered no less than a miracle and an inspiration for many newly industrializing countries. Its application for membership (and expected acceptance) into the Organization for Economic Cooperation and Development (OECD), open only to the richest nations in the world, is testimony to how this formerly impoverished country has emerged as a new global economic and political force.

In crossing the threshold to join industrialized nations, Korea also finds itself at a crossroads. In many respects, Korea's current challenges arise from its previous successes. In the wake of political and economic liberalization, many of its previous policies and enabling institutions are under siege. This book is an attempt to understand how Korea's collective entrepreneurial spirit—one that embodies its history and culture as well as its sense of national purpose—can renew itself in the face of daunting challenges.

While traditional economists and political scientists usually take the "outside-in" approach to the study of economic growth, applying conventional theories to the particular economy being examined, in this book, we examine Korea from the "inside-out"—that is, we use the Koreans' definition of their problems and challenges as the starting point of our analysis (although we do nonetheless use a number of theories to explain emerging patterns of growth and development). Within Korea, there are signs of maturity and age as it finds itself caught in the midst of complex and sweeping change. For the millions of Koreans who voted in the 1992 elections, the victory of President Kim Young Sam was a real changing of the guard. The change of regime was seen as significant not only in political terms but in economic terms, rooted in deep-seated beliefs about the need to redistribute income, to upgrade social welfare, to promote small and medium-sized companies, and to restructure Korean conglomerates.

While the economic reform under way encompasses all phases of Korean life, we focus here on the globalization of the Korean conglomerates, the *chaebols*. The old formula that propelled Korea to the top ranks of world competitiveness centered on making the *chaebols* the engines of growth and development. The new formula places demands on the *chaebols* to be competitive on the world front, while seeking more balanced growth and concentration of economic power during and after the transition. This book is an attempt to understand this dramatic enterprise.

TURBULENT TIMES IN THE LAND OF THE MORNING CALM

In November 1994, Korean President Kim Young Sam challenged his nation to embark on a new cultural revolution. In what has come to be known as the Sydney Declaration, President Kim articulated a new national goal for Korea: globalization. The Korean term for the globalization envisioned by Kim is *segyehwa* (pronounced se-gay-wha), and it has as much to do with effecting change within the country's borders as it does with increasing Korea's presence in world markets. Intended to reach all aspects of Korean society, including politics, economics, culture and the arts, education, and mass communication,[10] *segyehwa* embodies the country's goal not to copy foreign models but to "raise Korean standards in all these areas to the levels of the world's advanced economies."[11] The intended transformation commenced with the inauguration of Kim, and it is expected to continue for several decades. Koreans have in mind an ambitious program that will develop all sectors of Korean life in harmony with each other. While this program for change is widely acclaimed within Korea, it is not as well understood or appreciated by outsiders. Today, *segyehwa* is the Koreans' rallying cry as they anticipate the challenges they will face in the twenty-first century.

Once dismissed as a war-torn economy, Korea has become one of the most successful late industrializers. Whether recognized as a newly industrializing country (NIC), a so-called Asian tiger, or one of the "four dragons" (along with Taiwan, Singapore, and Hong Kong), Korea today has an economy that is the third largest in Asia, after Japan and China. South Korea's economic presence around the world is seen in the products of such companies as Samsung, Goldstar, and Hyundai, which have become household names. Korea is a significant player at the technological edge of the semiconductor and consumer electronics industry. And in 1995, Samsung became the world's largest manufacturer of DRAM chips, surpassing even the Japanese manufacturers that had dominated the market for the past two decades.

President Kim's election in December 1992 is considered by many to be a watershed event for Korea. His election marked the end of decades of military rule that were characterized by civil war, the toppling of South Korea's first republic headed by Rhee Syungman, the authoritative rule of General Park Chung Hee, the succession to power of General Chun Doo Hwan, and the presidential election of Chun's classmate and former general Roh Tae Woo.[12] When President Kim issued his challenge to globalize, he tapped into the nation's need to be recognized for its accomplishments. In fact, as a construct, *segyehwa*—the drive to achieve excellence and economic parity with the world's most advanced nations—has long been rooted in Korean consciousness. Indeed, many Koreans seem to base their modern sense of identity on the economic growth rates of their country.[13] Koreans from many walks of life take considerable pride in how much they have achieved in a relatively short time. Kim's call for globalization marked the public recognition of what had long been a commonly held goal for most Koreans.

In a fundamental way, President Kim's call for modernization signals the passing of one era and the birth of a new one. It also points to a host of new challenges facing contemporary Korea as it approaches the twenty-first century. Indeed, we argue that there are at least seven key challenges facing Korea today as it attempts to globalize and enter the new century as a stronger economic and political power. In this sense, Korea's decision to pursue *segyehwa* is not unlike that of letting the genie out of the proverbial bottle: once out, it is not easily managed or subdued. In many ways, Korean enterprise is entering the rapids of its economic development; it is no longer protected by a strong central government or high trade barriers, and it must compete in a global market against multinationals with considerably more resources, experience, and technology. The manner in which Korean companies meet this challenge will determine in large measure the economic—and perhaps the political—future of the country. *Segyehwa* is a necessity for Korea at this point of its development; it is also a major gamble.

There are clear and present risks in making this transition. In anticipation of OECD membership, Korea has to liberalize its financial and capital markets. At the same time, growing foreign capital inflows are beginning to place stress on its deficit. In his speech to the Asia Society in May 1996, Deputy Prime Minister and Minister of Finance and Economy Rha Woong-Bae framed the challenge: How can Korea adopt capital/market liberalization without suffering significant macroeconomic dislocations and without undermining the competitiveness of Korean industries?

While many of the advanced countries in the Western world would like to see a more open and liberalized Korean market now, the Korean government would like to manage the pace of liberalization. The government is aware that the Korean peninsula is a highly sensitive geopolitical region and that capital inflows and outflows can easily change in response to nonmarket factors such as North-South reunification. Moreover, the Korean government would like its small to medium-sized enterprises to be much more competitive as both foreign capital and competitors begin to enter the domestic market. In an attempt to regulate this pace of capital inflow and outflow, the government has stipulated that Korean conglomerates finance 20 percent of all investment overseas from their own internal funds—a move that could limit globalization initiatives.

As discussed in this chapter, the challenges facing Korea during this period of transition are complex and interrelated. The historical allocation of resources by the government in exchange for monitored corporate performance is now viewed as questionable in light of renewed demands for greater equity and social welfare. Because newly industrializing countries in Asia are forcing Korea to yield much of its advantage in low-cost production, both the government and *chaebols* appear to share the goal of transforming the focus of Korea's economy to high and midlevel technologies. Yet there is substantial disagreement over how to make Korean *chaebols* competitive. The government's current program calls for specialization. Unless these specialized *chaebols* are competitive internationally, however, they may find themselves squeezed in the middle between competitors from low-wage nations and competitors from more advanced, better-financed economies—an untenable position.

Popular sentiment favors small to medium-sized firms, but there is question as to whether they can be sufficiently competitive to survive in harsher environments, such as the liberalization of Korea's domestic market. In many industrial sectors, the professionalization of Korea's work force is a popular topic of discussion. In some contexts, this means greater liberalization (such as in the financial banking sectors); in other contexts, this means developing untested management structures and processes patterned after popular Western organizations (network organizations, matrix structures, horizontal firms). Although Koreans are considered to be among the world's hardest workers, some wonder whether their work habits will deteriorate once they are exposed to the comforts and luxuries of a more affluent lifestyle. Whether or not President Kim represents the dawning of a new age of political and economic liberalization in Korea, the arrival of his administration coincides with increased pressure on Korean society to meet these challenges.

While Kim's popularity ratings have remained high (especially compared with those of his predecessors), some observers remain nervous about reforms that are instituted by means of the same directive methods used by past dictators. While President Kim has called for economic liberalization and deregulation, his plans are issued as executive fiats; little effort has been made to reach political consensus. Some critics suggest that not much has really changed: government still calls the shots on what and how to reform.[14] And lurking in the background is North Korea—a foreboding presence since the Korean War. Although the two governments have affirmed their goal of unification, major obstacles remain. Indeed, there is little that is calm in Korea these days.

SEGYEHWA: JOINING THE GLOBAL COMMUNITY

President Kim's program incorporates three intertwined contexts for change: (1) political and social reform, (2) economic renewal, and (3) cultural development. These are captured in the segyehwa theme and provide a contextual background for understanding the seven challenges (to be listed shortly) facing Korean enterprises today. Moreover, Korea's Presidential Commission on the Twenty-first Century defines reunification with North Korea as a central issue, if not the top consideration, in setting the direction of development in the next century.[15] President Kim once said, "When all of us share the sacrifices and pain, we will succeed in making a great leap forward."[16]

Many of the current plans involve the dismantling of the system that made Korea a world power. As these changes involve risk, Kim believes that effective implementation of his policies will undoubtedly demand considerable sacrifice. As history shows, the willingness to sacrifice for the benefit of the country and for future generations is deeply ingrained in the character of the Korean people. Thus, in a fundamental way, Kim's belief captures the underlying meaning of *segyehwa.*

Political and Social Reform

In his inauguration speech, President Kim said: "Deep in my heart I have a vision of a New Korea. The New Korea will be a freer and more mature democratic society. Justice will flow like rivers throughout this land."[17] As powerful as these words are, a number of Koreans doubted their sincerity. After all, the likelihood of establishing true justice appeared remote in a system in which many government and business leaders had risen to wealth through misconduct and corruption. However, Kim has relentlessly pursued his "New Korea" policy aimed at eradicating corruption, or what he calls the "Korean disease." From Kim's vantage point, many Koreans had fallen prey to moral laxity, rampant misconduct, and an eroding work ethic—problems Kim believed would ultimately weaken Korea if not addressed immediately.

President Kim ruffled feathers in his own Democratic Liberal Party by appointing academics and technocrats to key cabinet positions, while ignoring long-time politicians. Following through with his stated reforms, he quickly disqualified three of his new appointees when allegations of ethical violations were raised against them. He also ordered members of the National Assembly and other government officials, including himself, to publicly disclose their personal and family assets. Parliamentary Speaker Park Jun Kyu, who disclosed assets of $14 million, was forced to resign. Any doubt of President Kim's resolve was put to rest when he launched the "real name" program by executive decree. In August 1993, Kim decreed an end to the use of fictitious names on personal financial accounts, then a commonly used means of hiding ownership and concealing cash derived from questionable sources. The removal of the so-called false name accounts made it more difficult to disguise improper financial transactions. The decree required all Koreans to close all accounts under false names by October 12, 1993, thereby putting an end to considerable tax evasion, funding of corrupt practices, illegal contributions, and illicit activities.[18]

The new administration's firm stand on corruption went as far as the arrest and detention of prominent government officials, including former presidents Roh Tae Woo and Chun Doo Hwan.[19] The head of two *chaebols*—Kim Woo Choong of Daewoo and Choi Won Suk of Dong-Ah—were summoned to explain their financial contributions to former president Roh.

President Kim indicated that he would make an example of the arrest of former president Roh to "cut the collusive links between politics and businesses and achieve clean politics." He continued by saying: "This is an unfortunate incident which must never be repeated."[20] Kim's anticorruption reforms also extended to the banking sector, where the industrywide audits he ordered resulted in the firing of the presidents of two of Korea's largest banks.

Economic Renewal

The performance of the Korean economy over three decades has been stellar, especially considering Korea's agrarian beginnings. From 1952 to 1962, per capita GNP increased by only 0.7 percent per year, or from $67 to $87 over the ten-year period. However, growth accelerated during the period 1962–1971, when per capita GNP increased from $87 to $278 for a growth rate of 13.8 percent per year (see table 1-1). In 1980, per capita GNP was $1,605, representing 6.1 percent growth per annum. Table 1-2 shows steady increases in per capita GNP, up to $8,483 in 1994. While not shown in the tables, the Korean economy grew at an average annual rate of almost 18 percent in nominal terms, from $2.3 billion in 1962 to $237.9 billion in 1990.[21] Note that Korea's GNP per capita is more than twice the combined GNP per capita of Thailand, Indonesia, and China. Even so, the performance of the Korean economy during the first half of the 1990s suggests that the decades of extremely high growth have passed and that the adaptability of the *chaebols*—as well as the small to medium-sized companies—will soon be tested.

In a recent long-term forecast, the Korean government projects that per

Table 1-1   Key Economic Indicators for the Korean Economy, 1953–1980

Year	Per Capita GNP	Exports
1953	$67	Negligible
1962	$87	$55 million
% annual change: 1953–1962	0.7%	—
1971	$278	$1.6 billion
% annual change: 1962–1971	13.8%	39.1%
1980	$1,605	$17.5 billion
% annual change: 1971–1980	6.1%	36.4%

Source: Korean Ministry of Finance and Economy, Seoul, 1994.
Note: All figures in adjusted U.S. dollars.

Table 1-2 Macroeconomic Indicators for Korea, 1980–1994

Year	GNP Growth Rate	Per Capita GNP	GDP Growth Ratio (%)
1980	−3.9	$1,597	−2.7
1981	5.5	1,741	6.2
1982	7.5	1,834	7.6
1983	12.2	2,014	11.5
1984	8.5	2,187	8.7
1985	6.6	2,242	6.5
1986	11.9	2,568	11.6
1987	12.3	3,218	11.5
1988	12.0	4,295	11.3
1989	6.9	5,210	6.4
1990	9.6	5,883	9.5
1991	9.1	6,757	9.1
1992	5.0	7,007	5.1
1993	5.8	7,513	5.8
1994	8.2	8,483	8.4

Source: National Statistical Office, Seoul, 1995.

capita GNP will reach $42,550 (in 1997 dollars) in the year 2010. If this projection is realized, Korea will reach parity with the G-7 of most industrial Western economies (Canada, France, Germany, Great Britain, Italy, Japan, and the United States) by the year 2020 with a GNP of $3.9 trillion. Naturally, forecasts depend on certain underlying assumptions, which are shown in table 1-3. These assumptions reflect the optimism the government shows concerning future economic performance.

Table 1-3 Korea's GNP Forecasts and Assumptions, 1994–2020

GNP Projections	1994	2001	2005	2010	2020
Per capita GNP ($)	$8,483	$20,570	$30,230	$42,550	$77,280
Total GNP ($ billion)	$376.9	$969.7	$1,464.0	$2,114.0	$3,909.0
GNP Growth Rate Assumptions		1996–2000	2001–2005	2006–2010	2011–2020
GNP growth rate, real term (%)		7.0–7.5	6.0	5.0	4.0
GNP deflator (%)		4.0–4.5	3.0	2.5	2.0–2.5

Source: Adapted from "Korea's per Capita GNP Could Rise to $42,550 by the Year 2010," *Kusec Newsletter* 16, no. 58 (August 31, 1995), 9.

Although Korea has clearly attained substantial economic heights, the climb has not always been an easy one. Exports provided the lifeblood of growth throughout the past three decades, but dropped precipitously in 1989. Perhaps more troubling from the Korean standpoint is the pattern of trade between Korea and the United States. Merchandise exports increased in real terms more than five-hundred fold during this period, accounting for 35 percent of GDP.[22] In 1994, for example, Korean imports of U.S. goods were worth about $16.5 billion, making Korea the sixth largest export market for the United States, but the overall U.S. share in Korean trade continued to decline. As shown in figure 1-1, Korea enjoyed a trade surplus with the United States until 1994; however, by 1995 this surplus turned into a deficit. Initial figures for 1996 show that this deficit is growing.

In 1991, South Korea's main commodity exports were (in order of value) apparel, semiconductors, ships, imaging equipment, synthetic textiles, iron and steel products, footwear, computers, automobiles, and audio equipment. Taken altogether, these accounted for 48 percent of total exports. In 1992, semiconductors and related electrical equipment replaced apparel as South Korea's leading export. Korea's imports in 1991 were crude oil, semiconductors, petrochemicals, iron and steel, computers, lumber, animal products, engines and generators, grain, and coke and coal. These accounted for

Figure 1-1   U.S.-Korean Trade, 1988–1995

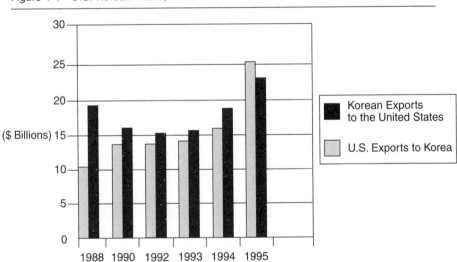

Source: U.S. Department of Commerce.

35.4 percent of total imports. Imports of machinery made up the largest composite group after raw materials, reflecting the government priority to upgrade Korea's industrial capacity, especially in high technology.[23]

This pattern reflects the transition in the Korean economy from low- and midvalue technologies to high-value-added, clean, capital-intensive industries. This transition comes at a time when there are also great demands on Korea to liberalize its domestic markets and on Korean companies to compete more effectively abroad. As part of a program of administrative decentralization, Kim's government has relaxed its grip on the economy. The shrinking of the government safety net that has protected companies in the past is another indication of a major shift away from a command-capitalist system into market orientation and guidance.[24]

Recognizing that the Korean economy might never regain the growth and vitality it has demonstrated during the past three decades, the government has focused on strengthening economic competitiveness by boosting exports and investments. *Vision and Development Strategy for the Korean Economy in the Twenty-first Century*, the long-term blueprint for Korea's economy prepared by the Korea Development Institute (KDI), expects per capita GDP to reach $80,000 (in 1995 dollars) by 2020. Korea will then be the world's seventh largest economy and about even with the G-7 of most industrial Western economies. To achieve these goals, the KDI seeks the urgent promotion of government efficiency, the encouragement of market forces, and the granting of autonomy to the private sector. Naturally, forecasts depend on underlying assumptions, some of which have been questioned.[25] These projected figures are shown in table 1-4. In any event, these projections reflect the government's optimistic outlook toward future economic performance.

Cultural Integration and Relations with North Korea

The third aspect of *segyehwa* focuses on cultural integration, reexamining what it means to be Korean. After years of foreign (Japanese) subjugation and dependence on external cultures (including the United States), Koreans have become alienated from their cultural roots and need to redefine their national identity. Weakened by such domination, Koreans tended to view their culture as an "embarrassing anachronism that has impeded modernization."[26] In the late 1960s, when economic growth began, Korean self-perception also changed, reflecting greater respect for traditional Korean values and a quest for cultural roots. Such confidence was bolstered by democratization and the success of the 1988 Seoul Olympics. An important

Table 1-4 Projections for the Korean Economy in the Twenty-first Century

	1995	2000	2010	2020
Population	44.8 million	46.8 million	49.7 million	50.5 million
GDP (in current prices)	$456 billion	$851 billion	$2,051 billion	$4,081 billion
World ranking for GDP	11th	9th	8th	7th
Per capita GDP				
In current prices	$10,163	$18,200	$41,300	$80,600
In 1995 constant prices	$10,163	$13,700	$22,000	$32,000
Trade volume	$251 billion	$416 billion	$1,105 billion	$2,441 billion
Ranking in world trade	13th	9th	7th	6th
Participation of women in the workforce	62%	64%	67%	68%
Industrial structure				
Agriculture, forestry, and fisheries	6.6%	3.9%	3.0%	1.6%
Manufacturing	26.9	27.4	26.9	26.8
Services	66.2	68.6	70.2	71.9

Source: Adapted from Korea Development Institute, *Vision and Development Strategy for the Korean Economy in the 21st Century* (Seoul: KDI, 1996).

aspect of *segyehwa* is making Koreans more aware and appreciative of their traditions, values, and heritage. It is no wonder that Park Jae Yoon, minister of Trade, Industry, and Energy, sees educational reform as an integral part of this effort.[27]

Part of establishing cultural identity, although not formally included in the definition of *segyehwa*, is a renewed effort to discover constructive means to reunite the entire Korean peninsula—economically and politically. Soon after President Kim opened up Korea's political process, he began making overtures to North Korea about developing a closer relationship.[28] Despite the harsh inflammatory rhetoric played out in the popular press, there appears to be a growing sense of urgency on both sides of the border to foster the development of greater humanitarian and economic ties.

Yet negotiations on these topics have been overshadowed by recent tensions over North Korea's nuclear potential. In 1993, conflict erupted when North Korea withdrew from the nuclear nonproliferation agreement and refused to allow international inspection of suspected nuclear sites. To the chagrin of South Korea's politicians, they were excluded in an agreement between the United States and North Korea in Geneva in October 1995. In what North Korea viewed as a diplomatic triumph, it pledged to freeze its entire nuclear program by agreeing to replace its graphite reactors with light-water reactors to be provided by the United States and South Korea. President Kim finally accepted the Geneva accord, reversing his initial opposition to it unless North Korea would first open up its nuclear facilities completely to outside inspection.

Beyond the nuclear issue, South Koreans generally fear the motivations of their northern neighbor, realizing that the North has engaged in a conventional military buildup since 1991, with most of this power amassed near the southern border. Observers attribute this development to Kim Jong Il, the son and successor of long-time ruler Kim Il Sung. The buildup, it is widely believed, was designed to placate or curry favor with the military establishment that had been resolutely loyal to Kim Il Sung but questioned his son's leadership capability. An alternative scenario that worries South Korean leaders is that North Korea, now nearly bankrupt, isolated from the world community and from its former communist patrons, might use a military assault to distract the attention of its populace from its destitute state.[29]

South Korea's government is not sure how best to handle its relationship with the post–Kim Il Sung regime, particularly concerning North Korea's eroding economy, political instability, and potential famine. Providing the help necessary to repair five decades of neglect under communist rule would be difficult. The scenario would be similar to that of the reunification of East and West Germany, but with far greater costs.

KEY CHALLENGES FACING KOREAN ENTERPRISE

Despite its success—or possibly because of it—Korea today faces serious economic and political challenges. Korea's recent history is replete with examples of political corruption, overconcentration of wealth and abuse of power, labor unrest, a lowered competitive position in world markets owing to increased labor costs, a lack of trained personnel in the more advanced industries, limited access to state-of-the-art technologies, and antiquated management structures. While Korea has clearly arrived as a newly industrialized country, these problems are seriously impeding its progress toward becoming a twenty-first century global power. *Segyehwa* is intended to help Korea and its firms overcome these problems. It represents an implementing vehicle that the current Korean government hopes will carry the country to a new level of economic prosperity, cultural development, and political freedom (see table 1-5).

Korea's desired end state, which it hopes to achieve early in the next century, is a country characterized by global industrial strength, continued economic growth and stability, technological prowess, political and economic democracy, and international respect as a leading nation of the industrialized world. To achieve this end state, however, Korea—both its companies and the nation as a whole—will have to meet what we have defined as seven key challenges. They are:

1. reframing industrial policy and developing a new economic covenant,

2. restructuring the *chaebols*,

3. enhancing the competitiveness of small and medium-sized firms,

4. meeting the requirements of globalization,

5. developing and acquiring new technologies,

6. developing new management structures, and

7. developing the human resources that will be needed in the twenty-first century.

We briefly introduce each of these challenges here and then develop them further as the book progresses.

Reframing Industrial Policy and Creating a New Economic Covenant

There is little question that the hallmark of Korea's growth and development has been its industrial policy, defined broadly as government intervention in the private sector designed to achieve the central goal of national economic development. What has historically distinguished Korean industrial policy from that of many other nations is the practice of allocating resources and subsidies based on the principle of reciprocity.[30] That is, the national government offered appropriate incentives to firms provided that the recipients of this support would, in turn, deliver on predetermined goals (mostly in the form of export targets). Government support for business was still

Table 1-5 Seven Challenges Facing Korean Firms

Late 20th Century	Implementing Vehicle	Barriers to Implementation	Early 21st Century
Korea as a newly industrialized nation			Korea as a global power
Emerging Problems	⟶ *Segyehwa* Movement	Seven Challenges to ⟶ Implementation	⟶ Targeted End States
Increasing labor costs	Political development	1. Reframing industrial policy	Global industrial power
Access to technology	Economic development	2. Restructuring the *chaebols*	Economic growth and stability
Labor unrest	Cultural development	3. Enhancing the competitiveness of small and medium firms	Technology leader
Political conflicts and corruption		4. Meeting the requirements of globalization	Political democracy
Concentration of wealth and power		5. Developing and acquiring new technologies	Economic democracy
Antiquated management structures		6. Developing new management structures	International political leader
Lack of trained personnel		7. Developing human capital	

necessary at the margin, protecting infant high-technology sectors from foreign competition and providing them with relatively cheap credit.

Despite significant economic progress—indeed, partly because of it—Korea today faces increased challenges on the economic front. From a macroeconomic standpoint, Korea needs to maintain a high growth rate to foster continued economic development. However, tension is increasing between Korea and its major trading partners over the trade imbalances resulting from Korea's economic success. In addition, many countries have accused Korea of failing to open its markets to foreign products and competitors. Indeed, when the Korean government reluctantly reduced some trade barriers (as it did for tobacco, movies, and some farm products), highly organized protests and boycotts erupted and kept up the pressure until the government relaxed its efforts. Such shortsightedness by special interest groups in Korea created additional tensions and increased the probability of overt actions by others. In the past decade, 35 to 45 percent of Korean exports have come under some form of foreign restriction, and this trend is likely to intensify unless corrective measures are taken.[31]

At home in Korea, there is a need to further develop internal markets and to satisfy the increased consumer demands of a more prosperous society. Korea has a growing middle class that is eager to see the fruits of its labor; to a large extent, future political stability rests with the government's ability to fulfill these expectations. Throughout the expansion of both their internal and external markets, Korean corporations will have to find new ways to secure the necessary financing for their growth because government-controlled sources have diminished significantly. Korean companies are highly leveraged, which places them in a precarious position. This vulnerability is seen in various appeals from the *chaebols* for government help. As the government moves toward more open capital markets, corporations will need to be much more responsive and competitive in their financial transactions. This internal and external challenge to develop a new economic covenant with its people and its neighbors is the topic of chapter 3.

Restructuring the *Chaebols*

The second major challenge facing Korea today is the need to restructure its corporate enterprise system. The economic size and concentration of the *chaebols* have been both a driving force and a consequence of Korea's rapid economic growth.[32] Even so, this growth has frequently taken the form of special treatment and protectionist policies. With globalization, there is need to reexamine extant policies of protectionism and economic concentration. Moreover, political democratization brightens the spotlight on the so-called *chaebol* issue, as many see the close relationship between the government and business to be less justifiable and sustainable in the future.[33]

The economic size and dominating reach of the *chaebols* has continued to disturb both inside analysts and outside observers. A major component of President Kim's economic program called for the thirty top *chaebols* to select a few core businesses for future development and to divest themselves of the rest. Following his rise to power after the assassination of President Park Chung Hee, President Chun Doo Hwan considered a similar plan. In a country where size is often equated with strength, however, challenging the *chaebols* was considered tantamount to placing the country's economic future at risk. Without the minimum amount of capital obtained through favorable credit policies and the requisite managerial resources and business skills, it would have been difficult for the *chaebols* to diversify into a number of areas and to have strengthened their market positions globally. Nonetheless, momentum continued to build for some effort to curtail the monopolistic behavior of the larger firms. In effect, *chaebol* reform emerged to parallel the political reform that Kim Young Sam so boldly implemented. This is the topic of chapter 4.

Enhancing the Competitiveness of Small and Medium-Sized Firms

Whether or not Kim Young Sam represents the dawning of a new age of political and economic liberalization in Korea, his administration coincides with increased pressure on the Korean economy. Long content to follow the Japanese model of development, Korea now finds itself at a crucial juncture in economic policy. What is the future trajectory of economic growth—export-led or globalized? Can the *chaebols* be reduced in financial size and concentration and still compete in higher-value-added industries with larger and better financed rivals? Moreover, what is the new role for the small and medium-sized firms that have been exploited in the past? Market liberalization as envisioned by Kim is tied to the competitiveness of just these firms. There is serious question as to whether they will be able to compete with foreign multinationals operating in Korea without either protection or assistance from the major *chaebols*. Developing the role of the small to midsized firm in the Korean economy represents the third major challenge facing Korea. It is discussed in chapter 5.

Meeting the Requirements of Globalization

Clearly a major challenge facing most Korean firms today is to keep up with—and hopefully get ahead of—the worldwide trend toward globalization in both production and marketing. As much as can be said about Korea's economic might, the Korean economy, like all others, has several vulnerabilities. On the positive side, Korea exhibits a competitive advantage in at least four areas: (1) textiles and apparel-related industries, (2) transportation equipment, including ships and automobiles, (3) consumer electronics, and (4) iron and steel.[34] Other pockets of strength include cement, semiconductors, and construction. However, Korean firms have little or no position in health care, chemicals and plastics, forest products, or most areas of food and consumer packaged goods. What emerges as a general pattern is strength in the manufacturing industries, mostly at the medium-technology level. But the breadth of even these competitive industries is rather narrow.[35] Moreover, Korean firms frequently lack the strong supplier-manufacturer linkage that is routinely seen in the *keiretsu* system in Japan (see chapter 2). Korea's emerging strength in semiconductors has grown out of its strength in consumer electronics, while its healthy position in transportation and automobiles is rooted in its traditional competence in steel.

For *chaebols* that have historically benefited from various forms of government assistance and support in the domestic market, globalization presents a different challenge. Restructuring efforts, enacted by the new government, are aimed at reducing the size and diversity of Korean firms—the very basis of their previous corporate strategies. While critics have contended that large diversified firms have been ineffective in world competition, this does not appear to apply for the Korean *chaebols*. Current plans for the *chaebols* to globalize—and the nature of problems they are bound to face once such plans are put into action—are of paramount concern as Korea approaches the new century.

A related challenge is the increasing competition from other countries. At the low end of the market, Korea is being seriously challenged by lower-cost manufacturers in China and Southeast Asia. For example, Korea's shoe factories, the world's largest only a few years ago, have nearly disappeared. In fact, many Korean companies that routinely employed between 10,000 and 20,000 employees in the mid-1980s are now bankrupt. At the high end, such as personal computers, where Korean firms emerged as formidable competitors in the 1980s, the triple challenge from Taiwan, Japan, and the United States has proven significant. Taiwan, with its reduced design and production times, began to dominate the PC market in the early 1990s. And although Korea still ranks as the world's second-largest producer of consumer electronics, behind Japan, its firms have competed principally on price, not product innovation. Consequently, these firms are now vulnerable to lower-priced producers from Asia and elsewhere. One ominous sign in this sector of the economy is the growth of wages, which from 1985 to 1990 jumped 143 percent in Korea while rising by only 18 percent in Japan.[36]

Taken together, these conditions could make for a convincing argument that this is the worst possible time for the large *chaebols* to reduce their size and economic concentration through highly diversified subsidiaries. While it is possible that smaller size will lead to increased flexibility and quicker market response, it is not clear whether Korean firms can compete effectively against Asia's lower-cost producers. Moreover, with reduced financial strength and increased risk, the *chaebols* themselves are beginning to question whether they have the staying power to compete against larger and better financed Japanese and American firms in higher-value-added industries. Korean firms are essentially sandwiched in the middle. We examine their quandary, as well as Korea's response to it, in chapter 6.

Acquiring and Developing New Technologies

The fifth challenge facing most Korean firms is accessing and/or developing competitive technologies, as we will see in chapter 7. Korea faces an increasingly complex technological environment. In the past, Korean firms found it relatively easy to acquire aging technology, either through joint licensing ventures or reverse engineering of products already on the market, and to compete in the international marketplace based on price. This is how Korean companies entered such markets as consumer electronics, automobiles, and household appliances. Today, however, as the half-life of technology-based products declines and labor costs escalate, it has become increasingly important for Korean companies to develop their own technology and to be the first to market. This puts these companies squarely in competition with American, Japanese, and European companies that have far greater resources to devote to research and development.

Korea's answer to date has been to combine leading-edge joint ventures with Japanese and Western companies to develop the required technologies with individual or consortium efforts within Korea to create what is needed. In many ways, Korea's success has also been its Achilles' heel. Japanese high-technology manufacturers, once an important source of Korea's technological know-how, have become increasingly reluctant to share new product knowledge with Koreans, fearing that their former suppliers may soon become formidable competitors. Even the most cursory examination of international joint ventures bears out a striking fact: despite their popularity, they fail more often than they succeed. Research studies indicate that seven out of ten such alliances experience major problems.[37] In one major study, the failure rate was over 50 percent.[38] It is now generally believed that only one out of three alliances succeeds over the long run and that management obstacles are formidable.[39] Whether Korean firms will be able to develop the requisite technological competence through strategic alliances or on their own is open to question, as is whether they can sustain their competitiveness in higher-value-added industries. Korea's latest projects, including the much acclaimed G-7 technology development project, will be discussed.

Because Korea's path to globalization takes it on a collision course with larger, better financed rivals, one potential scenario—one unfavorable to Korea—places specialized *chaebols* in the middle of the "sandwich" mentioned above; that is, stuck in the middle between low-cost competitors and larger and more experienced rivals. Another scenario shows technological advances simply creating more market niches that will vary in terms of value-added contributions, thereby allowing low-cost and highly differentiated firms to coexist. In this case, Korean firms could excel in memory chips (DRAMs), and even flash memories, while American and Japanese firms pursue more sophisticated circuitry. To achieve this end, Koreans will have to leverage their human resource management strengths into tangible and sustainable advantages in world competition.

Developing New Management Structures

For most companies trying to compete in the global marketplace, the 1990s have been years of tumultuous change. We have witnessed countless examples of corporate reengineering, downsizing, rightsizing, mergers, and bankruptcies. Corporations around the world have desperately sought new management technologies, such as flatter organization designs and total quality management (TQM), as if they were searching for a corporate version of the fountain of youth. And as we approach the twenty-first century, the depth and breadth of these changes—and the need for appropriate management responses—is likely to intensify. Megatrend forecasters see the next century as being characterized by significant changes in technology, business-government relations, manufacturing processes, employee expectations, environmental concerns, labor costs, financial markets, and political risk. All of these changes can be summed up in two words: increased competition. The new realities of a truly international economy place increased burdens on management to respond in a timely fashion to myriad unpredictable events and uncertainties. The manner in which corporate managers respond to these challenges will determine in large measure how well the companies perform and, indeed, whether they even survive.

Nowhere is this challenge more evident than in Korea. While traditional neo-Confucian management practices may have served Korean firms well in the past as they grew their companies within the walls of protective barriers, the new global marketplace will increasingly require professional managers and organizational configurations that can move swiftly and decisively to take advantage of available opportunities and to avoid possible threats to their survival. Thus, a clear challenge facing many contemporary Korean firms today is how to restructure their organizations so they will be ready for the next century. Underlying this challenge in Korea, however, is a paradox: How can Korean firms "modernize" management structures in ways that are necessary to their becoming global players without jeopardizing the cultural foundations on which their success is based? This issue is discussed in chapter 8 as we examine what may be called the New Confucianism. What we will find is that Korean firms have indeed been very active in recent years in experimenting with management structures designed to advance decentralization, flexibility, and individual accountability without sacrificing the core cultural traits that nurture their traditional motivation for success. They have also learned many lessons about how not to conduct labor relations. Indeed, the new pattern of industrial relations that is slowly emerging from Korea may provide lessons for other countries.

Developing Human Resources for the Twenty-first Century

The seventh and final challenge facing Korean firms today is how best to develop their human capital so they will have the intellectual resources to compete successfully in the twenty-first century. Some economists, such as Lester Thurow, argue that the quality of a firm's (and a country's) human resources will likely determine who succeeds and who fails under the new competitive rules. As many of the traditional bases of competition become either standardized or more readily available (for example, access to capital, raw materials, cheap labor), the quality of a firm's employees emerges as a key potential differentiator between competitors.

Many Korean firms are keenly aware of this challenge and have initiated a wide variety of plans and programs aimed at recruiting, training, and motivating employees at all levels in the hierarchy to help their corporation compete with other global players around the world. A new role is also emerging for women employees. These responses are based in large measure on Korea's traditional emphasis on education as a means of individual and group advancement. In chapter 9, we examine how Korean firms character- ize this challenge and how they are orchestrating their responses. This chapter focuses on exploring recent changes in the human resource manage- ment policies and practices of Korea's major firms and on the new role of the HR executive as a leader/educator/policy maker within the firm.

The seven challenges facing Korea and its business enterprises are daunting. Even so, in perhaps characteristic Korean style, government bureaucrats, business leaders, and even people at large seem to have taken them in stride, if not with some enthusiasm. While we have presented these challenges in a particular order, we do not mean to imply that one or the other has greater priority or that they have evolved sequentially. In fact, the challenges are very much intertwined and interrelated. The restructuring of the *chaebols*, for example, will have far-reaching consequences for their ability to become players in the global economy as well as for their efforts to develop their human resources.

Throughout this first chapter, we have tried to demonstrate the intercon- nectedness of Korea's past economic accomplishments and its future chal- lenges as it enters the next century. While Korean leaders and politics may change over time, the current shift toward globalization, market liberaliza- tion, and political democratization creates a long-standing and irreversible challenge that will occupy Korea well into the next century. Before we examine these issues in depth, however, it is useful to understand the origins of the major Korean firms and the way they grew and developed in a short period of time to become contenders on the world stage. This is the subject of chapter 2.

For the balance of the book we enter a more detailed discussion of the nature of the seven challenges and the actions Korean firms are taking to meet them. This is not a book about history, although history clearly plays a role in the development of successful Korean enterprise. Rather, it is a book about present realities: present challenges and current responses. We examine what Korean firms—and their government—are doing right and what they are doing wrong. Throughout, we endeavor to draw implications both for Korea watchers and policy makers and for Western managers faced with the challenge of competing against these new international rivals.

CHAPTER TWO

Building the Entrepreneurial Machine:
A Look Back

When native Korean Park K. C. went to work for IBM in the early 1980s to help develop liquid-crystal-display (LCD) technologies, he became increasingly frustrated by the pace of the company's investment in the project. Compared with its Japanese competitors, he felt that IBM was slow to put money into new technology development. Later, as head of IBM's multimedia unit in 1993, Park again became disillusioned by the timidity with which the company invested in the future. Later that year, the twenty-seven-year IBM veteran left the company, returning to Korea to become the new executive vice president of LG Electronics, a $6.5 billion unit of the former Lucky-Goldstar conglomerate. Park soon realized he had entered a new world. LG Electronics was rapidly establishing itself in memory chips, LCDs, and high-speed CD-ROMs, and it was committing more than $2.5 billion to R&D in these key areas over the next five years. In addition, LG was negotiating joint ventures with AT&T and Motorola, and Microsoft's Bill Gates and Oracle CEO Lawrence Ellison had recently made visits to LG's headquarters. Later LG would announce its takeover of American Zenith Electronics, thereby giving itself access to important new HDTV (high-definition television) and multimedia technologies. Park could hardly contain his excitement. Commenting on his move from IBM to LG Electronics and his new company's commitment to innovation, Park observed, "If we [LG] decide we need it, bang!—we go in. That's the way it has to be. No nonsense. That's what really excites me about Korea."[1]

Indeed, what typically differentiates many Korean firms from their international counterparts in the recent past is neither the financial strength and years of experience we see in many American firms nor the commitment to the long term that we see in many Japanese firms. Rather, it is their fervent commitment to entrepreneurship. Returning from a trip to North Korea in 1992, Daewoo Chairman Kim Woo-Choong observed, "I can smell money everywhere," even in bleak, economically bankrupt North Korea![2] Successful Korean firms like LG and Daewoo will do almost anything it takes to leapfrog the competition as a means to both survival and prosperity. It is the story of companies like these that we focus on in this chapter. Specifically, we will look at the emergence of major Korean conglomerates as the engine of growth for the country's economic development since the Korean War. As part of this assessment, we will take an in-depth look at the so-called Big Four—Korea's largest and most successful firms—as examples of Korean success stories. Finally, we compare the major Korean firms with their Japanese counterparts, the so-called *keiretsu*. Throughout, we attempt to learn what it is about these firms that makes them such fierce competitors in the global marketplace. First, however, we examine the meaning and origins of the *chaebol* as a means of doing business in Korea.

EMERGENCE OF THE *CHAEBOLS*

The major Korean firms are generally referred to as *chaebols*. A *chaebol* can be defined as a business group consisting of large companies that are owned and managed by family members or relatives in many diversified business areas.[3] In other words, it is a financial clique consisting of varied corporate enterprises engaged in diverse businesses and typically owned and controlled by one or two interrelated family groups. Hence, Hyundai is largely owned and managed by the Chung family under Chung Ju-Yung, while Samsung is largely owned and controlled by the family of its late founder, Lee Byung-Chull. LG Group (formerly Lucky-Goldstar) is largely controlled by the two interrelated Koo and Huh families. And so on.

Today, more than fifty *chaebol* groups of varying size exist in Korea. The ten largest, in terms of sales, are Hyundai, Samsung, LG, Daewoo, Sunkyong, Ssangyong, Kia, Hanjin, Lotte, and Hanwha. The names of these firms can sometimes be deceiving, or at least confusing. For example, the LG Group appears on first glance to be two companies: its chemicals and cosmetics are manufactured and sold under the Lucky label, while its electronics products use the name Goldstar. Even so, in reality, it is a highly integrated if diversified company. The Ssangyong Group is often confused with Sunkyong Group, its foremost rival. And one of the largest *chaebols*, Hanwha, recently changed its name because of continual misunderstanding about its product line; it used to be called Korea Explosives.

It is perhaps worth noting that for some the term *chaebol* has negative connotations, in much the same way as do the terms *zaibatsu* in Japan or *conglomerate* in the United States. This fact results in large part from the perception that some of the *chaebols* accumulated their wealth through unfair advantage or government connections. Moreover, some but certainly not all of these corporate giants have been accused of exploiting their employees for the sake of profits. It should be said, however, that most large-scale enterprises around the world—in the United States, Japan, and Western Europe—have been similarly accused. In fact, several of the major Korean companies, such as LG and Sunkyong, have received widespread international recognition for their positive approach and contributions to employee welfare and community development. Even so, the purpose of our study here is not to evaluate corporate social responsibility, in either Korea or elsewhere. Rather, our aim is to establish a better understanding of how the *chaebols* evolved and developed and of what makes them unique competitors in the international marketplace. In this sense, we use the term *chaebol* simply to mean what it says: a closely held, integrated, yet diversified corporate entity that produces a wide array of product lines for global consumption.

Large, diversified groups are not unique to Korea or Japan. In fact, developing countries such as Taiwan, the Philippines, Thailand, India, Brazil, Argentina, and Venezuela all have industrial groups as their common feature.[4] In Korea, the rise of the *chaebols* is closely associated with President Park Chung Hee, beginning in the early 1960s. Park thought that economic growth and consequent improvement of living conditions would help legitimize his military rule. Throughout his presidency, he determined to discourage wasteful activities and to encourage businessmen to invest in the productive economy of the country. His revolutionary fervor set the stage for intermittent crackdowns on various forms of real estate speculation, corruption, and black market activities. However, it was Park's decision to confiscate large shareholdings in banks, as well as his decision to place the Bank of Korea under the control of the Ministry of Finance, that secured his control over the entire financial system.[5]

At the end of the Korean War, two types of firms existed in Korea.[6] The first was specialized and oriented toward cotton weaving and spinning. Textile manufacturing encompassed by far the largest and most modern companies in the country. The second—the predecessors of the modern *chaebols*—involved entrepreneurs who had gained access to specific business lines confiscated from the Japanese or acquired using American-aid-related loans and foreign exchange. With one exception—the Sunkyong Business Group—Korean cotton weavers, despite their prominence, did not become the crucible for diversification in Korea. As textile manufacturing was largely labor intensive, firms generally did not invest as much in managerial capabilities; their standardized equipment did not warrant such investments.[7]

By contrast, greater capabilities were required for capital-intensive industries, given the needed investment in nonstandardized technologies that tended to be science based and more specialized. Harvard historian Alfred Chandler argues that the switch from labor-intensive to capital-intensive industries entails a totally new way of managing the firm that makes capacity utilization and the age of the equipment strategic concerns.[8] The initial activities of the *chaebols* were capital intensive and included sugar refining, soap manufacture, construction, steel manufacture, and metallurgy. Among the *chaebols* that engaged in textiles—most notably, Hyosung, Kohap, and Kolon—efforts focused on the manufacture of synthetic fibers that required more capital investment than pure cotton spinning and weaving. Today's most successful *chaebols* made the necessary investments, while the conservative textile firms did not.

But beyond capital investment, there is another reason why modern-day *chaebols*, and not specialized firms, dominate the present landscape. Three of these firms—Samsung, Hyundai, and Daewoo—have origins in the service industries, while a fourth, LG, started in chemicals.[9] Yet early on they began to pursue other industries. Hyundai moved into construction, for example, while Samsung moved into the import-export business. These activities provided them with a commercial bridge to other business activities. Hyundai's petition for a cement-making facility in the mid-1960s never led to its becoming a major Hyundai operation. Rather, it was pursued so the firm would have a stable source of cement for its construction; it also served as a pilot project so Hyundai engineers could learn about manufacturing processes. Hyundai not only purchased technology from a process specialist (Allis Chalmers) but also contracted technical consulting know-how for general engineering. At each sequential step, Hyundai bought less and less technical expertise from the outside. This learning pattern is also seen in Hyundai's experience in automobiles and semiconductor manufacturing. Whatever their origins, first and foremost Korean firms wanted to learn!

MIT economist Alice Amsden argues that the size of the *chaebols* afforded them the ability to diversify into related and unrelated industries.[10] Their broad diversification and central coordination, she notes, are products of late industrialization. Korea's business groups had no technical expertise to build on in related industries or in higher-quality product market niches. Thus, as with other late industrializing countries after World War II, Korean firms had to industrialize by borrowing and improving technology that had already been developed by experienced firms in more advanced economies. For all practical purposes, the only asset available to most late industrializers that have had to compete against firms from industrialized economies has been low wages. Thus it was that most Korean firms began their rise by combining reengineered technology and mass production with competitive labor costs.

KOREAN ENTREPRENEURS AND THE RISE OF THE "BIG FOUR"

While there are many Korean entrepreneurial companies, we will examine the four largest by way of illustration. As will be seen in the four case examples that follow, the growth and development of Korean firms invariably shows the strong hand and unremitting determination of their founders.

Lee Byung-Chull and Samsung

From its inauspicious beginnings in 1938 and its rebirth in 1951, the Samsung Group grew along with Korea, guided by Lee Byung-Chull (frequently referred to in the West as B. C. Lee). Immediately following the Korean War, the company focused its efforts on providing basic necessities to resupply a war-torn country. Cheil Sugar & Co. was founded in 1953, followed closely by Cheil Wool Textile Co. in 1954. Interestingly, several of Lee's initial ventures were named *Cheil* (meaning "number one" in Korean) to reflect the founder's desire to be the best. Lee once observed, "Money is not what I pursued. Instead, I have only striven to be the best in whatever business I chose."[11]

As Korea's standard of living began to rise in the 1960s, Samsung moved into the service sector with such businesses as insurance, broadcasting, securities, and department stores. By the end of the 1960s, Samsung had an annual turnover of $100 million. In the 1970s, the company entered electronics (initially black-and-white televisions) and heavy industries (ship-building and petrochemicals). By the end of the decade, Samsung's combined turnover had reached $3 billion. In 1986, Samsung Aerospace was designated by the government as systems integrator for the Korean-built F-16 fighter-plane. Throughout the 1980s, more emphasis was placed on high-technology ventures. Samsung Semiconductor and Telecommunications Co., established in 1978, became the first Korean company to manufacture the 64K DRAM chip, following shortly with the 256K and 1M chips. Today, the company is the largest producer of 4M DRAMs and is moving into 16M, 64M, and 256M DRAMs ahead of most Japanese and American firms.

Samsung has also achieved its goal of becoming a truly international corporation. In 1982, it opened a television assembly facility in Portugal with a capacity of 300,000 units for sale within the European Union market. This was followed in 1984 with a $25 million plant in New Jersey that produced 1 million televisions and about 400,000 microwave ovens per year. In 1987, another $25 million facility was opened in England with a capacity for 300,000 VCRs, 400,000 color televisions, and 300,000 microwave ovens. Further expansion is proceeding or anticipated throughout Southeast Asia, Latin American, South Africa, and Europe.[12] Samsung's current goal is to raise its offshore production to 40 percent by the year 2000.[13]

Since founder Lee's death in 1987, Samsung has been managed by his third son, Lee Kun Hee. Group sales in 1994 were $62 billion, making it the eighteenth largest firm in the Fortune Global 500. The firm's business fields can be divided into five key areas: electronics, engineering, chemicals, financial and information services, and consumer products and services (see figure 2-1). Clearly, the Samsung Group is a highly diversified and adaptive enterprise that competes effectively in the global economy. Even so, Samsung is transforming itself into a truly global company, hiring executives from other countries. Its goal is to become one of the world's top five electronics firms, with annual sales of $50 billion, by the year 2000.[14] In many ways, Samsung is also beginning to look more like a traditional Western corporation (see chapter 8). Recently, Chairman Lee issued a directive requiring employees at all levels to work fewer hours; he was convinced they could be more productive in fewer hours if they just put their minds to it. Lee repeatedly called on his managers to be more "professional," by which he meant more autonomous, independent thinking, analytical, and creative. However, through such directives, the continuing central power of the CEO-owner can still be seen. In 1995, for example, Chairman Lee decided that his executives were spending too much time in nonproductive activities, such as playing golf. In a company meeting he observed, very simply, "I do not play golf." The other executives got the message.

Figure 2-1   Major Companies of the Samsung Group

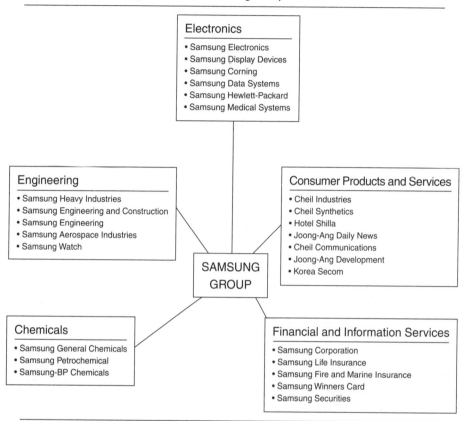

Source: Compiled from *An Introduction to Samsung* (Seoul: Samsung Group, 1995), and Ungsuh Park, "The History and Future of the Samsung Group of Companies" (paper presented at the University of Oregon, May 22, 1995).

Chung Ju-Yung and Hyundai

The story of Hyundai is the story of Chung Ju-Yung. Until about a decade ago, Hyundai was virtually unknown in the West. Then came the Hyundai Excel, the fastest selling import in both the United States and Canada when introduced. More—and better—cars followed. Now Western consumers are beginning to see new microcomputer products from Hyundai. But while name recognition for this and other Korean companies may be a recent phenomenon, the strength and diversity—and success—of the Hyundai Group go way back.

While Lee Byung-Chull was born to a reasonably wealthy family, Chung Ju-Yung was born to poor rural farmers in 1915. With little formal education, he set about learning various manual labor skills and in the 1940s established a truck and motor service business. By 1947, he had formed Hyundai Engineering and Construction Company, focusing on the construction of dams, roads, harbors, and housing projects. As the first Korean construction company to win overseas contracts, Hyundai undertook highway projects in Thailand, harbor dredging in South Vietnam and Australia, bridges in Alaska, and housing complexes in Guam. The name *Hyundai* (which means "modern" in Korean) was selected to emphasize the fact that the company used the very latest techniques in the business. As time went on, Hyundai became increasingly adept at completing larger and more complex projects and could always compete internationally by virtue of its cheap, hard-working labor and a tradition of timely completion dates.

In 1968, Chairman Chung decided to enter the automobile industry and established Hyundai Motor Company to assemble Ford passenger cars to be sold locally. With technical assistance from Mitsubishi, Hyundai thus designed and produced Korea's first integrated passenger car, the Pony. In 1983, the midsized Steller model was introduced, and by 1988 Hyundai was producing a luxury sedan, the Grandeur, under license from Mitsubishi. A redesigned version of the Pony Excel was introduced to Canada in 1986 and to the United States a year later. The Steller had also been sold in Canada. Since 1990, a newly designed Hyundai Sonata and other cars (Elantra, Accent) have been introduced to the North American market. The Sonata was designed as a more upscale, medium-sized car aimed at competing with many of the Japanese imports, such as the Honda Accord and the Toyota Camry.[15] In 1994, U.S. sales of Hyundai cars topped 125,000, a company record.[16]

In 1973, Hyundai Heavy Industries Co. was formed as a major shipbuilding enterprise, one of the largest in the world. With its highly skilled labor force and competitive prices, Hyundai was soon winning shipbuilding contracts away from Japan and Western Europe. Meanwhile, the company's construction business expanded significantly in the Middle East. This effort was highlighted by the completion of the $1.1 billion Jubail Industrial Harbor Project in Saudi Arabia in the early 1980s.

Because of the increasing size and opportunities facing Hyundai, many units were spun off as independent companies. These included Hyundai Engine & Machinery Co., Hyundai Electrical Engineering Co., and Hyundai Rolling Stock Co. Hyundai also acquired Inchon Iron & Steel Co. and Aluminum of Korea. In 1976, the Hyundai Corporation was formed as the corporate group's general trading company. As the 1980s approached, Hyundai Electronics Industries Co. was formed as Chairman Chung decided to take the company into high technology. And in 1984 Hyundai Offshore and Engineering Co. was formed to take better advantage of the increasing business in offshore drilling platforms.

Owing to Chung's interest in education, he established the Ulsan Institute of Technology in 1977 to increase the number of engineering students in Korea. Also in 1977, Chung donated half of his holdings in the parent company, Hyundai Engineering & Construction Company (worth $70 million), to his newly created Asan Foundation to help fund rural hospitals, educational scholarships, and social welfare programs. Chung has also served as a member of the Board of Directors of Korea University, where as a young man in the 1930s he had worked as a bricklayer.

Today, Hyundai is a thriving enterprise, consisting of forty-seven companies, with eighty-three branch offices in forty-six countries. Annual sales for 1994 reached $49 billion, and as of 1996 Hyundai employs more than 161,000 employees worldwide. A list of Hyundai's primary business interests is shown in figure 2-2.

Koo In-Whoi and Lucky-Goldstar

While Samsung's origins can be traced to general trading and Hyundai's to construction, Lucky-Goldstar's beginnings were in the field of chemistry. Founded by Koo In-Whoi in 1947, the Lucky Chemical Company (later simply Lucky) initially manufactured cosmetics. From here, the company branched out into plastics (including combs, toothbrushes, and plastic basins). After the Korean War, toothpaste and laundry detergent were also being produced by the predominantly home-products company. A trading company was established in 1953, followed by the creation of Goldstar Co. in 1958 to produce radios, refrigerators, and televisions. An oil refinery was established in 1967. From there, the company continued to grow as a "dual-track" entity, stressing product innovations in both chemistry (through Lucky) and electronics (through Goldstar Co.) and later adding services and public welfare to its areas of business.

Today, the LG Group, as it is now called, consists of 39 affiliated companies, 39 joint ventures, and 130 branch offices around the world (see figure 2-3). It is managed by the dynamic Chairman Koo Bon-Moo. Sales for 1994 totaled $25 billion, while employment currently stands at 100,000.

The LG Group differs in several important respects from most other Korean enterprises. First, while employees of the company are clearly proud of the achievements of founder Koo In-Whoi, there is little of the personality cult that typifies many other *chaebols*. Second, the group is in reality more

Figure 2-2   Major Companies of the Hyundai Group

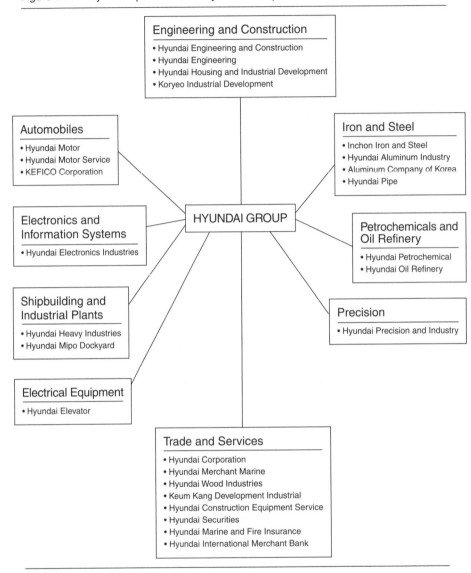

Source: Compiled from *Building a Better Future: Hyundai* (Seoul: Hyundai Corporation, 1994).

decentralized than many other such organizations. Significant efforts have been made to develop competent professional managers capable of overseeing the various businesses (see chapter 7). Major strategic decisions are still made in the office of the chairman, as would be expected, but within these guidelines individual companies are free to pursue their businesses as

Figure 2-3   Major Companies of the LG Group

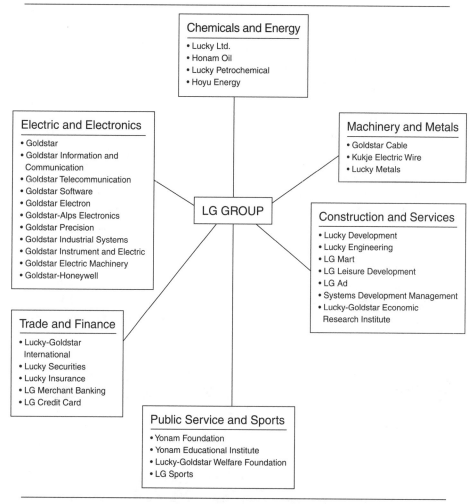

Chemicals and Energy
- Lucky Ltd.
- Honam Oil
- Lucky Petrochemical
- Hoyu Energy

Electric and Electronics
- Goldstar
- Goldstar Information and Communication
- Goldstar Telecommunication
- Goldstar Software
- Goldstar Electron
- Goldstar-Alps Electronics
- Goldstar Precision
- Goldstar Industrial Systems
- Goldstar Instrument and Electric
- Goldstar Electric Machinery
- Goldstar-Honeywell

Machinery and Metals
- Goldstar Cable
- Kukje Electric Wire
- Lucky Metals

LG GROUP

Construction and Services
- Lucky Development
- Lucky Engineering
- LG Mart
- LG Leisure Development
- LG Ad
- Systems Development Management
- Lucky-Goldstar Economic Research Institute

Trade and Finance
- Lucky-Goldstar International
- Lucky Securities
- Lucky Insurance
- LG Merchant Banking
- LG Credit Card

Public Service and Sports
- Yonam Foundation
- Yonam Educational Institute
- Lucky-Goldstar Welfare Foundation
- LG Sports

Source: Compiled from *Lucky-Goldstar Annual Report: 1994* (Seoul).

they see fit. Finally, LG is often described as a more conservative, perhaps more stable company that avoids risky ventures and stresses group harmony in all endeavors (the company motto is *inhwa,* meaning "group harmony"). In this sense, it has less of the "department store mentality" that characterizes some other groups that have tended to spread themselves thinly into many new and often unrelated areas. Most of LG's new ventures are logical extensions of an existing business. For example, as noted in interviews with senior executive Kwon Moon-Koo, the chairman has always stressed autonomous decision making for each company of the group.[17] Moreover, careful value-added analyses are done before new ventures are initiated. There is considerable emphasis on the sustainability of the overall group and its companies in all decisions. And, finally, Mr. Kwon emphasized the importance of competitiveness in all decisions affecting the marketplace; LG intends to grow and prosper.

The company maintains numerous research labs, but its major efforts are centered in the Central Research Institute (established in 1979) in Taedok, which undertakes research in chemical technologies and advanced material sciences, and in a major R&D complex in Anyang (established in 1985), which focuses on electronics research. A visit to the Anyang facility offers an impressive show of vitality and ambition on the part of the researchers. As early as 1988, Koo Cha-Hak, then vice chairman of the LG Group and CEO of Goldstar, noted, "Our goal is to become nothing less than the number 1 electronics manufacturer in the world, and we are striving to achieve this goal through strict attention to quality, a commitment to efficiency and through strategic management."[18] Its decision to implement a major corporate reorganization beginning in 1991, guided by McKinsey & Company, is testament to its commitment to succeed. LG wants to be a global player and battle the world's best technology companies. As current CEO Lee Hun-Jo recently observed, "We want to compete upward toward heaven. To compete downward is hell."[19]

Goldstar has also been aggressive in overseas production. In 1982, the organization opened what has become a major manufacturing plant in Huntsville, Alabama, which now manufactures 1 million color televisions and 500,000 microwave ovens annually for sale in North and South America. This was the first major manufacturing facility built in the United States by a Korean company. Rejection rates at the plant are described as one of the lowest in the world, and employee absenteeism is about 1 percent, compared with the U.S. national average of 5 percent.[20] A second facility was opened in Worms, West Germany, in 1987 with annual capacities of 300,000 televisions and 400,000 VCRs. Following the success of these two ventures, further international facilities emerged across Europe. In 1989, Goldstar built a television manufacturing facility in China, the first such venture for a Korean company. And in 1995, LG bought 58 percent of Zenith Television for $350 million. Zenith, despite recent financial troubles, has become a leader in the digital signal processing and transmission technologies required for the next generation of high-definition televisions. This acquisition gives LG access to both the technologies and the markets required for success in this area.[21]

Kim Woo-Choong and Daewoo

Founded in 1967 as a small textile trading company with an investment of $18,000 and four employees, Daewoo has grown in three short decades into a 100,000-employee organization with 19 domestic companies and 135 overseas subsidiaries. Sales for 1994 reached $31 billion, double the sales figures for 1988.

If we are looking for an example of entrepreneurship in a Korean firm, Daewoo is clearly a good place to start. Daewoo began its existence in 1967 by exporting fabrics to Southeast Asia. First-year sales were $580,000; two years later sales had reached $4 million. Soon the company was producing textiles and had developed a reputation for high-quality, low-priced merchandise. Sears, Roebuck became Daewoo's first major American customer, followed quickly by J.C. Penney and Montgomery Ward. By 1972, the company was awarded 30 percent of the total U.S. import quota for textile products. By 1975, Daewoo was one of Korea's most profitable companies.

From this firm manufacturing base, Daewoo (which means "great universe" in Korean) moved into its second phase of development by initiating a series of fourteen acquisitions. Throughout, the strategy was the same and throughout it was successful: take over an ailing company, improve the management system and product quality, and turn the company around. In fact, one of Daewoo's hallmarks is superior production capability. As one foreign observer for *Asia Finance* concluded, "Anyone who looks, for example, at Daewoo Electronics' TV production facilities at Gumi, the assembly lines at Daewoo Motor, the plants of the Korea Steel Chemical Co., or the shipyard at Okpo will have little doubt that here is production capability at its best."[22]

The first major takeover occurred in 1975, when Korean President Park asked Daewoo to acquire a state-owned machinery plant that had been losing money for thirty-seven years. Kim Woo-Choong, founder and CEO of Daewoo, changed the name of the company to Daewoo Heavy Industries and took personal charge of the new company. Within one year the company broke even and by the second year it began paying dividends. Shortly thereafter, President Park asked Kim to take over Okpo Shipbuilding Company, renamed Daewoo Shipbuilding and Heavy Machinery. Kim invested $500 million in completing the facility, which today ranks as one of the world's largest and finest shipbuilders. Finally, Daewoo took over Saehan Motor Company, renaming it Daewoo Motor Company, in 1979. Again, through Kim's efforts, the enterprise was transformed into one of Korea's three largest auto companies.

Today, many of Daewoo's companies are joint ventures. Daewoo teamed up with General Dynamics to manufacture fuselages and equipment for the F-16 and with Boeing to assemble fuselages and wing parts for the 737, 747, and 767. Forklifts and construction equipment are made with Caterpillar. Optical fiber, cable, and telephone-switching systems are built in partnership with Northern Telecom, while Daewoo Electronics builds motors for General Electric. Through this three-pronged strategy of company creation, company acquisition, and joint ventures, Daewoo continues to grow (approximately 20 percent per year) and is becoming one of the world's most dynamic companies. By 1994, it ranked thirty-third in the world in the Fortune Global 500. A listing of the principal companies within the Daewoo Group is shown in figure 2-4.

Figure 2-4 Major Companies of the Daewoo Group

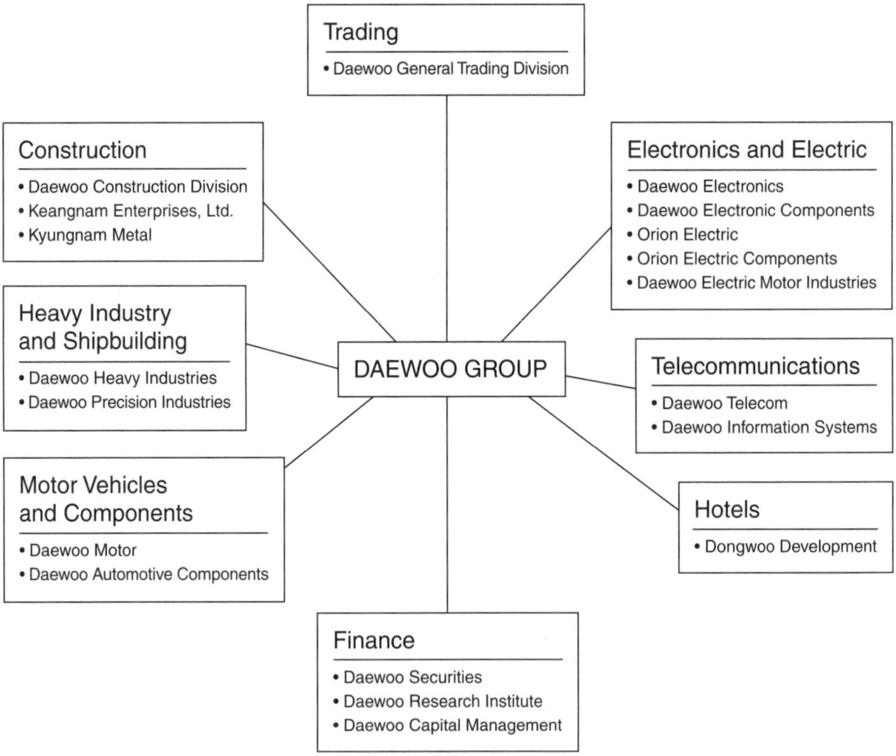

Trading
- Daewoo General Trading Division

Construction
- Daewoo Construction Division
- Keangnam Enterprises, Ltd.
- Kyungnam Metal

Heavy Industry and Shipbuilding
- Daewoo Heavy Industries
- Daewoo Precision Industries

Motor Vehicles and Components
- Daewoo Motor
- Daewoo Automotive Components

DAEWOO GROUP

Electronics and Electric
- Daewoo Electronics
- Daewoo Electronic Components
- Orion Electric
- Orion Electric Components
- Daewoo Electric Motor Industries

Telecommunications
- Daewoo Telecom
- Daewoo Information Systems

Hotels
- Dongwoo Development

Finance
- Daewoo Securities
- Daewoo Research Institute
- Daewoo Capital Management

Source: Compiled from *Daewoo Around the World* (Seoul: Daewoo Corporation, 1994).

Like many other Korean firms, Daewoo has focused intensely in recent years on overseas production. Today, Daewoo manufactures products in twenty-three countries and has sales operations in many more (see table 2-1). It is also interesting to note the interrelationships between the various companies in the group. Many Daewoo companies invest sizable sums in other Daewoo companies. The interlocking nature of this relationship, combined with the high rate of corporate borrowing, increases the risk

Table 2-1   Principal Daewoo Manufacturing Sites outside of Korea

Company	Product	Capacity (per year)	Investment (Millions of dollars)
Algeria			
Oil Development	Oil development	NA	$ 15
Belgium			
Euro-Daewoo	Excavators	900	20
China			
Daewoo Bag & Tent Co.	Bags, tents	300,000	5
Qingdao Daewoo Stone	Granite	NA	5
Shangdong Cement	Cement	2.4 million tons	300
Automotive Components Plant	Auto components	NA	2,000
Guilin Daewoo Bus	Buses	2,500	35
Daewoo Electronics	Car audios	600,000	3
Namwoo Glass	Glass panes	80,000 tons	28
Zhangjiang Yu-Qui Steel Products	Pipes	100,000 tons	29
Xianyang Daewoo Electronics	Deflection yokes	600,000	3
Jinan Daewoo Bus Co.	Buses	2,000	22
Daewoo Paper	Art paper	35,000 tons	16
France			
Daewoo Electronics	Microwave ovens	300,000	23
DEMSA	TVs	400,000	37
CPT Plant	CPTs	1,200,000	150
Daewoo Orion	Color CRTs	NA	138
Hungary			
MHB-Daewoo Bank	Loans, trusts	NA	50
Magyar Daewoo Securities	Securities	NA	10

Table 2-1 Continued

Company	Product	Capacity (per year)	Investment (Millions of dollars)
India			
CRB Securities	Securities	NA	NA
DCM Daewoo	Autos	NA	200
Indonesia			
PT Continental	Antennas	12,000	3
Iran			
Passenger Car Plant	Autos	50,000	600
Kazakhstan			
DAECO	Microwave ovens	100,000	4
Libya			
Passenger Car Plant	Autos	50,000	NA
Oil Development	Oil development	NA	60
Mexico			
DELMEX	TVs	600,000	20
Myanmar			
DEMCO	TVs, audios	410,000	9
Myanmar Daewoo	Shirts, blouses	165,000DZ	1
Myanmar Korea Timber	Plywood	2 million sheets	1
Pakistan			
PELDAEWOO	TVs	100,000	5
Philippines			
Passenger Car Plant	Autos	20,000	20
Poland			
Daewoo Electronics Polcand	TVs	200,000	4
Romania			
Romania Oltcit	Autos	200,000	320
Russia			
Natural Gas Exploration & Pipeline Project	Natural gas exploration and pipeline	NA	NA
RUSKO	Agrofishery	NA	0.4
Orion Plazma Research Co.	Display panels	NA	4
Sudan			
Nile International	Cotton spinning	NA	91
GTC	Leather	NA	16

Table 2-1 Continued

Company	Product	Capacity (per year)	Investment (Millions of dollars)
Taiwan			
Tuntex Daewoo	Cement silo	NA	200
United Kingdom			
DUEK	VCRs	500,000	42
Daewoo Securities	Securities	NA	15
United States			
Daewoo Securities	Securities	NA	12
Uzbekistan			
Uz-Daewoo Electronics	TVs, VCRs	200,000	10
Uz-Daewoo Motor Co.	Autos	200,000	635
Textile Mfg. Plant	Spindles	200,000	44
Vietnam			
Orion-Hanel Picture Tube	CPTs, TVs	1,600,000	170
Daewoo Vietronics	Cabinets	1,600,000	5
First Vina Bank	Securities	NA	10
VIDAMCO	Buses, trucks	20,000	32
KOSVIDA	Agrichemicals	1,200 tons	8
Daewoo-Bach Tuyet Paint	Paints	6,800 tons	6

Source: Data compiled from *Daewoo Around the World* (Seoul: Daewoo Corporation, 1994).
Note: This table includes only manufacturing facilities located outside of Korea and does not include
   international sales organizations.

of serious financial problems. For example, when Daewoo Shipbuilding experienced financial difficulties in 1988–1989 and sought government assistance, the consequences could be felt by Daewoo Heavy Industries, Daewoo Corporation, and the government's Korea Development Bank—all of which had substantial investments in Daewoo Shipbuilding.[23]

In the case of Daewoo, as in the case of most of the *chaebols*, the success of the company can be traced rather directly to the drive, skill, and entrepreneurial spirit of its founder, Kim Woo-Choong. Chairman Kim was born in 1936 in Taegu and was raised during the period of both the Japanese occupation and the Korean War. He is known in Korea as perhaps the hardest working executive in the country. He sleeps only four hours a night, works one hundred hours per week, and travels more than two hundred days per year. By his own admission, he hasn't taken a vacation in thirty years.[24] Indeed, he once noted, "I certainly expect Daewoo people to work hard. But most of them know that in the 21 years since I founded Daewoo, I have taken no time off—except for the morning of my daughter's wedding."[25] He is up every morning at 5:30—"Breakfasting with my family is very important to me,"[26] he observes—and prefers Sunday morning meetings so as not to interrupt productive working hours. He doesn't drink or play golf or tennis. And in the early 1980s, he turned over all of his personal business assets (estimated at between $40 million to $50 million) to an independent cultural and medical foundation. Because of such exploits, and because of his business success, Chairman Kim is an oft-cited role model and folk hero for many Korean managers both inside and outside Daewoo.

In his approach to management, Kim frequently refers to the "Daewoo spirit." This spirit (often written in calligraphy and hung on the walls of Daewoo executives) consists of three elements: *creativity, challenge,* and *sacrifice.* Daewoo employees will tell the outsider that this is more than an empty slogan; it is a heartfelt set of beliefs that guide employee behavior. During this period in Korean economic development, these three qualities are believed to be essential if the company and the country are to attain their aspirations. Kim also talks about Daewoo's emphasis on *coprosperity.* By this he means that every company has a responsibility to deliver equitable benefits to workers, customers, suppliers, partners, and the government. In this way, harmony is preserved and every sector of the culture benefits.

Kim attributes the success of Daewoo to three related attributes. First, the company is market driven. "At the time of our founding as a textile trading company," he notes, "I saw tremendous international possibilities. When I entered the American market, I decided to go directly to independent retailers and chain stores. I avoided Japanese middlemen, which was an uncommon practice for Koreans at that time. I also learned the benefits of market research and innovation. We developed new styles and fabrics, rather than passively meeting buyer demands. I believe that pioneering new markets is as important as creating new technology."[27]

Second, Kim describes Daewoo as a company that is "flexible, ready to adjust, and innovative. . . . We have not waited for things to happen. We have capitalized upon changing opportunities."[28] Daewoo, like many other Korean companies, exhibits a capacity to accommodate environmental changes such that it often seems to be ahead of the trends. When people were getting out of oil, for example, Kim bought an oil refinery in Belgium. He then proceeded to increase his business in underdeveloped nations, where he could trade his products for crude oil. Since he had his own refinery, he was less susceptible to price changes on the world spot market, thereby increasing both his security and his profitability.[29]

Third, Kim is known as a risk taker (like Chairman Chung at Hyundai). In Korean, *risk* translates into a word that combines the characters for *crisis* and *chance*. In other words, any crisis facing a company can also be thought of as an opportunity if handled correctly. When many Korean companies were engaged in construction work in the Middle East, for example, Kim believed he would find greater opportunities (and less competition) contracting in Africa. As Kim notes, "Of course, the African market was smaller and less stable, both financially and politically. But the greater the risk, the greater the chance for accomplishments and profits."[30] As a result, Daewoo ended up with $2 billion in construction contracts in Libya. If there is no risk, says Kim, there is no money. Indeed, his 1992 book, *Every Street Is Paved with Gold*, has as its theme the idea that most anyone can become wealthy if only he or she becomes a true entrepreneur.[31] The question, according to Kim, is how one manages the risk. And the way one manages the risk in Libya is to require payment in advance. As a result of this approach to doing business, Daewoo has accounted for nearly 10 percent of Korea's exports over the past twenty years.

These brief histories of the founding and development of Samsung, Hyundai, LG, and Daewoo illustrate how Korean managers and employees, working in concert, can contribute to rapid industrial progress through hard work, initiative, and the willingness to seize opportunities when they present themselves. To be frank, no one in the world of commerce gave the Koreans anything. Instead, as a result of their unbridled zeal to achieve, Koreans and their companies strove to demonstrate their worth and earn respect through competitive success.

KOREAN *CHAEBOL* VERSUS JAPANESE *KEIRETSU*

Westerners frequently assume that few, if any, differences exist between the major Korean conglomerates and their Japanese counterparts (the *keiretsu*). Indeed, both exist in East Asian countries and both are influenced by similar cultural and religious roots. Moreover, many of today's Korean companies and government agencies were established during Japanese occupation. And both represent huge concerns that are highly diversified in their holdings. This latter point is evidenced in two typical large firms, Mitsubishi from Japan and Samsung from Korea. Each company represents its country's largest firm. Each is monumental in size and diversity.

Despite such similarities, however, it would be a mistake not to acknowledge the distinct differences between the *keiretsu* and the *chaebol* (summarized in table 2-2, based on the examples of Mitsubishi and Samsung). First and foremost, there are significant differences in size. The typical *keiretsu* is substantially larger than the typical *chaebol*. Mitsubishi Group, for instance, consists of twenty-nine *kinyo-kai*—or "president's council"—companies, each of which is a conglomerate in its own right. In addition, Mitsubishi owns 160 smaller companies and controls numerous other smaller "independent" subsidiaries. All told, Mitsubishi has 146 companies that are large enough to be listed on the Tokyo or Osaka stock exchange. Annual group sales in 1995 were $433 billion, with group employment topping 400,000 people. Mitsui and Sumitomo, Japan's other giants, are not far behind. The Samsung Group, by contrast, consists of about fifty companies with annual group sales of $62 billion in 1995. Samsung employs 150,000 people world-

Table 2-2 Comparison of the Korean *Chaebol* and the Japanese *Keiretsu*

Characteristics	Korean *Chaebol*	Japanese *Keiretsu*
Size*		
Annual sales of largest group	$62 billion	$433 billion
Number of affiliated companies of largest group	50	189
Number of employees in largest group	150,000	400,000
Nature of ownership	Predominately family held	Predominantly publicly held
Centralization of power	Highly centralized	Moderately decentralized
Professionalization of management	Early stages of development	Clearly established
Business-government relations	Partnership among unequals; government over firms	Parternship among relative equals
Nature of financing	Almost exclusively external financing	Large percentage of internal financing
Approach to human resource management	Employees as variable cost of production	Employees as fixed cost of production

*For purposes of size comparison, Japan's largest *keiretsu* (Mitsubishi) is compared with Korea's largest *chaebol* (Samsung) as of 1995.

wide. Hyundai, LG, and Daewoo, Korea's other giants, are not far behind. Clearly, then, Japanese firms are larger by an order of magnitude than Korean firms.

Second, there are differences in the nature of ownership of the *chaebols* and *keiretsus*. As mentioned above, in Korea most companies are closely held by family members. While many large business groups in Japan are also family enterprises (especially those founded before World War II, when such conglomerates were referred to as *zaibatsu*), the percentage of family shares in contemporary Japanese conglomerates is now typically much smaller. Moreover, the definition of *family* is different in Japan and Korea. In Korea, family members are determined by blood relationships (consanguinity), while in Japan there are two different definitions of family, one based on blood relationships and one based on household or clan relationships.[32] In most cases, it is this clan relationship, not blood, that determines inheritance and succession. In Korea, family members typically own a larger share of the company because fewer people are considered to be a part of the family. Hence, we see a greater concentration of wealth or assets in fewer hands.

As a result of this difference, a third emerges, namely, the increased centralization of power in the hands of the CEOs in Korea compared with Japan. Korean CEOs are seldom challenged, however politely; their decisions are absolute. This characteristic often allows Korean firms to move more quickly and decisively than their Japanese counterparts because they can devote less time to consensus building among people at various levels of the organization. By the same token, they are more likely to make strategic errors because decisions may be made too quickly or without adequate information. Based on our observations, executives from both countries collect an incredible amount of information about business events; however, Japanese executives tend to make greater use of this information than their Korean counterparts.

Also as a result of greater family ownership of Korean enterprises, a greater proportion of top managers in Korea are family members. Hence, the percentage of professional managers who worked their way to the top is considerably higher in Japan than in Korea. Much of this difference, however, can be attributed to the relative newness of the Korean companies (that is, many of the founders are still alive, while many of the major Japanese companies are several hundred years old), and, as we will see later, Korean companies are moving rapidly to increase the number of professionally trained managers on their staff.

A fifth difference is the nature of business-government relationships. As seen earlier, this relationship has historically had a decidedly superior-subordinate character in Korea as opposed to Japan (with government essentially dictating business strategy in many cases), although this too is changing slowly under the new government. In Japan, this relationship (especially with the Ministry of International Trade and Industry), while not equal, is at least a little less one-sided than it has been in Korea.

Because of this, a sixth difference can be noted, namely, the nature of financing. Until very recently, the source of most borrowing for new ventures in Korea was the government, while in Japan far more borrowing is from group-affiliated banks. Indeed, most of the major *keiretsu* own their own banks and several own multiple banks, thereby easing credit and borrowing issues. In Korea, during the military regimes, the banks were controlled by the government. Only recently have most of the banks been privatized, and now several of the *chaebols* are following the Japanese example of buying a bank or other financial institution. Still, with rare exception, the major *chaebols* do not own banks. This gives Japanese concerns far greater financial freedom than their Korean counterparts.

Finally, while many similarities exist in the approaches Japanese and Korean conglomerates take to human resource management, several differences should be noted. Many of these can be historically characterized by Korean firms treating employees more like a variable cost of production—much like in the United States—and Japanese firms treating employees more like a fixed cost of production. If employees are treated as a variable cost, management's responsibility is to minimize such costs to enhance return on investment. Such a strategy suggests that employees are not a highly valued input in the production process. On the other hand, treating employees like a fixed cost (or fixed asset) implies that it is important for managers to tend these resources well, making prudent investments where appropriate. Differences here include corporate attitudes toward lifetime employment guarantees, training costs, bonus payments, and retirement policies, all of which will be discussed in greater detail in chapter 9. As we will see, the approach to human resources taken by Korean firms is undergoing a major transition that will affect their ability to compete successfully in the global marketplace.

CHAPTER THREE

Industrial Policy and the New Economic Covenant

Ever since political scientist S. M. Lipset argued that democracy is a product of economic development, two opposing views have existed concerning the relationship between political systems and economic well-being.[1] One view sees authoritative regimes as more effective in insulating nations from particularistic pressures and selfish group interests and as, therefore, better at mobilizing savings for economic development. The alternative view posits that dictatorships by definition act in self-interest and that democracies are therefore by definition superior in allocating resources. The transformation of Korea from a war-torn economy into a modern industrial enterprise was facilitated by almost four decades of interventionist government policies, often under the direction of highly authoritarian regimes. It is now recognized that this highly successful system of government control may have to change if Korea is to meet the external demands of a global economy and the internal demands for greater political liberalization. That is, to become more adaptable to these changing conditions—and to meet the goal of parity with the world's advanced nations (*segyehwa*)—Korea must take on the formidable challenge of determining how best to manage the transition from an authoritative regime to a democratic one.

In this chapter, we discuss the changing direction of industrial policy in Korea. Historically, industrial policy has encouraged rapid growth, and Koreans were generally asked to make sacrifices to support its requirements. *Chaebols* were protected and nurtured because they were considered the drivers of economic development. During the late 1950s through the mid-1960s, political and security issues dominated relations between Korea and the United States. Even when Korea emerged as a major supplier of basic manufactured goods to the U.S. market in the early 1980s, there were a few significant trade disputes. For as long as Korea accounted for a small portion of world imports, its trading partners ignored the lack of openness in the Korean domestic market. Korea's emergence as an economic power, however, symbolized by its application to the OECD (with approval expected by 1996), has called into question the continued validity of these protectionist policies. Mounting internal pressures are directed at correcting the undesirable correlates of rapid growth—inequities in income distribution, imbalances in regional and sectoral growth, and inequities in the treatment of large *chaebols* and small companies.[2] *Chaebols* have generally welcomed this free-market initiative but resisted government reform aimed at reducing their size and scope of diversification.

Given the complexity of any assessment of industrial policy, we have organized our discussion into several sections. The first part of this chapter reviews industrial/economic policies during the 1962–1992 period. The second begins an examination of Korea's current industrial policy, commonly referred to as President Kim's "Five-Year Plan for the New Economy." Because the new plan encompasses several important areas, we have further divided this discussion into three parts. First, globalization and the initiatives to change the infrastructure embodied in the new plan are discussed. Next, in chapter 4, we review recent directives aimed at reforming the *chaebols*, along with their implications for economic development. Finally, in chapter 5, we conclude our discussion of economic policy with a look at the role of small and medium-sized firms in Korea's economic development initiatives.

THE CONDUCT OF KOREAN INDUSTRIAL POLICY

A review the events leading up to the current situation in Korea will provide some perspective on recent proposed changes in industrial policy. Even the staunchest critics of Korea's industrial policy are hard pressed to deny that the country's economic success was due in large measure to centralized planning and effective government intervention. While this "simple" and conventional explanation of effective government is generally acknowledged, there is emerging work suggesting that the effectiveness of government intervention varied across different industries as well as in different time periods. Some of these works are reviewed in this chapter, but the reader is advised to refer to specific works for in-depth treatment.[3]

Korean industrial policy has been embodied in a series of national economic five-year plans classified into three stages:[4]

- The outward-oriented industrialization phase of 1962–1971.

- The shift from general export promotion to heavy and chemical industries of 1972–1981.

- The trade and market liberalization phase of 1982–1992.

Prior to the enactment of a formal industrial policy in the early 1960s, Korea was largely a closed agrarian economy, with about two thirds of the working population engaged in agriculture.[5] The Korean War had largely destroyed its industrial base. About three out of every five Koreans lived on a farm, with most being subsistence farmers.[6] Because of rural poverty, industrialization could not be funded from surpluses in agriculture. This bleak assessment of Korea's prospects had been held even before the Korean War, when an American general said: "Korea can never attain a high standard of living. There are virtually no Koreans with the technical training and experience required to take advantage of Korea's resources and effect an improvement over its rice-economy status."[7]

During the 1950s, government policy emphasized import substitution of nondurable consumer and intermediate goods behind a wall of protective tariffs and quotas. Because of the small size of the domestic market and the large amount of capital infusion required, the limits of import substitution were quickly realized. The lack of an adequate infrastructure and capital investment precluded long-term economic development. In fact, between 1954 and 1959, more than 70 percent of all reconstruction projects were financed by aid from other countries, notably the United States.[8] As a consequence, economic policy stressed meeting the immediate demand for consumer goods and easing distribution bottlenecks rather than fostering long-term economic development. Urban development and unemployment exacerbated Korea's early economic difficulties. Population growth had reached 3 percent per annum in 1955. Some held the influx of North Koreans during the Korean War responsible for South Korea's socioeconomic problems, such as increased unemployment, high demand for consumer goods, low capital formation, housing shortages, and sociopolitical unrest. On the positive side, educational facilities were greatly expanded, with enrollments at all levels increasing rapidly. Reflecting the high priority placed on education, the number of college students increased from 8,000 in 1945 to 100,000 by 1960, while the literacy rate improved from 22 percent to 72 percent during the same period.[9] From 1953 to 1962, per capita GNP increased from $67 to $87. Meanwhile, U.S. aid increased from $194 million to $232.2 million.[10]

Phase 1: Outward-Looking Development Strategy (1962–1971)

Because of Korea's poor endowment of natural resources and its small domestic market, it developed an outward-looking strategy at a rather early stage. Initially, the intention was to capitalize on its comparative advantage in labor-intensive manufactured goods. Following the downfall of the Rhee government in 1960, a new policy, largely promulgated by President Park Chung Hee, promoted the inflow of foreign resources of all types and the development of Korea's exports. The takeoff phase featured wide-ranging interventions in export promotion, industry finance, and protection. Because all other government objectives were either consistent with this goal or deemed secondary to it, this was considered a strategy of national economic development. Some key reforms included fiscal and monetary policies aimed at increasing public and private savings, the establishment of a uniform exchange rate, and the operation of a free-trade zone beginning in 1970.[11] The spectacular growth of Korea's export of goods from $50 million in 1962 to $1.07 billion in 1971 reflects the successful implementation of these strategies. Domestic savings also increased from 26 percent in 1962 to 60 percent in 1971. This remarkable growth in trade was accompanied by changes in sectoral composition. The share of primary products exported declined from 73 percent of the total in 1962 to only 14 percent in 1971, whereas that of industrial products increased from 27 percent to 86 percent.[12] The outward-looking strategy served to expand labor-intensive manufactured exports, which increased employment opportunities, significantly improving the economic conditions of millions of Koreans at the lower end of the income scale.

In *Korea's Competitive Edge*, Rhee Yang Soo, B. Ross Larsen, and Garry Pursell provide reasons why the Korean government was able to control the actions of the private sector during the takeoff stage and the ensuing period of intervention.[13] First, the government was a major stockholder in domestic banks and had the power to appoint bank managers. Second, it controlled the inflow of foreign capital, which was the principal source of corporate loans in Korea. Third, through the Bank of Korea and the Ministry of Finance, the government controlled the interest rates in the formal banking sector. This rationing of bank loans gave the government considerable leverage in promoting its export-growth policies. In addition to these conventional methods, other mechanisms of control included a system of setting export targets and the practice of holding monthly national trade promotion meetings, which were attended by no less than President Park Chung Hee himself. He set the tone with his commitment to what he called "nation building by export." These sessions provided the principal forum through which the various parties could informally negotiate product mixes and levels of administrative incentive as well as resolve thorny problems in export expansion.

Effective policy making was also facilitated by a strong and competent economic staff comparable with that of Japan's Ministry of Trade and Industry. In Korea, this task was assumed by the Economic Planning Board (EPB), whose minister was also the deputy prime minister and was accountable only to the president. In 1994 the EPB was merged with the Ministry of Finance and became the Ministry of Finance and Economy. The EPB was entrusted with special powers and responsibilities, such as developmental planning, budgeting, foreign cooperation and investment promotion, and preparation of five-year economic plans. While the EPB was not directly responsible for specific industrial policies, it was designated to conduct macroeconomic planning. Industrial policy was designed mainly by the Ministry of Trade and Industry in consultation with the Ministry of Finance, which was in charge of tax and financial policy.[14] To ensure success, all plans were consistently backed up with solid budgets and financing from various ministries. The probability of successful implementation was further enhanced by linking implementation with the career advancement of the bureaucrats.

Certainly, a good part of Korea's economic success was due to the entrepreneurial skills of Korea's top business leaders (see chapter 2). It is no secret that Park Chung Hee was favorably disposed to entrepreneurs, such as Chung Ju Yung of Hyundai and Kim Woo-Choong of Daewoo. Both of these men were hard-driving, dynamic, and enterprising leaders of their organizations and impressed Park with their commitment to nation building. When President Park once paid a surprise visit to a Hyundai construction work site, he was surprised to find Chung, who had slept on the site with his crew, working with them at dawn.[15]

Still another version of Korea's success story stresses the sacrifices made by Korean workers in the name of nation building. President Park put into place brutally long work hours, high rates of saving, and an authoritarian system that rewarded those who cooperated and punished those who did not.[16] Park once proclaimed: "The people of Asia today fear starvation and poverty more than the oppressive duties thrust upon them by totalitarianism."[17] While Park was a disciplinarian with the ability to squelch most dissent, he was also pragmatic enough to make sure that Korean companies were competitive and to oversee the financing of industrial expansion by foreign banks and foreign companies.[18]

Phase 2: Sectoral Policy (1972–1981)

Following the general export promotion phase came a new period that featured more typical, sector-oriented import substitution initiatives. The impetus behind this movement was to support large-scale, capital-intensive industries, such as heavy and chemical industries. The decision to move in this direction was formalized in the five-year economic plans, which stated where the government expected the economy to be headed, which industries were "strategic" to this direction, and which industries were not. Special incentives were granted to strategic industries—including tax exemptions, custom rebates, access to foreign exchange, and other forms of protection or enhancement—so that these industries could be competitive at a world level. Credit, especially at very low interest rates, was provided by the Korea Development Bank, the Korea Exchange Bank, and a host of commercial banks that were controlled by the government. Informally, considerable pressure was exerted on industries to comply with government directives, including occasional visits from President Park.

Consistent with the argument presented in *Korea's Competitive Edge*, the lack of capital or access to capital during the early developmental period bolstered the power of government.[19] Korean businesses depended on the government for financial assistance, giving the government more leverage in implementing its export goals. Another reason for government dominance was Korea's shortage of skilled entrepreneurs. Because the Japanese had dominated commercial enterprise during their long occupation, Koreans did not have many opportunities to develop their talents, except in a few select industries. Hence, Korea's selection policy was based on the government's desire to quickly fill the entrepreneurial gap by supporting those individuals who were most promising. This policy of selecting and supporting particular individuals led to the growth and prominence of the *chaebols*. In the 1970s, government-assisted *chaebols* became the leading agents of export of capital goods and related services. The *chaebol* groups have been instrumental in spurring growth in steel, shipbuilding, consumer electronics, petrochemicals, and industrial construction. To achieve the necessary economies of scale in a limited domestic market, the government allowed monopolistic production in a number of these *chaebols*.

After the general export promotion phase, a new period began (1973–1979) that featured more typical sector-oriented import substitution initiatives. The impetus behind this movement was a desire to accelerate changes in Korean comparative advantage, and attention was directed at supporting large-scale capital-intensive industries. From 1971 to 1980, per capita GNP increased from $285 to $1,605. Exports rose from $1.07 million to $17.5 million, representing a 36.4 percent increase for the nine-year period.[20] At the beginning of 1979, Korea faced enormous problems that were to continue into the 1980s. There was mounting criticism that sectoral policy was overly ambitious and had led to serious misallocation of resources. The protection and import substitution of heavy industries led to economic inefficiency and the overconcentration of power in the hands of a few *chaebols*.[21] The adverse consequences of other macroeconomic missteps surfaced: middle-class consumers were priced out of the housing market and began to spend more on consumer goods, causing shortages and pushing up inflation; bank savings were penalized by low interest rates during inflationary periods; land prices doubled and property prices soared to new heights; and, as the domestic market roared ahead, exports started to fall.[22] The second oil shock (1978–1979), which was prompted by significant oil price increases, had led to a world recession. Finally, the assassination of President Park in 1979 created considerable political uncertainty. Accordingly, Korea embarked on a more cautious path to liberalization beginning in 1979.

Phase 3: Economic Stabilization and Market Liberalization (1982–1992)

Beginning in the early 1980s, Korean firms faced both internal and external problems.[23] The free-trade environment that characterized world markets in the 1970s was yielding to increasing protectionism. Internally, there was pressure to alleviate the problems caused by the overexpansion and overconcentration brought on by past sectoral policies. It was at this time that the first stirrings in favor of greater market liberalization were felt. The shift in philosophy underlying Korea's industrial policy had been evolving since the later years of President Chun Doo Hwan's administration. The aftermath of Korea's investment in heavy industries and chemicals during 1979–1982 led to economic difficulties. This prompted government officials to move away from interventionist policies, in which the state played a critical role in allocating resources for economic development, and toward a greater emphasis on the market as a means of regulation. In December 1984, new regulations stipulated that the government would withdraw support from the *chaebols* in favor of small and medium-sized firms that were seriously undercapitalized, underdeveloped, and underfunded.

Implementing these policies proved a daunting task. The *chaebols* continued to seek government assistance for pet projects and government protection against the deleterious effects of their business failures. Despite limitations on their market activities, the *chaebols* continued to grow and diversify, increasing public antagonism toward them. Citing the traditional subordination of individuals to the greater good, these firms aggressively resisted workers' demands for higher wages and better working conditions. Initially, it was held that the absence of political democratization undermined these efforts.[24] However, when such democratization occurred in the late 1980s, the relaxing of dictatorial controls led to demands for wage increases far in excess of productivity.[25] The unwillingness of the *chaebols* to specialize, the continued problems of small and medium-sized firms, and the difficulty of balancing wage increases with productivity undermined efforts to develop and implement new industrial policies.

Following in the footsteps of President Park Chung Hee, General Chun Doo Hwan, who was elected president on August 27, 1980, maintained this posture on continued economic growth. The government's new development strategy then focused on three interrelated goals: price stability, market liberalization, and balanced economic growth. To stabilize prices, a series of tight monetary and fiscal measures were introduced to bring inflation under control. The government also controlled aggregate demand through a restrictive monetary policy that limited the annual money supply expansion rates and, in 1983, introduced a fiscal austerity program. Other government measures included the selling of commercial banks to private shareholders, the establishment of new financial institutions, increases in interest rates, reductions in interest rate subsidies for particular borrowers, and the enactment of liberalized trade control measures. To more evenly distribute economic power, the Monopoly Regulation and Fair Trade Act was introduced in 1982, and credit restraints were applied to slow down the acquisition of equity and land by weaker financial conglomerates. The act also attempted to eliminate cartel arrangements, price fixing, and other monopolistic practices. At the same time, incentives were directed at promoting a more equitable distribution of income and balanced development in all industrial sectors. Financial incentives for research and development, marketing, and industrial expansion of small and medium-sized firms were also provided. Per capita GNP increased from $1,592 in 1980 to $6,518 in 1991. After 1985, the Korean economy began to improve, with the GDP growth rate in double digits in 1986 (12.4 percent), 1987 (12.0 percent), and 1988 (11.5 percent).[26]

Domestic developments provided another stimulus for market liberalization initiatives. Increasing demands for more equitable distribution of wealth—occasionally expressed passionately in student demonstrations—had brought on severe labor disputes since the late 1980s. Between 1987 and 1992 wages rose at an average annual rate of 18 percent, with some employers claiming an even higher rate because of the inclusion of benefits and work rules. It is argued, for instance, that actual costs increased by more than 500 percent during this period.[27] With higher wages today, Korean firms have become vulnerable to competition from Malaysia, Thailand, Indonesia, and the Philippines—countries with substantially lower labor costs—for the first time in Korea's economic history.[28] Another emerging concern is that Koreans have the longest workweek in Asia (47.9 hours on the average), prompting questions as to why their standard of living is not as high as that of other nations.[29] In the past, Koreans were asked to sacrifice for the sake of the country.

For the Korean economy, the year 1991 was an ominous one. Problems were manifest in almost every measure: a slowdown in growth, continued inflationary pressures, and widening trade deficits. The GNP growth rate of 8.4 percent, down from 9.2 percent in 1990, was largely the result of overheated construction investment and private investment. The country's trade deficit hit an all-time high in 1991 of $8.73 billion—the highest in Korea's modern history. However, the situation began to improve in 1992, with continued low growth coupled with low inflation and an improved balance of payments. The GNP growth rate was at 4.8 percent in real terms, considered the lowest in twelve years.[30] The government's stability-oriented policy, aimed at cooling down the overheated economy, was one of the main reasons for this improved pattern of performance.

Some even felt that the famous Korean work ethic had begun to wane among workers and entrepreneurs alike. After seven years in power, President Chun Doo Hwan stepped aside for his military classmate, Roh Tae Woo, who was elected president on December 17, 1987. President Roh presided over the 1988 Summer Olympics and started the gradual movement toward political democratization.

ASSESSING KOREAN INDUSTRIAL POLICY

Early explanations of Korea's economic miracle emphasized neoclassical causes, such as getting fundamental policies right, and not industrial policy per se.[31] Strong linkages with international markets, high rates of investment in physical and human capital, and vigorous private enterprise were regarded as the pillars of international competitiveness. But while these explanations are credible, they are also limited; they do not entirely account for the vigorous pace of industrial development by Japan or for the success of late industrializers such as Korea.[32] Mainstream economists still explain the success of Japan and Korea in terms of neoclassical economic models, but a very different explanation has received increased attention. The fact that Japanese and Korean firms have succeeded in a wide range of industries—as opposed to a particular industry—suggests the presence of enduring institutions that create competitive advantages for them in international competition. Broadly defined, these institutions include elite autonomous bureaucracies responsible for aggressive government policies that encourage the flow of resources into selected sectors, for preferential credit allocation and direct subsidies, and for educational policies.[33]

Korea's success in industrial policy is consistent with an argument made by Stanford economist Paul Krugman, who says, "At least under some circumstances, a government by supporting firms in international competition can raise national welfare at another country's expense."[34] In a related work, he postulated four questions to ask in evaluating the effectiveness of any strategic trade policy:

1. Can strategic sectors be identified?
2. Can a strategic policy be pursued successfully?
3. Can the government be trusted to use the policy wisely?
4. How will other governments respond?[35]

Can Strategic Sectors Be Identified?

In this context, the government must know what its national interest is, and its definition of that interest must be beneficial. The Korean government—not unlike the Japanese ministries during the early stages of industrialization—targeted key sectors in which the country had a comparative advantage. As these sectors were already prevalent in the world market, making them targets for rapid technology transfers was not problematic. Perhaps one questionable area of focus was heavy industry and machinery during 1972–1981. But even this criticism can be debated. Detractors often argue against what they perceive to be *overinvestment* in these sectors (and therefore the powerful *chaebols*), not against the direction of the investment. Certainly, the success in these areas, specifically in the steel industry, paved the way for the development of large-scale production capabilities—an area that Koreans successfully leveraged in their entry into high technology.[36]

But government intervention by itself does not constitute the sufficient condition for successful industrialization. Both the British and the French had fashioned their brand of industrial policy with somewhat deleterious results, far below those attained by the Japanese and the Koreans.[37] Both the content and intent of these countries' industrial policies differed. British and French interventions appeared at later stages of the life cycle of certain products, after a period of intense competition during which so-called national champions had emerged. Japan and Korea favored a kind of "infant-industry protection" policy. Moreover, the organizational structures that supported the British and French governments' industrial policies also differed from those in Japan and Korea. A late industrializing firm is unable to protect itself by innovating further around a core technology; rather, it protects itself by routinizing a strategy of wide diversification into many technologically related mature product markets.[38] The organizational structure that evolves from this is a network or collection of technologically isolated firms. While the logic of "unbundling" technologies appears to run counter to that of vertical integration, the benefits of networking are beginning to emerge in recent discussions of networks and virtual organizations.[39] But the ability to effectively control vast networks of unrelated technologies comes in part from paternalistic control, as exemplified in the *chaebols* and in the complex webs of shared ownership that are part of the Japanese *keiretsus*.

Can a Strategic Policy Be Pursued Successfully?

Partly because of its authoritative regime, Korea was able to control competing sectors that did not benefit from government targeting. Many observers also relate Korea's successful implementation of industrial policy to its prevailing capital structures.[40]

As indicated earlier, the success of the outward-looking strategy was facilitated by tight credit allocation. The rise of the *chaebols* is associated with the regime of Park Chung Hee, which emerged following tumultuous social changes accompanying the decline of the agrarian economy in the 1950s. Early in his presidency, Park summoned ten businessmen who had been threatened with jail and the confiscation of property. He offered them exemption from criminal prosecution in return for their agreement to establish new corporations in accordance with government guidelines and to donate all of their shares in the corporations to the government.[41]

While many of these corporations were not built, this action set the pattern for a close, albeit stormy, union between government and business. Park hoped that economic growth and the improvement of living conditions would legitimize his military rule. Throughout his career, he was determined to discourage wasteful activities and to encourage businessmen to invest in the productive economy of the country. His revolutionary fervor set the stage for intermittent crackdowns on certain forms of real-estate speculation, corruption, and black-market activities. However, it was Park's decision to confiscate large shareholdings in banks, as well as to place the Bank of Korea under the control of the Ministry of Finance, that secured his control over the entire financial system.

In this context, money was channeled to productive investment. In the absence of well-defined financing alternatives, this all but ensured the effective implementation of Park's targeting policies. For example, a favored firm, such as one producing textiles for the export market, would receive subsidies or funding at favorable rates, while those businesses with a low priority, such as the manufacture of noodles, would have to rely on retained earnings or loans from the curb market, which were more expensive.[42]

Another key institution that supported the previous industrial policies was the emphasis placed by Korean companies on shop-floor production operations.[43] Alfred Chandler argues that big business succeeds in a new environment by making a three-pronged investment: (1) it must invest in plants large enough to realize economies of scale, (2) it must invest in distribution channels after these plants have been established, and (3) it must invest in management—both at the top of the organization and in the middle rung of each operating unit.[44] Korean firms did all three.

The plants they invested in were large, and most business groups emphasized human resource development of the middle and lower managers at the plant level where foreign technology had to be infused, adapted, and improved to become a competitive weapon. Korean firms established corporate cultures that were conducive to the adaptation and assimilation of foreign technology. First, the professional middle managers they hired tended to have technical backgrounds. Between 1960 and 1980, the number of engineers rose by a factor of 10:2, the number of general managers by 2:2.[45] Second, management generally kept in close contact with the ranks. The differences in managerial layers between large and small enterprises are narrow, suggesting the effectiveness and utility of shop-floor operators who needed far less supervision than their American counterparts. In the case of the Pohang Iron and Steel Company, Ltd. (POSCO)—a state-owned integrated enterprise created in 1968—its best managers were assigned to line rather than to staff positions. Moreover, POSCO emphasized on-the-job training for all technical managers. Newly recruited engineers were required to work on all three shifts so as to become familiar with every operation. The staff of the quality control department had to work in the plant for three months.[46]

Can the Government Be Trusted to Use Policies Wisely?

MIT economist Alice Amsden distinguishes early industrialization, based on invention and innovation, from late industrialization, based on learning.[47] Specifically, she contends that industrialization without the competitive asset of novel products and processes creates a common set of institutions in countries as diverse as Korea, Taiwan, India, Brazil, Mexico, and Turkey. As in the case of Japan, the government of Korea has consistently intervened in the private sector to promote its goals. This form of intervention through subsidies is undertaken deliberately to distort market prices for the sake of stimulating economic activity. Conventional developmental theory posits that latecomers industrialize by "getting the prices right"—that is, by allowing supply and demand to determine prices. In this context, government intervention is justified on the basis of market failure—that is, imperfect competition, external economic factors, or uneven distribution of information that hinders the efficiency and competitiveness of the marketplace. In fact, successful late industrializers such as Japan and Korea used subsidies to lower production to get prices "wrong"—that is, to prevent market forces from determining prices so as to overcome the handicap of the absence of any proprietary technology. Therefore, a necessary condition of industrialization in the twentieth century has been a systematic and well-coordinated government intervention that promotes manufacturing investment.

For Korean *chaebols*, the belief was that they had the support of government because of its vision of industrialization fixated on size and market power. Amsden argues that the Korean government had to intervene and provide subsidies because the competitive weapon of lower wages had been all but undermined by the higher productivity levels of the advanced countries. The full argument goes as follows:

The Korean government offered generous subsidies to stimulate exports, including subsidizing long-term loans to targeted industries and firms that are not included in calculations of the "effective exchange rates." . . . The Korean government offered generous subsidies first as a response to the political demands of the spinners' and weavers' cartel, later as an article of faith in an industrialization strategy. . . .

> *The subsidy serves as a useful symbol of late industrialization, not just in Korea and Taiwan but also in Japan, the Latin American countries, and so on. The First Industrial Revolution was built on laissez faire, the Second on infant protection. In late industrialization, the foundation is the subsidy—which includes both protection and financial incentives. The allocation of subsidies has rendered the government not merely a banker . . . but . . . an entrepreneur, using the subsidy to decide what, when, and how much to produce.*[48]

But how does this distinguish Korea from other countries that also had the benefit of government subsidy? Two points are noteworthy here. First, the Korean government disciplined all recipients of aid, including friendly political allies, by imposing performance standards. Ties of reciprocity developed between the government and business; the delivery of export goals ensured continued financing. Second, Korea, at the time, had supporting infrastructures that facilitated compliance with these government policies. These supports included tight restrictions on credit and capital for industrial expansion, strong bureaucracies and technocrats, relatively controlled wage increases, and a focus on shop-floor engineering that placed a premium on learning and reverse engineering.[49]

How Will Other Governments Respond?

Korea's success was also facilitated by the United States, which helped Korea for geopolitical reasons, and by Japan, which exported technology to Korea. At the time, both viewed Korea as a fledgling state in need of developmental support. The end of the Cold War, however, shifted the focus of policy from a political/military agenda to an economic one. Trade relations between nations became more significant, and they were characterized by feverish protectionist policies.[50]

The declining competitive position of the United States and Japan's continued economic success focused attention on government intervention (that is, import targeting) in Japan's private sector—considered by critics to be a form of nontariff barrier. Because Korea pursued similar policies, it also became a target of criticism.[51] The 1993 Uruguay Round agreements and the formation of the World Trade Organization (WTO) in 1994 as a unified structure to settle international disputes have been significant developments in the world trading system.[52] According to Associate Secretary Lee Hong-kyu, the WTO requires member nations to drastically remove import barriers and to abolish direct industrial subsidies within a given grace period.[53] Lee adds, "Instead of providing directly tax and financial incentives to industries, the [Korean] government can now only assist industrial development indirectly through investment in technology, human capital and infrastructure."[54]

CURRENT CHALLENGES AND THE "FIVE-YEAR PLAN FOR THE NEW ECONOMY" (1993–1997)

At the onset of the 1990s, new challenges emerged that threatened to undermine Korea's success in industrial policy. As described earlier, protectionism among trading nations became prevalent. Regional blocks that threatened the free multitrading system of the past three decades emerged. And the income distribution in Korea, which had been relatively equitable, began to widen, creating labor problems and fomenting social unrest.

A new alignment between business and government called for less government intervention and more business autonomy. The policy of "internal liberalization" was introduced to minimize government interference and to free the private sector to be guided by market incentives. In the early 1990s, the Korean government abolished several laws for promoting strategic sectors, such as the machinery and electronic industries. Tax and financial incentives were also curtailed. The second thrust, called "external liberalization," opened up the domestic market to greater foreign competition and stimulus.[55]

In 1992, Kim Young Sam became Korea's first directly elected civilian head of state in more than thirty years. His government moved early in 1993 to shift Korea's industrial policy from producer capitalism to market efficiency.[56] The intent was to enhance Korea's industrial competitiveness. Four main strategies were to be pursued: (1) promotion of technological innovation and the establishment of a system promoting the efficient flow of information; (2) modification of education and training systems; (3) enhanced efficiency of the private sector and industrial organizations, through the strengthening of small and medium-sized companies; (4) expansion of the infrastructure, such as the transportation system. Korea's problems and its plans for resolving them were incorporated into President Kim's "Five-Year Plan for the New Economy" in 1993. The major elements of this plan are presented in table 3-1. Under this new policy, the government is to assist industrial adjustment only indirectly, through investment in technology, human capital, and infrastructure. In lieu of direct taxes and financial incentives to industries, the Korean government has launched a wide-ranging program of deregulation, with the aim of facilitating industrial adjustment by eliminating entry barriers, streamlining socioeconomic regu-

Table 3-1 Goals of the 1993–1997 Five-Year Plan for the New Economy

1. Enhancing Growth Potential

- Promotion of industrial structural development
- Establishment of rules for fair competition
- Promotion of technology development
- Facilitation of informatization
- Development of small and medium-sized firms
- Human resources development and reform of industrial relations
- Balanced regional development
- Expansion of SOC and reform of infrastructure
- Efficient use of energy and resources

2. Strengthening Internalization

- Active participation in the world economic order
- Facilitating inbounding and outbounding investments
- Enhancing international competitiveness and cooperation
- Economic cooperation between South and North Korea

3. Improving the Living Environment

- Enhancing housing supply
- Protection of environment
- Alleviation of transportation problems
- Improvement of social welfare
- Protection of consumer rights

Source: Adapted from Hong-kyu Lee, "Industrial Success and Business Concentration" (speech given at the Lundquist College of Business, University of Oregon, May 22, 1995). Reprinted by permission.

lations, simplifying administrative procedures, and inducing foreign competition. Achievement of these goals, however, hinges on changing the mentality of frontline government officials with respect to the role of public service.[57] In summary, the goals of Korea's most recent economic five-year plan are to: (1) create a healthy economy characterized by economic vibrancy and national competitiveness, (2) achieve a "just" economy in which efforts to improve the competitiveness of all firms—large and small—are rewarded, and (3) develop a forward-looking economy that anticipates future global changes and prepares for future unification with North Korea.[58]

Although the restructuring of the *chaebols* is not formally articulated in the plan, it is an important part of achieving greater competitiveness across all sectors. The *chaebols'* quest for globalization that is leveraged from a highly diversified structure is challenged by the government's intent on making the *chaebols* more specialized. (This issue is addressed in chapter 4.)

The new industrial policy is also intent on fostering small and medium-sized industries and stimulating regional economies. The objective is to alleviate the long-standing structural and regional disequilibrium of the Korean economy. The purpose of promoting small and medium-sized companies is to foster their competitiveness in areas once dominated by large, highly concentrated conglomerates. In more developed economies, small and medium-sized companies act as key suppliers of intermediary inputs, such as specialized parts and components, to large assembling industries operated by conglomerates. Many Koreans have viewed small and medium-sized companies as contributing to a decrease in industrial competitiveness in the assembly industries. The weakness of the parts and components industry, in particular, has been a crucial factor in Korea's chronic trade deficits with Japan. It is believed that a significant trade imbalance with any major trading partner is counterproductive to the sustained growth of Korean exports. Some economists point out that the trade structure should be reshaped from the present triangular relationship of trade deficits with Japan and trade surpluses with the United States, as is common among Asian countries. It is hoped that a dynamically competitive and diverse population of small and medium-sized firms will revitalize the economy. (The content and implications of this policy are developed further in chapter 5.)

The Korean government believes that it can restore balanced bilateral trade with Japan by improving the technological competitiveness of its industries, aggressively penetrating Japanese markets, and creating an environment for diversifying imports. In this context, the recent sharp increase in the value of the Japanese yen against the dollar represents a favorable factor for import diversification. Since the mid-1980s, various supportive measures have been institutionalized. Efforts have focused on providing existing firms with tax and financial supports and increasing the number of new start-ups of competitive smaller firms. The government has also attempted to make supporting measures more effective by consolidating them and by increasing their linkage effects, including the dissemination of industrial and technology information (as discussed in chapter 7). The Economic Planning Board's projections, based on the above assumptions, are shown in table 3-2.

To summarize, the success of previous industrial policies was facilitated by the proper identification of strategic sectors, the ability of the Korean

Table 3-2 Government Projections for the Korean Economy

	1996	1997	1998
Growth Rate			
GNP	7.3%	7.2%	7.1%
Total consumption	6.3	6.3	6.3
Fixed investment	7.6	9.0	9.3
Exports	9.1	8.3	8.2
Imports	7.7	8.3	8.6
Balance of International Payments ($ billions)			
Exports	$115.8	$129.7	$145.0
(% increase)	12.5%	12.0%	11.8%
Imports	$107.0	$118.3	$131.2
(% increase)	10.0%	10.6%	10.9%
Trade balance	$8.8	$11.4	$13.8
Per Capita GNP ($)	$11,030	$12,681	$14,506

Source: Korean Ministry of Finance and Economy Report (Seoul: Ministry of Finance and Economy, 1995).

government to implement these policies, the performance restrictions imposed by the government on the *chaebols* to comply, and the indifference of other governments to Korea's "infant-protection" and trading policies. The winds of change threaten such institutions. Institutions that had supported Korea's policies in the past are no longer functional. The changing structure of credit allocation, specifically the deregulation of the banking sector, limits the government's ability to intervene in the private sector. Moreover, foreign governments are no longer content to allow Korea to pursue past practices, particularly its restriction of foreign entry into its domestic market, and are more likely to respond with protectionist measures of their own should past practices continue. As Korea moves away from export-led industrial policies to the twin goals of globalization and liberalization, the challenge is to pace the rate of developments arising from them in ways that will maximize the benefits of global reach and minimize macroeconomic dislocations at home. Such issues are developed further in the next chapters.

CHAPTER FOUR

Restructuring the Chaebols

When Academy Award–winning filmmaker Steven Spielberg joined forces with producers Jeffrey Katzenberg and David Geffen to form the DreamWorks production company in 1995, the largest single investment—more than $300 million—did not come from New York, London, Tokyo, or even Hollywood. It came from Seoul and was made by Miky Lee, the granddaughter of Samsung founder B. C. Lee. The funds were transferred to DreamWorks through Cheil Foods and Chemicals Company, a Samsung Group company. Insiders wondered if Korea had discovered Hollywood, much like the Japanese had a decade earlier. Rumors circulated about other possible Korean investments in film companies, such as Columbia or MCA. What were the Koreans up to, investors wondered. In point of fact, the Korean firms were doing what they had long been doing: making huge investments in somewhat risky ventures in the hope of reaping major financial returns.

Samsung is not alone in attempting such endeavors. Indeed, a principal characteristic of the major *chaebols* is a strong entrepreneurial orientation that encourages risk taking on a grand scale. This is combined with a tradition of family control of the management of the firms to ensure that the owners' wishes are strictly followed. However, as Korean firms move to join the global economic community, both internal and external forces are at work that are changing the way they do business. The traditional high-risk "bet-your-company" mentality characterized by making quick decisions based on gut instinct is giving way to a more thoughtful and analytic approach to investment strategy.

These changes have several sources of influence. They are influenced by government shifts in industrial and economic policy, combined with an increasing reluctance of the government to underwrite corporate risks; by increasing pressures for "fair trade" from Korea's major trading partners; and by shifts in management strategy and corporate governance patterns. Whatever the reason, however, the traditional Korean *chaebol* is evolving fairly quickly into a new form of competitive machine. This rapid evolution represents both a threat and an opportunity for such firms. We identify it here as the second major challenge facing contemporary companies in Korea.

TRADITIONAL CHARACTERISTICS OF THE *CHAEBOL*

To understand the changes in Korea's economic policy and the ways in which these changes will influence the ability of the *chaebols* to become true global competitors, it is first necessary to consider how such firms evolved structurally. Until recently, the typical *chaebol* structure resembled the early Japanese *zaibatsu* model in place before World War II. Indeed, *chaebol* and *zaibatsu* share the same Chinese characters when written. Korean firms were closely held and managed in a paternalistic manner by male family members. Indeed, if we look inside a typical Korean firm, several key characteristics stand out, including reliance on family control and management, an entrepreneurial orientation, strong paternalistic leadership, centralized planning and coordination, close business-government relations, and the importance of strong school ties (see figure 4-1). Let us look at each of these factors briefly.

Family Control and Management

Following Confucian tradition, the family or clan plays a central role in contemporary Korea. Family members are keenly aware of their lineage and help one another when needed. Above all, the family acts as a unit and supports its members steadfastly. It is therefore not surprising that many companies organized and managed over the past several decades have been family owned and controlled.

Unlike their Japanese counterparts, many Korean companies are tightly controlled by families through stock ownership. An example is Hyundai, where most of the companies that make up the group are at least 50 percent owned by the founder and his family or by other companies controlled by the founder.[1] A review of other major Korean companies reveals similar

Figure 4-1 Traditional Characteristics of the *Chaebol*

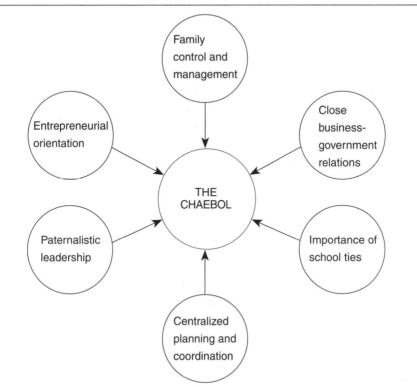

patterns of ownership and control. This finding, too, is not surprising in view of the relatively short history of the *chaebols* and the traditional Korean allocation of family responsibility (eldest sons typically inherit most family property as well as responsibility for it and the family).

In addition to family ownership, there has also been active family participation in company management. While there is a recent trend toward recruiting more executives from outside the family, "management by family" remains a strong tradition. Thus, when Hyundai reorganized in 1995, founder Chung's sons emerged in key administrative positions in most of the group's companies. Still, it is important to note that a major consequence of the management revolution of the early 1990s (see chapter 8) has been a reduction in both the number and power of family members in executive positions. Ability—not relationships—is becoming more critical in determining career success than it was just a few short years ago.

Entrepreneurial Orientation

The second traditional characteristic of Korean firms is their distinct entrepreneurial bent, which can be traced to the personalities of the founders
and the nature of Korean society. Because of the drive and ambition of
founders such as Chung of Hyundai, Lee of Samsung, and Kim of Daewoo,
and because of the unique nature of business-government relations in Korea
(see chapter 3), the conditions conducive to entrepreneurial efforts were
clearly present. During the past thirty years, many Korean businessmen
attempted to start new companies. What separated the successful businessman from the unsuccessful was often entrepreneurial talent. As Kumho's
former President Park noted in an interview, "We [Korean entrepreneurs]
would try new things and fail and sell the business and try again. . . .
Hunger. Drive. Only entrepreneurs take the necessary risks to succeed."[2]
    Several characteristics are typical of this entrepreneurial flair:

- *A clear-cut vision.* Most successful founders began their companies
  with a fairly clear-cut vision of what they wanted their businesses
  to be. In many cases, these efforts were initiated with government
  support and encouragement. Business leaders sought opportunities
  in the marketplace, chose their product lines carefully, and implemented highly developed business plans designed to meet these
  objectives.

- *Solid political skills.* Successful founders exhibited keen political skills.
  They had to convince the Korean government that their plans had
  merit and would contribute to economic development. Without this
  key support at the highest levels of government, the *chaebols* would
  never have received the necessary financing for new ventures. The
  vast majority of new financing came from the government or government-controlled banks, not from stocks or venture capitalists.

- *Active pursuit of the business.* Successful founders and their managers
  pursued their businesses aggressively and relentlessly. The entrepreneurs who founded the "Big Four" *chaebols* described in chapter 2
  illustrate this point.

- *Keen insight.* It has been argued that the founders of successful ventures
  had keen insight, which led them to make appropriate decisions
  and to hire and promote the right people. As one executive we
  interviewed observed, "We Koreans are as sophisticated as the Americans and other international competitors, but we tend to follow our
  instincts much more."[3] This is not to imply that Korean executives

tend to make hasty decisions; rather, this seemingly impulsive behavior is borne of years of watching and observing business markets around the world.

- *Good fortune.* As might be expected, at least some of the success of these entrepreneurs can be traced to good fortune. Economic opportunities that emerged were quickly exploited, often leading to new opportunities. For example, in the mid-1980s, one frequently heard about the "age of the three lows," meaning low oil prices, low currency valuation, and low interest rates. Because of this, and because of the concomitant rise in the value of the Japanese yen, Korean companies were able to move quickly into Western markets and capture considerable market share.

An example of this entrepreneurial drive can be seen in Chairman Chung of Hyundai. In the early 1970s, Hyundai set out to build Korea's biggest shipyard. The company had no experience building ships—not even a rowboat—and experts were certain the venture would fail. However, Chung had made up his mind. "A ship has an engine inside and an exterior made of steel. . . . Ships resemble power plants, which Hyundai has built many times," he observed.[4] With these words he inspired his subordinates and went on to accomplish the task. Chung succeeded for many reasons. He had market knowledge and a business plan, he had capable employees willing to work long hours to make the venture succeed, and he had government support that allowed for financing and a quasi-monopolistic business environment. However, in addition to this, he had an entrepreneurial drive and the instinct to recognize an opportunity and plan accordingly. This story is repeated over and over in the history of modern Korean business enterprise.

A second example is Lee Byung-Chull of Samsung. In his autobiography, published shortly before his death in 1987, Lee described his continual struggle to overcome the many obstacles he encountered in his quest to build a major enterprise. Founded in 1938 with a total capital of $2,000 and forty employees, the Samsung (meaning "three stars" in Korean) Company was enjoying limited growth as a small trading company when the 1950 communist invasion into the South forced Lee to leave his major operations in Seoul. His inventories were stolen (by soldiers and politicians on both sides of the conflict, according to Lee), and he was left with practically nothing. Retreating back to Taegu, where the company had been founded, Lee met with the manager and staff of his last remaining enterprise, Choson Brewery. When he told of his plight, the manager replied simply, "Mr. President, there is nothing to worry about. We have some savings and with these funds you can start the new business that you want."[5] Moving to Pusan in 1951, Lee used the funds to create Samsung Trading Co., and within one year corporate assets increased twenty-fold.

The company continued to prosper as it moved increasingly into manufacturing. In 1965, Lee determined that his next project would be the building of the largest fertilizer company in the world. (Fertilizer was in short supply and high demand as Korea's agricultural sector was expanding.) With loans of $42 million and licensed technology and technical assistance from Mitsui of Japan, he quickly received government approval for the project and selected Ulsan as a building site. Many people from different walks of life—including many business leaders—felt the venture was too risky. After all, how could "little Korea" attempt to build such a major enterprise? But Lee set about his new project with characteristic vigor. He personally selected the project manager, and for the next eighteen months the manager slept and ate with construction crews, leaving his family at home. When construction was nearly 80 percent complete, the government charged Samsung with smuggling illegal goods from Japan to finance its construction costs. While the company argued that the sale had been a clerical oversight, the government (and government-controlled newspapers) did not ease up their pursuit of a scandal. Lee's second son was arrested by the government. (What was not brought out until much later was that Lee had been approached before the scandal by a high-ranking politician who asked for—but did not receive—a "donation" of 30 percent of Korea Fertilizer's stock.) Talk of the scandal continued until Lee agreed to a proposal to donate the entire fertilizer plant to the government after first completing the facility at his own expense. The scandal dissolved, and his son was released from jail.

About the same time, Lee also decided to enter the mass communication business. As he tells it, "I consulted with [Korean] President Park about this and he gave his consent on the spot. Immediately, he telephoned Mr. Hong Jong-Chull, the Minister of Culture and Information, and directed him to support me positively on this project. Thus, Radio Seoul began its broadcast."[6] Shortly thereafter, a television station, Tongyang Television Broadcasting Corporation (TTBC), was added, followed by a daily newspaper, the *Joong-ang Daily News*. Working under the credo "The best facilities, the best treatment, and the best people produce the best quality goods," all three ventures proved highly successful. However, the editorial policies of these news outlets were not always to the government's liking. While not confronting the government directly, Lee's telecasts and publications advocated morality in government, a message not lost on many people. Shortly after President Park was assassinated, President Chun took control, and the government declared that all private television stations would be merged into the government-owned Korean Broadcasting System. TTBC and the new ten-story building Lee had just finished building were turned over to the government on November 30, 1980.

Thus, three times in his career Lee had experienced a major setback and financial loss. Yet each time, Chairman Lee recovered and with a loyal cadre of employees went on to build Samsung into an even bigger and stronger company than it had been.

The stories of Hyundai's Chung Ju-Yung and Samsung's Lee Byung-Chull illustrate a fairly typical pattern of growth and development for other major companies, including LG, Daewoo, Ssangyong, and Sunkyong. Such examples are vivid evidence of the dedication and achievement of Korean entrepreneurs. They also show how conditions for growth were created to some extent by supportive government policies and close business-government relationships. Finally, because of a unique set of circumstances that were present in Korea, stories like Hyundai's and Samsung's also present evidence that Korean companies are in many ways distinct from most companies in the West.

Paternalistic Leadership

A third feature of many *chaebols* is that they are managed by one central, paternalistic figure. The CEO, often the founder, typically assumes personal responsibility for the performance of every aspect of the firm. Consequently, he is likely to centralize decision making and authority to ensure tight controls. Moreover, such a leader usually assumes a personal interest in the welfare and development of his employees. This facet of Korean management follows naturally from the Confucian values of the society; the CEO is a quasi-father figure and as such is to be obeyed in all matters.

In most *chaebols*, the chairman meets regularly with his group of presidents. For example, at Hyundai, the chairman meets every Monday and Friday morning with the forty or so presidents. The chairman asks each president a series of questions concerning corporate activities and settles pressing issues on the spot. At Daewoo, the group presidents' meeting is attended by the chairman, two deputy chairmen, and about ten presidents in charge of the more important business fields, such as foreign trade, construction, shipbuilding, electronics, automobiles, and so forth. And at LG Group, a management committee reporting to the chairman meets regularly to make primary strategic decisions for the company. Hence, this "presidents' group" emerges as a central vehicle through which the group chairmen discuss corporate activities and issue directives regarding present and future activities of the company. Throughout this process the role of the chairman is usually paramount.

Centralized Planning and Coordination

Partly because of the nature of family-based management and strong authoritarian leadership, the fourth characteristic of most Korean corporations has historically been the existence of a central planning function whose representatives work closely with the group chairmen in reaching decisions and developing strategic plans for future corporate actions. This function has also served to effectively coordinate resource allocation across the various enterprises in such a way that highly complex ventures typically meet with success.

Most *chaebols* have a planning group, known variously as the planning and coordination office, the central planning office, or the office of the chairman. The size of this group varies considerably, with Hyundai's consisting of approximately forty managers and Samsung's having more than two hundred. Typically, the planning group resides organizationally in the nucleus company, such as Hyundai Construction Co., and as such often appears to be an organ of that particular company instead of the *chaebol* as a whole. The cost of maintaining the planning group is apportioned to all companies in the *chaebol*, and the planning group is typically headed by its own "president." Senior members of the office staff often carry the title of senior managing director or managing director.

The primary function of the planning group historically has been to collect, analyze, and present useful information to the chairman for future decision making. Typically, the representative from each member company explains to the president of the planning group what his company has accomplished and what it plans to do. This information is then organized and passed onto the chairman prior to the next presidents' meeting. At this meeting, then, the chairman can ask questions of the various presidents from a position of current (and, it is hoped, accurate) knowledge, and relevant decisions can be made. Other responsibilities typically assigned to the planning office include conducting regular and unscheduled visits to all companies; planning new business ventures, formulating group strategy; and conducting public relations, advertising, and legal activities on behalf of the whole group. All of these activities are conducted under the close scrutiny of the chairman.

Finally, the planning group often plays a major role in personnel decisions. At Hyundai, for example, the Personnel Affairs Committee is chaired by the president of the Planning and Coordination Office. This committee is largely responsible for screening, hiring, and assigning all new college graduates hired by the company, thereby ensuring continuity and quality across the various units. Other companies have similar practices. This committee is usually also responsible for transferring personnel between the various companies and for overseeing the overall salary and bonus system. Hence, in most Korean corporations, centralized planning, coordination, and decision making are of great importance.

Close Business-Government Relations

Until recently, the economic foundations of modern Korea rested firmly on a close and mutually beneficial relationship between business and government. While the strength of this relationship is clearly diminishing, the fact remains that a key to the *chaebols'* success has been their usefulness to the government as an instrument for economic development. The government used its power through preferential loans and interest rates, through licensing authorizations, and through inclusion of certain companies in its recurring five-year economic development plans to select and then guide those chosen for success. To be successful, it was thus essential for the *chaebol* to be well-connected. Being well-connected meant having to support the incumbent political party, make donations to the right causes, and succeed with government-sponsored ventures. Failure to do any of the above could—and sometimes did—lead to a termination of financing and sometimes bankruptcy. At the very least, it could land a company and its chairman in court.

A recent example can be seen in the conflict between Hyundai and the government in the early 1990s. When former Chairman Chung Ju-Yung formed the United People's Party and ran for president of Korea against Kim Young-sam in 1992, he allegedly made use of corporate funds and employees to help run his campaign. During the campaign, Chung criticized Kim and his Democratic Liberal Party for not reducing Korea's trade deficit and for interfering with business operations. After winning the election, President Kim immediately initiated a tax audit of Hyundai and its founder.

Chung was convicted of tax evasion and given a three-year suspended sentence. A short while later, when Chairman Chey of Sunkyong also criticized the government's economic policies, he too was investigated by Kim's government until he quickly recanted his position. Likewise, Samsung's Chairman Lee Kun Hee was punished by President Kim's administration in 1995 when he publicly criticized the Korean government for being "second-class."[7] In response to Chairman Lee's public statement, the Korean government immediately stopped all government loans to Samsung, blocked a public fund-raising initiative, and temporarily derailed Samsung's high-profile bid to buy controlling interest in the American firm AST Research. Thus, even today, in a more democratic Korea, companies and their powerful chairmen can pay dearly for criticizing the national government.[8]

One way Korean companies try to stay in the government's good graces is to hire retiring key government employees into the company as executives. Since government retirement age has historically been fifty-five and corporate retirement age among top executives is somewhat more flexible, this practice benefits both parties—the company gets a well-placed and well-connected bureaucrat and the bureaucrat continues to earn income. Many other countries, including the United States, engage in similar practices of hiring key government employees, most notably in the defense industry. However, this practice is clearly waning in Korea as corporations require more professional managers to meet the increasing demands of global competition. Even so, a fairly close relationship between business and government remains a hallmark of many of the major *chaebols*.

While observers have often called this close business-government relationship "Korea, Inc.," as in "Japan, Inc.," a clear distinction between the two countries is necessary. In Japan, the relationship between business and government is typically one of mutual consensus among relative equals on policy decisions. In Japan, for example, many major firms have their own banks as part of their organizational structure and are thus assured of a reliable source of credit; they do not require government financing. In Korea, by contrast, it has been the government that sets the policies and the businesses that typically follow. And Korean firms have not been allowed to own banks until recently. As a result, the Korean government has traditionally controlled the firm's access to capital. It is certainly not an equal partnership. Government disfavor, brought on for whatever reason, can bring about a loss of credit and financial ruin, even in today's changing environment. As a result, it is sometimes said that Korea represents an unusual blend of free enterprise and state direction.[9]

Importance of School Ties

A final characteristic of many of Korea's major companies is the importance they place on educational credentials. In South Korea, the university—and to a lesser extent the high school—one attends is crucial to one's later advancement in a career. While there are a number of excellent schools and universities in Korea, the more prestigious the institution, the better it is for one's career (which is not very unlike the situation in the United States). Clearly, the three most prestigious universities are Seoul National University, Yonsei University, and Korea University. Graduation from one of these schools typically guarantees a student a job with one of the best companies. This link between going to the "right" school and success can be seen in the case of Daewoo, where more than half of the top executives (including the chairman) all went to the prestigious Kyunggi High School; most also attended Yonsei University, as did the chairman. Similarly, at Sunkyong, Seoul National University graduates currently occupy 50 percent of the group's directors and high-level officials.[10] In fact, one study conducted in 1988 found that 62 percent of the top executives in seven leading companies (excluding founders and their successors) attended Seoul National University.[11] When Yonsei and Korea Universities were included, this percentage increased to 84 percent. These three universities provide more than four out of five of Korea's top managers. This same trend can be seen in the middle and lower echelons of management, although the percentages decrease.

When Korean managers first meet, one of their first questions concerns where the other person went to school. The discovery that they both went to the same high school or university—even at different times—often creates a tie and brings a feeling of closeness. These ties help define who the employee is in the organization and indicate a degree of status. Such ties benefit a person throughout his career.

THE NEW CORPORATE CHARTER: FROM COMMAND LEADERSHIP TO MARKET DISCIPLINE

Clearly, the success of Korea's major firms has been influenced by the six traditional characteristics just described, many of which have their roots in neo-Confucianism. However, while it is important to understand this basis for past successes, it is also important to realize that the basis for future competition is rapidly changing. And therein lies the second major challenge facing Korean firms. An important imperative that arose from President Kim's "Five-Year Plan for the New Economy," as discussed in the previous chapter, is the need to reform the structure of the *chaebols* so they can better contribute to Kim's overall plan for *segeyhwa*. Change is indeed coming in the way Korean firms conduct business.

The emerging *chaebols* were the engines of growth in Korea's postwar economy. They are viewed as a major institution in the late industrializing stage.[12] Because of their dominating presence, the *chaebols* have been associated with excessive market power and regarded as a significant obstacle to the development of small and medium-sized firms. Not surprisingly, policies to mitigate or curb the power of the *chaebols* have been justified on the basis of either efficiency and growth or equity and fairness.[13] The dilemma facing Korea is that the growth of the *chaebols* and national economic performance are closely linked. Thus, restructuring policies were eased during times of economic recession, only to be strengthened again during times of growth.[14] While favorable *chaebol* performance often results in good economic periods, the growth and perceived power of these organizations have aroused anti-*chaebol* sentiments among the Korean people, as reflected in presidential campaigns in 1987 and 1992.

The growth of the *chaebols* and their ensuing economic power have aroused the public ire and provided the impetus for reform. Although economic concentration is the salient issue, Koreans are also concerned about the *chaebols'* paternalistic management, which they believe to be the source of the *chaebols'* inner-directedness and alleged lack of concern for the general welfare of the people. Owing to the economic centrality of the *chaebols*, reforming them through increased specialization and professional management has broad implications for Korea's new economic program.

Economic Concentration and Paternalistic Management

The economic concentration of *chaebols* presents the possibility of deleterious social effects.[15] It is estimated that the top thirty *chaebols* accounted for about 30 percent of the country's GNP manufacturing sector alone[16] and for about 35 percent of Korea's total shipments in 1990.[17] In terms of revenue, the top thirty *chaebols* were equal to about 80 percent of Korea's GDP in 1992.[18] The pattern of economic concentration shared by the top thirty *chaebols* does not appear to have changed significantly over time. In fact, the concentration shared by the top five *chaebols* has been increasing, from 9.1 percent of total employment in 1977 to 9.9 percent in 1987, and from 15.7 percent in the concentration of shipment in 1977 to 22 percent in 1987.[19]

This pattern of economic concentration has abetted the popular perception that the *chaebols* have benefited considerably from government subsidies but have not shared their wealth with the rest of society. Given this concentration of wealth, the *chaebols* are expected to take some responsibility for the employment and social welfare of Korea's citizens. Most Korean companies, unlike their American counterparts, are controlled by families through stock ownership. Mentioned earlier in the chapter was the example of Hyundai, where sixteen of the twenty-four companies that make up the group are at least 50 percent owned by the group founder or by other companies directly controlled by the founder.[20] As of 1995, the in-group shareholding ratio for Hyundai was 61.3 percent; it averaged about 42.7 percent for the top thirty *chaebols*. Current policies are directed at reducing the cross-holdings among firms within the *chaebols* as well as the family shareholding ratio.

Because of their high concentration, *chaebols* are also associated with being monopolistic—a concern for the Korean public. In 1995, for example, 316 firms in 138 markets were designated as market-dominating firms.[21] Market-dominating firms are annually designated by the Fair Trade Commission under the criteria of market size and market share, and their abusive practices are prohibited by the Fair Trade Act. Many of the market-dominating firms in various sectors of the economy are, in fact, affiliates or subsidiaries of the major *chaebols*. Noncompetitive conduct by the *chaebols* includes mutual forbearance, reciprocal dealings, and other unfair methods of competition based on a *chaebol's* intragroup transactions of commodities and financial resources.

Although these activities are of concern to the Korean government, many argue that these arrangements can be justified in terms of the *chaebols'* efficiency and of the protection they offer against foreign takeover. Even though multimarket monopolistic behavior is possible, the *chaebols'* individual market position in world sectors appears small and highly vulnerable. Indeed, many argue that Korean companies are not particularly large when compared with other world-class firms, especially in Japan and the United States. In fact, size is simply one of many determinants of a firm's competitiveness. Simple statistics cannot explain the success of Samsung Electronics and Hyundai Motors.[22] Whether the Korean people agree seems to be another matter.

Risk and Diversification

Large, diversified groups abound in other countries as well.[23] Compared with these groups, however, Korean *chaebols* are distinctive in terms of their degree of diversification and economic concentration. Alice Amsden argues that the *chaebols'* size has enabled them to diversify into related and unrelated industries.[24] The diversification patterns of the *chaebols* into related and unrelated industries are compared with those of their American and Japanese counterparts in table 4-1.

Korean, American, and Japanese groupings are distinguished by their unrelated diversified industries; in the Korean *chaebols*, for example, the average number of industries within each *chaebol* is thirty. Despite the unrelatedness of their diversification strategies, Korean *chaebols* exhibit performance patterns different from those of their American and Japanese counterparts. While the most successful *chaebols* are highly diversified, they also exhibit higher profitability. In fact, some of the specialized *chaebols* of the 1960s and 1970s went out of business.[25] This contrasts with the experience of American conglomerates.

The current administration's guidelines for reforming the *chaebols* put their historical role in the country's development in sharp focus. In the mid-1980s, *chaebols* cooperated with the government because its support and protection were the keys to successful operation. However, with the rapid growth of *chaebols* after the heavy and chemical industry drives of the 1970s, and ensuing liberalization directives, the relationship between government and *chaebol* has been significantly altered. By far the most important role of the government in the past was that of underwriter.[26] The government has traditionally feared the bankruptcy of *chaebols*. Accordingly, in the era of government-led support, this function of insurer was regarded as a return for the support provided by business. Many believed that government was responsible for the failure of *chaebols*. In the current situation, the *chaebols* may perceive the national economy as hostage to

Table 4-1 International Comparison of Diversification by Business

Type of Diversification	Korea	Japan	United States
Related industry	6.1%	39.9%	45.2%
Unrelated industry	57.1	6.8	19.5

Source: Adapted from Seong Min Yoo, "Korean Business Conglomerates: Misconceptions, Realities, and Policies," in *Korean Economy 1995* (Washington, D.C.: Korea Economic Institute of America, 1995), 16.

possible failures. One way out of this vicious cycle is for government to abandon its role as an insurer and let ailing firms fail.[27] The *chaebols*, meanwhile, should attach the greatest importance to improving efficiency and worldwide competitiveness.

Initiative to Specialize

President Kim presented a bold plan to restructure the *chaebols*, aiming to transform them from highly diversified export-driven conglomerates into lean, highly focused international competitors. The plan calls for the thirty top *chaebols* to select between three and four core businesses for future development and to divest the rest. This initiative responds to three principal government concerns:

- First, the sheer size and diversified structure of *chaebols* were viewed as harmful to the development of small and medium-sized Korean enterprises. In effect, the *chaebols* were becoming highly monopolistic, with predictably negative consequences.

- Second, because of their massive size, the *chaebols* were seen as being uncompetitive in global markets. Observers based this opinion partly on the experiences of large American businesses, such as AT&T, IBM, and Ford, which had lost ground to more nimble and focused competitors.

- Finally, popular public sentiment and growing concern over the distribution of income mitigated against the *chaebols'* goals to become bigger and more diversified.

From the government's perspective, firms have to be lean and flexible to succeed in intensely competitive information-based industries such as semiconductors, computers, and consumer electronics.[28] While the economic performance of American conglomerates and Korean *chaebols* is different, the prevailing belief is that the *chaebols* must specialize to become more competitive. A secondary concern reflected in the new policy is that of limiting the traditionally fierce competition among the *chaebols*. Already, Korea has three struggling car manufacturers; Samsung has recently joined this overcrowded market. The government has assumed that when *chaebols* concentrate on their core businesses, the delineation of new goals will reduce domestic competition.

This government initiative evolved over time. Initially, the government used guidance and incentives. It proposed that each *chaebol* select three designated core businesses, for which it would get greater access to government loans. The government also announced a plan to cut permitted loan guarantees made on behalf of other companies in a group. It also set forth plans to reduce cross-shareholdings from the current average of 40 percent of net asset value to 25 percent. To ensure implementation, the government threatened to deny approval of royalty payments for technology transfers. It also threatened to liberalize, or open up, the Korean domestic market to curb the power of *chaebols*. In a written response, *chaebol* officials called the policy a "gamble," since the government did not provide guidelines concerning which industries they should select. Nor did the government give the *chaebols* any assurance as to their fate once they settled on a particular industry. In effect, *chaebols* questioned what would happen if they put their money on the wrong industries. At the time, Hyundai Chairman Chung openly stated that each and every *chaebol* in his group was considered a main strategic industry.

New Patterns of Specialization

After some reluctance and much deliberation, Korean *chaebols* selected their areas of specialization. With the lack of sufficient guidelines, it is not surprising that the major *chaebols* selected businesses with high potential, which may lead to crowding and overcompetition in the future. As reported by the Korean Ministry of Trade, Industry, and Energy, a majority of the companies selected distribution-delivery, storage, and wholesale/retail activities. Other businesses included electronics, chemicals, automobiles, and food and beverages. Among the top four *chaebols*, three—Hyundai, Samsung, and the LG Group—selected electronics. Hyundai also selected automobiles and energy; Samsung selected machinery and chemicals, and LG selected chemicals and energy. In contrast, Daewoo chose automobiles, machinery, and distribution-transportation.

The top ten *chaebols* showed a strong preference for capital-intensive industries such as chemicals and energy (preferred by five *chaebols*), automobiles (preferred by four), electronics (preferred by three), and machinery (preferred by three). The same report reveals that five conglomerates chose the transportation sector, where domestic firms lag far behind their U.S. counterparts in terms of competitiveness. The next twenty *chaebols*, which were asked to designate two core areas, showed greater diversity in selecting chemicals (six), food and beverages (five), steel (three), nonferrous metals (three), and electronics (two). In terms of the number of selected companies, chemicals was the most popular choice, drawing twenty-two firms, including petrochemicals (thirteen), synthetic fibers (six), and rubber and other chemicals (three). Food and beverages ranked second to chemicals in terms of selection (eleven). Automobiles drew nine firms, as did energy, machinery, and electronics, while nonferrous metals drew five. In the nonmanufacturing sector, the trade distribution field attracted twenty-four firms. Nine plan to specialize in trading, seven in wholesale and retail activities, and eight in transportation. The construction industry attracted twelve firms. These areas of specialization are shown in table 4-2. While these patterns might change as a result of negotiations between the *chaebols* and the government, there is little question that the direction is slanted toward less, not more, diversification.[29]

In essence, the conflict between the government and the *chaebols* represents a disagreement over the comparative benefits of scale and specialization as applied to higher-value-added, technology-based competition. Moreover, government interests also reveal the fear of monopoly, which many identify in the pattern of *chaebol* growth and diversification. Interestingly, while scale and specialization lead to competitive advantages, these are viewed as polar opposites by the Korean government and the *chaebols*. For the *chaebols*, the economies of scale and scope are paramount, particularly in high-technology competition. Most *chaebols* have already increased their investment in research and development; the average increase in R&D in 1991 alone was 57 percent. Moreover, Samsung spent $70 million (U.S. dollars) in advertising, including a special project to place the Samsung name on every baggage cart in every airport around the world. Daewoo completed its acquisition of Leading Edge Computers, and Hyundai and Goldstar have set up subsidiaries in the United States.[30] Behind these sizable investments is the firm belief in scale economies and diversification. Given the enormous financial power of *chaebols*, they are able to make these investments. Moreover, investments in different industries (diversification) essentially serve as a natural hedge against unfavorable business conditions evolving in other sectors.

Despite their diversification, Korean firms have been able to maintain their unity of command through paternalistic management and extensive information-sharing networks. By contrast, American conglomerates have justified diversification on the basis of marketing and financial synergies. They give mere lip service to human synergies, or to the benefits derived from the enhancement of human resources across the entire conglomerate.[31] Because U.S. firms generally regard employees as disposable assets (that is, variable costs), any synergy derived from their interactions are generally subservient to financial or marketing interests. Thus, by attending closely

Table 4-2 Patterns of Specialization for Selected *Chaebols*

Group	Selected Core Industries
Hyundai	Automobiles Electronics Energy
Samsung	Electronics Machinery Chemicals
Daewoo	Automobiles Machinery Distribution and transportation
LG	Electronics Chemicals Energy
Ssangyong	Nonferrous minerals Automobiles Energy
Kia	Automobiles Steel
Sunkyong	Energy Chemicals Distribution and transportation
Hanjin	Distribution and transportation Machinery Construction
Hanwha	Chemicals Energy Distribution and transportation
Lotte	Food and beverages Distribution and transportation Chemicals
Kumho	Distribution and transportation Chemicals
Daelim	Construction Nonferrous minerals

Source: Adapted from *Business Korea,* February 1, 1994, 34–35.

to the human factor and establishing human synergies, the Koreans and Japanese have succeeded where the Americans failed.

This American preoccupation with marketing and finance over human factors contrasts sharply with beliefs that have prevailed in the Japanese *keiretsus* and the Korean *chaebols*. As one Samsung executive mentioned, "We don't even like the word, human resources. . . . We view the entire organization as one human organism . . . one family."[32] This echoes a sentiment earlier pronounced by Japan's industrialist Mitshiyoda Matsushita, who argued that the Western world would never overtake the Japanese because of its propensity to value financial assets more than human beings. All in all, the Korean experience suggests that diversification is not associated with inefficiency, when in fact the obverse is largely true. Diversification—related or unrelated—will work if proper attention is paid to the development of the human resources needed to sustain it. As such, the adoption of policies intent on restructuring the *chaebols* based on the pattern of the American diversified firm alone may be largely misplaced.

To summarize, the debate over the future form of the *chaebol* is likely to continue over time—a debate that is locally represented as a choice between "diamond" and "mud."[33] As "mud" Korean firms represent little separation between owners and stockholders, blurred lines of responsibility, flexibility, and responsiveness, and a minimal role for outsiders. In contrast, diamondlike Western companies are characterized by clear role definitions between owners and stockholders, well-defined lines of responsibility, clear lines of specialization, and a more pronounced role for outsiders. *Chaebol* executives see their mudlike corporate structure as facilitating quick responses to the market environment and have criticized the government for pressuring them to adopt a structure untested in Korea. But the government is equally adamant in its desire for change, particularly when confronted with abuses of the old system, as evidenced by the implication of all thirty major *chaebols* in the bribery scandals of former presidents Chun Doo Hwan and Roh Tae-Woo. Ministry of Financial Economy (MOFE) Director General Choi Jong-Chan adds that unless the *chaebols* change their management style to make their corporate management more visible and understandable to outsiders, they will not be able to withstand escalating public cynicism.[34] Restoring the balance between owners and shareholders by checking management pits market forces against social equity, at least in the short term, and constitutes a major challenge for Korea's economic and political liberalization initiatives.

CHAPTER FIVE

Developing Local Entrepreneurs

In 1992, Ku Chon-Soo, a fifty-one-year-old head of a small auto parts company, committed suicide, leaving this note: "I decided to commit suicide to reveal the contradiction of the society which lets small businesses go bankrupt with malfunctions in the operations of technological, economic, financial systems."[1] This story, augmented when two other owners of small businesses killed themselves for similar reasons at about the same time, galvanized the country. Ku's suicide symbolized the sad plight of the small business. During the 1992 presidential election campaign, his case became the focal point for pledges to create an economic environment in which small to medium-sized firms would thrive.[2]

Ku's suicide came as a particular shock in that he was regarded as one of the most successful small businessmen of the time. A graduate of a prestigious university, Ku passed the highly competitive CPA examination with the highest score in Korea. Not one of Korea's traditional labor-intensive businesses, his firm, Korea Gas Industry Co., embodied an exemplary response to the government's call for technology development, having successfully developed a gas-filled shock absorber. Up to the time this product was built by Ku in 1990, Korea had been completely dependent on foreign nations. The invention garnered Ku the prestigious government award for outstanding small businesses in 1992. But things were not well in Ku's company. Despite its fast growth, the company had entered a serious cash bottleneck on account of a $6.3 million debt it had incurred to finance ongoing technology development. When Ku was not able to pay the interest or principal at the prescribed period, he was harassed and threatened by lenders. Ironically, this occurred at a time when falling interest rates had greatly improved Korea's liquidity, prompting financial institutions to scramble and find borrowers.[3]

The story of Mr. Ku reflects some of the fundamental problems facing Korea's small to medium-sized firms in the 1990s. The fast growth in the membership of Palgi-hoi, a private organization founded in 1992 to help small businesses in trouble, also signaled that the problems of smaller firms had become a widespread social concern.[4] Palgi-hoi, borrowed from the Korean proverb "to fall down seven times and recover eight times," held weekly Saturday sessions during which businessmen were encouraged to share their difficult experiences, offer comfort to members going bankrupt, and exchange relevant information. While these businesses struggled to respond to changing economic conditions, the prevailing belief was that they did not receive sufficient support from the government, that the government's policy toward small businesses was generally inappropriate, and that the government's commitments to and plans for small businesses were unfulfilled promises. Despite antitrust laws and pressure from the government to constrain the expansion of the *chaebols*, they had continued to expand across the economy, driving many small firms out of business.[5] The emphasis of Korean economic development policy had been almost exclusively on the economic growth and development of these *chaebols*, not on the balanced growth of businesses of many different sizes.

Undoubtedly, the weak economic and technological base of small to medium-sized firms poses a major threat to future growth of the economy. Korea's entry into high-tech fields demands a flexible and swift system of management able to overcome the problems that emerge from shorter product life cycles. While small to medium-sized firms are generally limited by their lack of advanced technology, capital, and managerial capabilities, they are entrepreneurial by nature and can be a positive force for competitiveness. In this regard, it is widely believed that the Japanese auto makers' competitive strength is due largely to the contribution of their small but flexible subcontractors. And Taiwan's robust economy, founded on many prosperous small businesses, may provide a useful lesson for Korea. An economy led by only a few major conglomerates will inevitably dull Korea's competitive edge unless such firms are supported by a lean and flexible supplier system made up of smaller firms.

In this chapter, we discuss the economic plight of small to medium-sized firms, new economic policies to improve their competitiveness, and more recent activities they have undertaken to meet this goal. It focuses on the dynamic role of small and medium-sized firms in the Korean economy, with special attention to the nature of the problems they face in the new global environment and the paths they must follow if they are to prosper.

THE HISTORY OF KOREA'S SMALL AND MEDIUM-SIZED FIRMS

Small to medium-sized firms contribute to industrialization by providing flexible specialization—in other words, by serving as a base of operations from which large-scale firms can grow.[6] Small businesses are often referred to as the backbone of economic growth. Indeed, in most circumstances, sustained national growth is possible only when a country's economy is founded on strong and stable small to medium-sized organizations. Historically, Korea's smaller businesses have been weak and so were frequently exploited during the period of rapid industrialization. However, these firms are slowly being recognized as an integral part of Korea's efforts to attain sustainable competitiveness and continuous growth into the next century.[7] A brief recent history of Korea's small to medium-sized businesses will help illuminate their role in the economy today.

Declining Fortunes (1962–1976)

The historical path of small to midsized firms is closely tied with the five-year economic plans initiated in 1962. A study from the Korea Institute for Industrial Economics and Trade (KIET) posits three distinctive stages of development, the first being 1962–1976. This period represents one of decline for the smaller business. During the take-off period of Korea's industrialization (1962–1971), when economic policies directed resources into export-oriented activities and import substitution, and during the period of sectoral development (1972–1981), small to medium-sized firms received little government support. *Chaebols* were flourishing, while small to midsized firms were substantially constricted. Between 1963 and 1973, the proportion of small to medium-sized firms, as a percent of all firms, declined from 98.7 percent to 95.5 percent in number of establishments, from 66.4 percent to 39.4 percent in number of employees, and from 52.8 percent to 27.2 percent in value added (see table 5-1).[8] Notably, the value added by small to medium-sized firms shrank to almost half of the initial level, reflecting a substantially reduced role for these firms in the mid-1970s.

Government Support and Protection (1977–1988)

The second stage in the development of smaller enterprises, 1977–1988, was represented by a period of enlightenment and growth in Korea. After

Table 5-1 Trends in Korea's Small to Medium-Sized Manufacturing Firms

		Number of Establishments	Number of Employees (In thousands)	Gross Output (In millions)	Value Added (In millions)
1963	Small to midsized firms	18,033 (98.7)	267 (66.4)	$ 125 (58.5)	$ 42 (52.8)
	All firms	18,310	402	213	79
1973	Small to midsized firms	22,256 (95.5)	457 (39.4)	1,240 (26.2)	480 (27.2)
	All firms	23,293	1,158	4,733	1,768
1975	Small to midsized firms	21,914 (96.2)	649 (45.7)	3,126 (30.7)	1,116 (31.7)
	All firms	22,787	1,420	10,179	3,523
1976	Small to midsized firms	23,474 (94.1)	646 (37.6)	3,369 (22.5)	1,238 (23.7)
	All firms	24,957	1,717	14,958	5,220
1980	Small to midsized firms	29,779 (96.6)	1,000 (49.6)	14,412 (31.9)	5,193 (35.2)
	All firms	30,823	2,015	45,198	14,771
1985	Small to midsized firms	42,950 (97.5)	1,368 (56.1)	34,017 (35.4)	12,532 (37.6)
	All firms	44,037	2,438	95,971	33,309
1988	Small to midsized firms	58,610 (97.8)	1,804 (57.8)	65,919 (39.4)	25,562 (42.4)
	All firms	59,928	3,120	167,355	60,226
1990	Small to midsized firms	67,679 (96.1)	1,864 (61.7)	94,326 (42.7)	39,159 (44.3)
	All firms	68,872	3,020	220,899	88,361
1991	Small to midsized firms	71,105 (98.5)	1,853 (63.5)	114,313 (44.6)	49,290 (45.8)
	All firms	72,213	2,918	256,269	107,599
1992	Small to midsized firms	73,657 (98.6)	1,845 (65.8)	129,416 (45.8)	56,888 (47.6)
	All firms	74,679	2,801	282,578	119,623
1993	Small to midsized firms	89,568 (98.9)	2,017 (68.8)	154,335 (48.0)	69,280 (50.5)
	All firms	90,530	2,933	321,270	137,063

Source: Compiled from *Report on Mining and Manufacturing Survey, 1995* (Seoul).
Note: Figures in parentheses indicate percentage of total firms.

the industrial restructuring of the mid-1970s, heavy and chemical industries stimulated more active involvement from small to medium-sized firms. These firms went through a lively expansion of production facilities to keep pace with the fast-growing economy. As the economy shifted from labor- and scale-intensive industries to technology-intensive industries, product life cycles became substantially shortened, consumer demands became more diverse, and product innovations became more frequent. Highly segmented markets evolved with these changes. In this environment, small to midsized firms were able to secure market niches because of their inherent flexibility. Unable to compete effectively against flexible foreign competitors, the *chaebols* found themselves in need of help from smaller local businesses and spun off large parts of their operations to them as subcontractors. The new cooperative relationship with the *chaebols* hastened the expansion of small to medium-sized firms throughout the 1980s. Through such spin-offs, it was intended that small to medium-sized firms would reduce the *chaebols* ever-increasing dependence on foreign components and materials, mostly from Japan.[9]

During this stage, the government was active in passing various laws in support of smaller firms. These included legislation to facilitate the purchase of goods produced by smaller firms (1981), to reserve certain businesses for small to medium-sized firms (1982), to provide finances for these firms (1983), to guarantee fair trade in subcontracting (1984), to support localization of machinery, components, and materials (1986), and to encourage new ventures (1989). As a result of this legislation, more than 30 percent of such firms received protection and various financial and tax benefits by 1992.[10] This was a prosperous era for small to medium-sized firms and led to the increasing significance of their role in Korea's industrialization. Not surprisingly, between 1976 and 1988 the proportion of small to medium-sized firms grew from 94.1 percent to 97.8 percent in number of businesses, from 37.6 percent to 57.8 percent in employees, and from 23.7 percent to 42.4 percent in value added.

Sink or Swim (1989–present)

At the close of the 1980s, small to medium-sized firms began to experience unprecedented difficulties, moving into a time of struggle for survival. This third stage (1989–present) is regarded as a transformational period during which small to medium-sized firms have gone through a structural adjustment from labor-intensive to high-margin businesses. Since the late 1980s, small to medium-sized firms have been under great pressure from the high costs of labor, land, and capital. Despite higher costs of labor, these firms have not been able to recruit the most talented employees. Korea's young people still prefer to work for the *chaebols*, which are believed to offer brighter long-term prospects. Because small to medium-sized firms have had great difficulty competing outside of Korea, in recent years their profitability has declined significantly and their bankruptcy rate has increased. Labor productivity (value added per capita) in small to medium-sized firms fell from 16 percent in 1991 to 12 percent in 1993, while comparable data for the large conglomerates remained unchanged (15 percent in 1991 and in 1993).[11] In 1993, the gap between smaller firms and large corporations in terms of employment cost to gross value added became much wider (65 percent for small to medium-sized firms, 47 percent for large conglomerates), reflecting a higher cost burden on smaller firms. In 1992, approximately twenty-five small and medium-sized firms declared bankruptcy each day, and this number climbed to thirty-five per day in 1995.[12] Reports of suicides among small business owners have not been uncommon in the 1990s.

In the early 1990s, the former protection-oriented government policies began to shift toward a new policy intended to foster self-reliance among small to medium-sized firms, thereby helping them to meet the challenges of market liberalization and globalization. The new policy places special emphasis on the transition to high-margin businesses from labor-intensive operations, facilitating technology development, automation, and data management systems. In 1993, small to medium-sized firms were responsible for 98.9 percent of total manufacturing businesses in number, 68.8 percent of total employees, 48.0 percent of gross output, and 50.5 percent of value added. The gross output by small and medium-sized firms reached $154 billion, of which $69.3 billion was value added (see table 5-1). Despite the turmoil since the late 1980s, small to medium-sized firms have continued to grow in size and in strength. In 1994, production and exports by such firms recorded double-digit growth rates, and the trend continued in 1995. The normal operation rate has also been increasing, amounting to 85 percent in 1994.

Despite this rapid growth, the bankruptcy rate of small to medium-sized firms has continued to rise since the late 1980s, even though it has been declining in the manufacturing industry. China's entry into the Korean domestic market with cheap-priced commodities was one important factor in the increasing rates of bankruptcy. As in the case of textiles and footware, cheaper imported products also led to the migration of labor-intensive industries to other developing countries. The higher bankruptcy rate in the service industry reflects the entry of large-scale, well-organized Western firms and suggests that there have been more rapid defaults of weaker businesses in these sectors. This recent increase may be partially explained by new ventures, which have had a higher rate of entry than exit. Table 5-2 reflects the recent trends in Korea's small and medium-sized firms.

Historically, Korea's smaller firms have been family-owned enterprises, but recently there has been a noticeable transition from the traditional individual enterprise to the corporation. The proportion of corporations almost doubled between 1980 and 1992, rising from 19 percent to 37 percent.[13] This reflects the growing sophistication of such businesses, which have come to require a higher level of managerial professionalism. Even so, Alice Amsden suggests that Korean firms—unlike Japanese small and medium-sized firms, which have historically been export oriented—have been primarily marginal exporters even when they accounted for a large share of employment.[14] Korean small to medium-sized firms typically exported 10–20 percent of their output in the late 1970s.[15] With Korean firms becoming more internationalized in the 1980s, small and medium-sized firms have come to account for just below 40 percent of Korea's total exports since 1989, reaching their highest rate—43 percent—in 1993. (See

Table 5-2 Recent Business Indexes for Korea's Small to Medium-Sized Firms

Index	1992	1993	1994	1995 (Jan.–June)
Growth rate	5.7	2.6	12.2	10.3
Normal operation	83.7	83.4	84.9	84.5
Export growth	8.4	14.6	17.5	18.3
Investment growth	5.4	9.6	20.1	16.5
Bankruptcy rate	.12	.13	.17	.21
Number of businesses (A)	10,769	9,502	11,255	6,559
Individual enterprises	7,055	6,100	6,752	3,801
Corporations	3,714	3,402	4,503	2,758
Manufacturing (%)	30.3	30.0	27.8	24.9
Construction (%)	10.5	11.9	10.7	11.9
Service (%)	25.7	26.8	33.1	38.9
Number of new ventures (B)	13,702	11,998	16,723	8,634
New ventures/bankruptcy (A/B)	1.27	1.26	1.49	1.32

Source: Korea Federation of Small Businesses, *1995 Major Statistics of Small and Medium Industries* (Seoul).

table 5-3.) Also, in 1990, exports of small and medium-sized firms approached 26 percent of their total production value, showing a substantial increase from the 10–20 percent range of the 1970s.

The increasing role of small to medium-sized firms in international activities is further evidenced by the recent surge of their foreign direct investment. Between 1985 and 1994, such investment increased from $37 million to $1.5 billion. Also, the average size per firm of these foreign investments almost doubled during the same period, from $231,000 to $437,890. By 1994, more than 20 percent in amount and 65 percent in cases, or instances, of Korea's foreign direct investment was made by small and medium-sized firms (see table 5-4). In other cases, Korean firms sought to invest in countries characterized by lower labor costs. Even though the primary reason for the recent surge in foreign direct investment was to look for cheap and easily accessible labor, a recent survey of small to medium-sized firms shows detoured exporting to developing nations and foreign market expansion as other significant motivations.[16]

Table 5-3   Export Performance by Korea's Small to Medium-Sized Firms (Millions of dollars)

	Total Exports (A)	Small and Midsized Enterprises (B)	Large Enterprises	B/A (%)
1985	30,283.1	8,413.5	20,641.9	27.8
1986	34,714.5	12,299.8	21,109.6	35.2
1987	47,280.9	17,812.2	27,234.5	37.7
1988	60,696.4	22,998.2	37,583.8	37.9
1989	62,377.2	26,054.8	36,221.6	41.8
1990	65,015.7	27,382.0	37,545.8	42.1
1991	71,870.1	28,287.0	43,445.9	39.3
1992	76,631.5	30,676.0	45,873.4	40.0
1993	82,235.9	35,168.7	46,947.4	42.8
1994	96,013	40,701.0	55,167.0	42.4
1995 (Jan.–June)	58,328	22,637.0	35,551.0	38.8

Sources: National Statistical Office, *Korea Statistical Yearbook* (Seoul: 1995) and Korea Federation of Small Business, *Major Statistics of Small and Medium Industries* (Seoul: 1995).

Table 5-4   Foreign Direct Investment by Small to Medium-Sized Firms (Millions of dollars)

Foreign Direct Investment		1985	1990	1991	1992	1993	1994
Total (A)	Amount	461	2,297	3,324	4,421	5,432	7,497
	Cases	433	1,226	1,646	2,109	2,725	4,132
Small and Midsized	Amount	37	286	483	721	1,027	1,517
Firms (B)	Cases	78	455	731	1,086	1,596	2,715
Ratio (%) (B/A)	Amount	8.1	12.5	14.5	16.3	18.9	20.2
	Cases	18.0	37.1	44.4	51.5	58.6	65.7

Source: Bank of Korea, *Overseas Direct Investment Statistics Yearbook 1995* (Seoul).
Note: Amount indicates total accumulated net investment by the end of a year.

CHALLENGES FACING SMALL AND MEDIUM-SIZED FIRMS

After being largely ignored throughout the 1970s, small and medium-sized firms grew substantially during the 1980s, along with the *chaebols.* Since the late 1980s, small to medium-sized firms have emerged as the primary source of new employment; the portion of employment by these firms has increased from 50 percent in 1980 to 69 percent in 1993 (as shown in table 5-1). Small to medium-sized firms now also play a stronger role in the economy; the value added by small and medium-sized firms grew from 35 percent in 1980 to 51 percent in 1993.

Despite their more significant role in the economy, Korea's small to medium-sized firms continue to face daunting challenges. As discussed in the previous section, the 1990s is seen as a "sink-or-swim" period of structural adaptation for them. To alleviate the long-standing structural and regional disequilibrium in the Korean economy, President Kim's new economic plan, begun in 1993, supports small to medium-sized businesses and stimulates regional economies. Yet even with the government's pledge of support, and with the increase in their portion of value added and employment, small and medium-sized firms continue to be highly vulnerable.

Volatile Financial Performance

Indicators of the vulnerability of small to midsized firms are the increasing banknote default rates and cyclical overcapacity. Based on a sample of about 20,000 small and medium-sized firms, a recent KIET study[17] reported that the banknote default rate between 1989 and 1991 was less than .07 percent and that 86 percent of small to medium-sized firms were holding normal operations.[18] The overall default rate jumped to 12 percent in 1992 and to 21 percent in 1995, while the normal operation rate fell below 85 percent from 1992 to 1995 (see table 5-2). During 1995, more than thirty-four small to medium-sized businesses defaulted on their bank loans each day, one of the highest rates in recent decades.

As more small to medium-sized firms go into bankruptcy—especially the larger ones—the overall bankruptcy rate is expected to snowball. A default by one major company can hurt other small to medium-sized firms that receive the company's notes. The snowball effect was apparent when Nonno, a major apparel retailer, defaulted on its loans in 1992.[19] The highest default rate, in 1995, has been explained by the bankruptcy of the Duksan Group. When these major companies went bankrupt, many of their affiliates and subcontractors faced the same fate. Smaller firms are always vulnerable because they do not have sufficient resources to absorb temporary financial setbacks. The default rate has increased substantially in recent years in terms of the size of the losses. The default rate in amount (defaulted amount/total financial transaction) for small to medium-sized firms declined to 20 percent in 1990 from a higher rate in the mid-1980s, then quickly rose to 38 percent in 1991 and to 74 percent in 1992.[20] Even though the bankruptcy rate in the manufacturing industry slowed down in 1994, along with that in construction, manufacturing remains the primary source of the dramatic upswing in the bankruptcy rates throughout the 1990s.

Several interrelated factors are largely responsible for this increase, including a decline in the competitiveness of previous core businesses, increases in the costs of key resources (labor, land, and capital), distortion in the capital markets, abuses of subcontractors by large corporations, ineffective government policies, and mismanagement by small to medium-sized firms.

Declining Global Competitiveness

Because of their significantly lower labor costs, Korea's small to midsized firms have generally been able to sustain their global competitiveness in labor-intensive industries. After the labor movement in the late 1980s, however, labor costs increased dramatically for all companies, including the smaller ones. Table 5-5 shows that wages per employee in small to medium-sized firms increased almost two and a half times in the five years since 1987. This trend was similar for large conglomerates, but small to medium-sized firms felt the impact more because they were already operating under tight cost constraints in price-sensitive industries.

Also, with the entry of China and other newly industrializing countries,

Table 5-5   Average Annual Wages for Small to Medium-Sized and Large Manufacturing
Firms, 1975–1992

	Small to Midsized Firms (A)	Large Firms (B)	Percentage by Which Large Firms Exceed Small to Midsized Firms 100 − (A/B)
1975	$ 497	$ 653	23.9
1980	1,944	2,415	19.5
1981	2,268	2,874	21.1
1982	2,536	3,265	22.3
1983	2,745	3,638	24.5
1984	3,071	4,056	24.3
1985	3,288	4,385	25.0
1986	3,474	4,684	25.8
1987	4,003	5,545	27.8
1988	4,663	6,837	31.8
1989	5,777	8,709	33.7
1990	6,877	10,397	33.9
1991	8,419	12,542	32.9
1992	9,759	14,639	33.3
1993	10,653	16,155	34.1

Source: Korea Federation of Small Businesses, *1995 Major Statistics of Small and Medium Industries* (Seoul).

Korea's small to medium-sized firms have experienced increasing pressure in the global market. Many of Korea's small to medium-sized firms have begun to face barriers in exporting and OEM (original equipment manufacturing) operations in labor-intensive areas and to lose their global competitiveness. Since the *chaebols'* move during the late 1980s into technology-intensive fields, small to medium-sized firms have realized that they, too, must move in this direction. Unfortunately, because of limited resources and a lack of expertise and trained personnel, they are not in a position to make this transformation into high-margin areas as easily as have the *chaebols.* The declining growth in paper, apparel and fur, leather and footwear, rubber and plastic products, and nonmetallic mineral industries reflects the weakening competitiveness of Korea's small to medium-sized firms. Table 5-6 presents manufacturing production indexes by small to medium-sized firms, holding 1990 as the base year.

The decline in global competitiveness is also seen in exports, as shown in table 5-7. For small to medium-sized firms, exports have declined or experienced only minimal growth in similar industries, such as primary products, plastic, rubber, leather products, and ordinary goods. The growth rate of exports by small to medium-sized firms failed to meet these companies' production goals. Table 5-7 also shows that export activities by Korea's smaller firms are heavily concentrated in labor-intensive, declining industries, such as primary products, textile and apparels, and ordinary goods. More than 45 percent of total exports by such firms have come from these

Table 5-6   Trends in Small to Medium-Sized Firm Manufacturing Production, 1990–1994

	1990	1991	1992	1993	1994
Food products and beverages	100.0	105.7	116.7	118.3	122.0
Textiles	100.0	103.6	110.3	113.1	129.7
Wearing apparel and fur articles	100.0	106.5	111.5	106.2	110.4
Leather, bags, and footwear	100.0	104.9	112.4	112.4	105.8
Pulp and paper products	100.0	106.2	106.3	100.6	113.5
Publishing, printing, and recorded media	100.0	105.0	114.0	125.1	146.4
Chemicals and chemical products	100.0	115.0	124.0	122.0	138.0
Rubber and plastic products	100.0	99.9	110.0	105.7	119.1
Nonmetallic mineral products	100.0	99.9	100.5	101.5	101.5
Basic metal	100.0	112.2	114.6	127.6	146.2
Fabricated metal products	100.0	108.9	113.8	126.8	149.5
Machinery and equipment	100.0	112.6	114.7	124.6	146.3
Other electrical machinery and apparatus	100.0	105.9	111.4	116.6	145.5
Radio, TV, and communications equipment	100.0	104.5	112.0	113.3	140.8
Motor vehicles and trailers	100.0	114.9	127.9	136.3	164.7
Overall small and medium production	100.0	107.4	113.4	116.4	130.6

Source: Korea Federation of Small Business, *1995 Major Statistics of Small and Medium Industries* (Seoul).

Table 5-7 Exports by Small to Medium-Sized Firms (Millions of dollars)

	1988	1989	1990	1991	1992	1993	1994
Primary products	$2,241	$2,319	$2,061	$2,261	$2,249	$2,312	$2,593
	(26.1)	(3.5)	(−11.1)	(9.7)	(−0.5)	(2.8)	(12.2)
Chemical industry products	425	516	761	716	980	1,403	2,019
	(−13.9)	(21.4)	(47.5)	(−5.9)	(36.8)	(43.1)	(43.9)
Plastic, rubber, leather products	1,392	1,996	1,937	2,138	2,529	2,249	2,648
	(37.7)	(43.4)	(−3.0)	(10.4)	(18.3)	(−11.1)	(17.7)
Textile wearing apparel	7,858	9,612	9,409	9,310	10,122	10,854	12,353
	(19.9)	(22.3)	(−2.1)	(−1.1)	(8.7)	(7.2)	(13.8)
Ordinary goods	3,615	3,648	3,986	3,881	3,288	2,842	2,837
	(22.2)	(0.9)	(9.3)	(−2.6)	(−15.3)	(−13.6)	(−0.2)
Iron and steel, metal products	1,263	1,361	1,644	1,350	1,507	1,612	2,089
	(9.8)	(7.8)	(20.8)	(−17.9)	(11.6)	(6.9)	(29.6)
Electric and electronic products	3,694	3,698	4,413	5,387	6,357	9,330	10,981
	(52.4)	(0.1)	(19.3)	(22.1)	(18.0)	(46.8)	(17.7)
Machinery and transportation equipment	1,617	2,012	2,097	2,279	2,642	3,243	3,655
	(112.9)	(24.4)	(4.2)	(8.7)	(15.9)	(22.7)	(12.5)
Miscellaneous	893	883	1,075	960	998	1,321	1,526
Total	22,998	26,046	27,382	28,287	30,676	35,169	40,701
	(29.1)	(13.3)	(5.1)	(3.3)	(8.4)	(14.6)	(15.7)
Percentage of the total exports	37.9	41.8	42.1	39.3	40.0	42.8	42.4

Sources: National Statistical Office, *Korean Statistical Year Book* (Seoul: 1995), and Korea Federation of Small Business, *1995 Major Statistics of Small and Medium Industries* (Seoul). *Note:* Figures in parentheses show yearly growth rates.

declining industries. This explains the series of bankruptcies of OEM-based apparel manufacturers like Daedo, Shinhan International, and Usang, which failed when their exports declined markedly owing to weak price competitiveness.

This trend is even more apparent in the footwear industry, which exports more than 75 percent of its final product. In 1991 alone, more than thirty major manufacturers went bankrupt and more than two hundred of their subcontractors followed. Moreover, in low-end electronics, such as cassette recorders and car stereos, a majority of the major producers have gone into bankruptcy since the end of 1980s. For example, in the car stereo industry, more than thirty of the sixty manufacturers went bankrupt because of difficulty in exporting after a dumping claim by the European Union.[21] Borneo International Furniture, one of Korea's best-known medium-sized firms, with a long history of success, also went into bankruptcy because it could not recover its losses in the global market in the late 1980s.[22]

Korea's small to medium-sized firms are at a point where they have to switch to higher-value-added fields by developing independent technologies and by moving away from OEM into the exporting of products with their own labels. Despite government and industry efforts to persuade local companies to increase overall benefits from their export products by developing their own brand names, small companies prefer to do business under OEM arrangements, choosing not to get involved with overseas marketing activities. While larger companies have actively pursued the development of their own brand names, with 54 percent of their products being exported under their brands in early 1995, small to medium-sized firms exported only 27 percent of their products under their own brands.[23] In particular, small to medium-sized firms intended to continue operations on an OEM basis, citing the difficulties in establishing and marketing their own brands.

Recent market liberalization policies of the Korean government have perhaps worsened an already difficult situation for those firms in labor-intensive fields as well as for firms in fields that have been operating under government protection. The domestic market has also become flooded with cheap foreign products, putting more pressure on local firms. While large corporations can afford a period of initial losses, smaller businesses typically cannot. As table 5-8 shows, Korea's smaller firms have not been able to make even a reasonable amount of investment in research and development. R&D investment rates have been mostly below 0.25 percent of sales until recently. In 1992, although there was a sharp increase in R&D to 0.42 percent of sales, there was also a substantial decrease in the number of firms that made any R&D investment compared with the late 1980s. In 1988, almost 17 percent (9,821 businesses) of small to medium-sized firms made an investment in R&D, while by 1993 this percentage had declined to only 6.3 percent (5,645 businesses).

Distortions in Financing and Subcontracting

While Korean financial markets have improved and interest rates have been stabilized since the end of 1991, as the story of Ku Chon-Soo's suicide reflects, most owners of smaller firms feel that their financial situation has

Table 5-8   R&D Investment by Small to Medium-Sized Manufacturing Firms

	Number of Firms with R&D Investment	Total R&D Investment (In thousands)	Average R&D per Firm	R&D Expenditures as % of Sales
1978	2,610	$10,339	$3,961	0.12
1979	2,847	14,184	4,982	0.11
1980	2,982	19,622	6,580	0.13
1981	5,175	22,755	4,397	0.11
1982	2,388	48,337	20,242	0.20
1983	6,031	86,483	14,340	0.28
1984	5,780	77,079	13,335	0.22
1985	5,630	81,374	14,454	0.22
1986	6,664	119,858	17,986	0.25
1987	7,522	137,759	18,314	0.22
1988	9,821	209,976	21,380	0.29
1989	5,962	151,728	25,449	0.19
1990	6,758	239,566	35,449	0.24
1991	3,653	264,097	72,296	0.24
1992	4,821	313,881	65,107	0.26
1993	5,645	546,692	96,845	0.42

Sources: National Statistical Office, *Korea Statistical Yearbook* (Seoul: 1995), and Korea Federation of Small Business, *1995 Major Statistics of Small and Medium Industries* (Seoul).

worsened. In a 1990 survey by the Federation of Small to Medium-Sized Firms, more than 50 percent of the respondents indicated that they were suffering from significant financial burdens and were not optimistic about the future, even after the liberalization of the financial markets.[24] A similar study conducted by the Industrial Bank of Korea in 1992 shows that the number of financially troubled small to medium-sized firms has continued to climb.[25] As explained above, the declining competitiveness in the domestic and international markets became a major reason for these financial difficulties. The survey by the Federation of Small and Medium-Sized Firms also shows that delays in payment (particularly for the smaller firms working as subcontractors to large corporations) and difficulties in accessing support from financial institutions worsened their financial situations.

In the basic metal and fabricated metal products industries, most small to medium-sized firms operate as subcontractors. The financial stress experienced by the large *chaebol* groups since the late 1980s has often led to delays in payments to subcontractors (the small to medium-sized firms). In Korea's subcontracting relationship, payment is normally made in long-term corporate bonds. Even when large corporations win lucrative government contracts, which pay on a cash settlement basis, their payments to small subcontractors are still typically made in banknotes. The legislation to protect subcontractors adopted in 1984 stipulates that bonds are to be cleared within sixty days of issue. However, according to an investigation by Korea's Fair Trade Commission of 101 large corporations in 1991, about 46 percent of the bonds were not cleared within the legally specified period. And more than 11 percent of the bonds were left uncleared for more than ninety days.[26] In an interview with *Business Korea*, one businessman said, "From the time of order to the actual payment stage, it can take anywhere from seven to nine months when dealing with big companies."[27] And as Amsden notes, Korea's large corporations often work closely with subcontractors to improve quality and lower costs on the basis of a just-in-time inventory system.[28] However, Korea's decades-long frantic drive for economic growth has resulted in a more power-based relationship between parties, in which the financial burdens of large corporations are passed onto small subcontractors.

The problems of Korea's small to medium-sized firms are compounded by the attitudes of the *chaebols* toward them. The *chaebols* have been criticizing the government policy requiring them to spin off large parts of their operations and to involve small to medium-sized firms more actively. The *chaebols* believe they can perform the service provided by the small to medium-sized firm more effectively and efficiently because of their abundant resources and experience. Accordingly, the roles of Korea's small and medium-sized firms have not been so critical—at least in the eyes of the *chaebols*—leading to substantial imbalances of power. To maintain cost-based competitiveness in the global market, large corporations often cut the prices of the products delivered by small to medium-sized firms when their production costs surge. *Business Korea* points out that unfair practices by large companies still prevail despite repeated government attempts to root them out.[29] It is not uncommon to see large corporations entering the fields reserved for small to medium-sized corporations. Consequently, large corporations cover a wide range of operations, from semiconductors to stuffed toys. When small to medium-sized firms confront the *chaebols*, they cannot possibly compete, considering the wide gap in capital and in management and marketing skills.

Inadequate Funding

One reason Korea's small to medium-sized firms have not been able to get sufficient funding from the direct capital markets (for example, the stock market) is because of their relatively short history and limited assets. Even though the number of corporations is increasing, most small to medium-sized firms are still individual enterprises. Therefore, they are heavily dependent on commercial banks, and they are affected more immediately by increases in capital costs. At the end of 1994, about 59 percent of the total loans made by banking institutions in Korea were made to small to medium-sized firms. Despite the heavy dependence of these firms on commercial loans, banking institutions have not been a friendly source of financing. Korea's banking system has traditionally favored the major *chaebols*, often extending loans to smaller firms only because of the mandatory loan requirements specified by Korean law. Indirect financing through commercial banks, accounting for about 78 percent of the total balance of loans for small to medium-sized manufacturing firms as of 1992, has been more costly for small to medium-sized firms than for large corporations.[30] Banks normally charge higher interest rates for smaller enterprises because of their lack of credit or collateral. This difference in interest typically runs about 1.5 percent, a major impediment to competitiveness.

In addition, the worsening financial picture for Korea's smaller firms is tied to their declining sales. With sales falling since the late 1980s, small to medium-sized firms have been further squeezed for not having enough cash and capital in hand to use as collateral. In Korea, loans are extended on the basis of collateral, not credit. Small to medium-sized firms often could not fund their R&D or facility expansion because they lacked cash and collateral. It has become a vicious cycle for such firms; as their competitiveness slips away, they are forced to make structural adjustments into high-margin fields by upgrading technological capabilities. However, a lack of cash and collateral does not allow them to secure the necessary funding from banks to make such conversions.

Ineffective Government Policy

As the late Mr. Ku complained, the government incentive system has often been an empty promise for small and medium-sized firms. In 1992, these firms could not utilize many of the special funding programs offered by the government because they did not have sufficient collateral needed for government loans.[31] They also had to meet highly burdensome requirements to make use of these support measures. For example, to receive special tax favors, they have to register their books with the tax office, an unfamiliar practice for most Korean firms. As a result, such firms complain that in reality government subsidies are too difficult to secure to make them a viable source of support.

Other government policies designed to protect small to medium-sized firms have also proved less than effective. For example, the laws designed to prevent large corporations from moving into certain business fields and to maintain fair trade in subcontracting have not been effectively implemented. Another major criticism of government policy toward smaller firms has been its short-term orientation. Government policies have largely targeted only urgent issues instead of working on a long-term plan to correct the fundamental problems plaguing smaller firms.

Recently, the Korean government has been somewhat more active in its efforts to help these firms. In 1993, for example, the government set up a special fund of about $37 million to stabilize the management of technologically oriented small and medium-sized firms. Low-interest loans were given to small businesses with growth potential that were in financial trouble at the time. The government has also extended the rediscount period and lowered rediscount rates for small to medium-sized firms.[32] In 1995, the Kim administration also announced a series of new plans to support small to medium-sized firms, including the offer of various financial benefits and exemption from tax auditing for 340,000 promising small to medium-sized firms for the next two years.[33] Whether such remedies will be of substantive assistance or simply too little too late remains to be seen. *Han-kuk Ilbo*, a Korean daily newspaper, points out that most small to medium-sized firms are not even aware of these new benefit plans and that such repeated announcements of new policies simply reflect the overall ineffectiveness of government efforts in this area.[34]

Lack of Qualified Employees

Korea's small to medium-sized firms have problems attracting highly qualified employees. The attractions of stability, status, and pay have traditionally drawn talented young people to work for large corporations. Smaller firms are always vulnerable to the vagaries of the economy. A large part of the large corporation's appeal is the relative job security it offers.

Because of the Confucian influence, status remains an important element in Korean society. Traditional Confucian society was divided into several classes in the civil service system. A screening system, something like today's bar examination, allowed young people to enter into different classes according to their talents. Therefore, young people worked hard to reach the highest level by passing the most competitive entrance examination into the class. This Confucian value of status has been transformed in modern society into the practice of entering into larger, more prestigious firms.

The wage gap between large corporations and small to medium-sized firms has also widened in recent years. As shown in table 5-5, the average wage per worker was 25 percent higher in large corporations in 1985, but this difference had grown to 34 percent by 1993. According to a report by the Korean Ministry of Labor, the shortage of employees in production areas for small to medium-sized firms represents a serious concern; in 1983, small to medium-sized firms had a 4 percent shortage rate, not dissimilar to the 3 percent rate of the larger corporations.[35] By 1989, this shortage rate had grown to almost three times the rate of larger corporations. Not surprisingly, a recent survey by the Industrial Bank of Korea reveals that employee morale at smaller firms has fallen substantially in recent years compared with that of the mid-1980s.[36]

Poor Management

Adding to the difficulties experienced by Korea's smaller firms is one final problem: poor management. Many of Korea's smaller firms failed to develop self-reliance while they were protected by various government policies throughout the 1980s. The law, initially intended to reserve businesses for small and medium-sized firms, was to encourage such firms to develop technological capabilities and human capital and to eventually improve their competitiveness in the global market. However, many of these firms often exploited this protection by initiating price collusion and other unfair practices.[37] They failed to improve quality or productivity, thereby causing problems for their customers. As Paul Chung, executive director of corporate planning for Sunkyong, notes, "The problem was not the structure, i.e., the government, but the small firm managers' mindset to always pursue new and bigger opportunities. They should focus on the strength they have, but they are too eager to get ahead, looking for opportunities. They never stick to their own strength. Therefore, they have never been able to build their own strength over time."[38]

The government's economic development policies were also intended to improve global competitiveness by forcing the *chaebols* to spin off their noncore businesses and work more closely with small to medium-sized firms on a complementary basis. Since smaller firms were not successful in developing internal competence, owing to the external constraints described above and to managerial incompetence, they were hardly perceived as beneficial partners by the *chaebols*. Professor Cho Dong Sung of Seoul National University points out that if the *chaebols* were forced to work with small and medium-sized firms that were substantially lacking in competence, it would hurt national competitiveness in the global market.[39] Sunkyong's Paul Chung also notes that "The government has interfered with the *chaebols* in building global competitiveness. We do not have the competitive basis that comes from the small to medium-sized firms." Another Korean *chaebol* executive noted: "I do not understand why the government tries to protect small to medium-sized firms. They can grow without protection. The *chaebols* understand that they cannot do everything, so they will spin off. However, the government should make a tough and competitive environment for small, entrepreneurial firms. They have to be exposed to the competitive environment. So, small to medium-sized firms should work on competence building, not on money-making and short-term deals."[40]

The survival of Korea's small to medium-sized firms requires significant determination, entrepreneurial spirit, and leadership, backed by reliable financing and a supportive government. Many small to medium-sized firms in Korea are family managed, and they lack these leadership and managerial skills. An exception is the success story of Nam Jae-Woo, president of the Rajon Wool Textile Company and founder of the Palgi-hoi.[41] It is not a coincidence that President Nam created the organization. Nam Jae-Woo experienced bankruptcy himself in 1984. However, surviving this difficult time led to his developing a reputation among Korea's small to medium-sized firms. Without his leadership and the employees' determination, the company would have failed. Since the employees believed in their leader and felt he always treated them like a family, they returned their salaries to the company and worked days and nights for months. Nam started all over again by distributing equity among his employees. Today, Nam's company is one of the most successful small businesses in Korea, with an average annual growth rate approaching 25 percent.

THE GROWING ECONOMIC SIGNIFICANCE OF SMALL AND MEDIUM-SIZED FIRMS

Korea's decades-long, growth-driven economic policy has created an unbalanced dual economy of large conglomerates and small to medium-sized firms. As Korea strives to become a more active player in the global market and to sustain its competitiveness into the twenty-first century, this weaker contributor to the economy must be strengthened, not eclipsed. Without the support from small to medium-sized firms, Korea's new economy in high-tech fields will be built on a less-than-ideal foundation, and will likely yield major sectors of its value-added economy to foreign suppliers, such as Japan. Small to medium-sized firms can provide the base on which to build increasing independence and self-reliance in high-tech fields by supplying large corporations with critical intermediary products. Indeed, small to medium-sized firms could meet these diverse and small-scale demands more effectively than large corporations.

In addition to offering a solid foundation for economic growth in high-tech fields and creating new employment opportunities, small to medium-sized firms may introduce equality into the Korean economy. Despite the major contributions by the *chaebols* to Korea's economic growth, they have often been viewed contemptuously by the general public because of their concentration of economic power and their occasional exploitation of small and medium-sized firms. The continued growth and prosperity of small to medium-sized firms would help to justify the presence of *chaebols* and allow more sustainable growth for the Korean economy. In the following section, we elaborate on these two important sources of contribution from small to medium-sized firms in the Korean economy.

Providing a Foundation for National Competitiveness

In moving from the labor-intensive 1960s and 1970s to the capital-intensive 1980s to the technology-intensive 1990s, Korea has made dynamic adjustments to improve its national competitiveness. In recent years, however, its dependence on foreign technologies has intensified. In 1990, for example, Korea's dependence on foreign technologies in the electronics industry was more than six times that of Japan (see chapter 7). There has been continued growth of Korea's trade deficit, particularly with Japan, in technology-oriented industries, mostly in intermediary products. Considering that the history of Korea's large corporations centered around manufacturing and assembling final products, Korea has been relatively weak in intermediary and capital-goods industries. This has created a hollow economy in which a major part of Korea's value added in the electronics and machinery industries is based on Japanese or American technology. In the late 1980s, the import rate of intermediary and capital goods (35 percent) far exceeded the import rate of overall manufacturing industry (22 percent).[42] This high import dependency in the intermediary goods industries has been discussed as one of the most critical strategic concerns for Korea's future. Without lowering this dependency, Korea will not be able to build sustainable competitiveness in the global market, giving up a large part of the value added to Japan and other foreign countries.

Korea will not be able to reduce its dependence on Japan without improving small to medium-sized firms, whose role as intermediate suppliers has been largely supplanted by Japanese firms. A KIET report shows that in 1990 Korea had a trade deficit with Japan in the machinery and equipment industries of about $8.5 billion, amounting to 1.4 times the total deficit in manufacturing industries ($5.9 billion).[43] The major source of this deficit was in the general machinery and components industries, which was about $5 billion, or almost 60 percent of the total manufacturing deficit. Because small and medium-sized firms contribute more than 50 percent of gross domestic production in these industries, their importance in helping to make for an unfavorable balance of trade seems indisputable. Korea's small to medium-sized firms contribute 30 percent of the overall production in the machinery and equipment industries, which are heavily dependent on Japan. In general machinery and components and in other machinery industries, small and medium-sized firms provide between 50 and 80 percent of total shipments. The automobile component industry is also heavily dependent on small to medium-sized businesses; these firms account for 47 percent of total shipments to the industry. It is clear that developing national competitiveness in technology-intensive fields should start with building competence in small to medium-sized firms. Otherwise, Korea's economic activities run the risk of being further hollowed to the detriment of the entire nation.

Adjusting the Inequalities in Korea's Economy

Korea's long path to economic independence has produced a critical social concern: the concentration of economic power in the hands of a few *chaebols*. In the name of industrialization, the Korean government routinely neglected small to medium-sized firms, and, in the past, the nation as a whole tolerated it. However, Korea now has reached a point at which small to medium-sized firms can no longer be treated lightly for economic as well as social reasons. As described above, small to medium-sized firms should be more actively involved in value creation to strengthen national competitiveness in global high-tech fields. President Kim's new economic policy puts a special emphasis on the promotion of small to medium-sized firms, with the intent of alleviating the historical structural and regional disequilibrium in the Korean economy. This trend toward equitable economic growth has been hastened in recent years by the rapid pace of democratization in Korean politics.

The current weakness in Korea's small to medium-sized firms is largely due to the economic policies that were so greatly skewed toward large corporations. While such policies resulted in rapid industrialization of the country, they also created a great deal of social inefficiency because of the reduced competition in many industries. The recent growth of small and medium-sized firms has helped substantially in loosening the concentration of economic power in a few *chaebols*. However, despite the government's efforts since the late 1980s to reduce the economic concentration of the *chaebols*, there was no substantial improvement by the mid-1990s. Indeed, in 1994, Korea's Fair Trade Commission reported that the economic concentration of the *chaebols* had not been significantly reduced and that the problem had grown more acute among the top five conglomerates: Samsung, Hyundai, Daewoo, LG, and Sunkyong. In 1993, these *chaebols* accounted for 66 percent of the overall turnover of the thirty top business groups and 90 percent of their net profits.

THE FUTURE OF SMALL AND MEDIUM-SIZED FIRMS

Korea's rapid economic growth has created an economy dominated by a few major firms. Small to medium-sized firms have grown rapidly in size over the 1980s as the *chaebol*-led economy continued the expansion. In the mid-1990s, the value added by small to medium-sized firms has surpassed more than 50 percent of the total value added in Korea. Despite such expansion in quantity, Korea's small to medium-sized firms have reached the point at which their survival requires a fundamental reorientation of their businesses. As the nation moves into the high-tech competition of the global market, small and medium-sized firms have the opportunity to become a vital part of the economy. Furthermore, Korea's enriched democratization in recent years has accelerated the need to adjust social inequality. However, Korea's long-term, growth-oriented economic policies have left small and medium-sized firms with little self-reliance. The government's policies toward small and medium-sized firms have been largely ineffective in terms of improving their competitiveness in the new areas of global competition. The *chaebols* have also failed to cooperate in helping small and medium-sized firms improve their competence. Whether Korea's small to medium-sized firms are able to carry out the structural adjustment and adapt to the new global competitive order remains open to question.

Facing the new challenges of Korea's globalization in the 1990s, the government has adjusted its policy for small and medium-sized firms from protection oriented to market oriented. Today, the economic concern is not to protect these firms from the threat of large corporations but to help them grow as a vital source of national competitiveness. Current government policy is attempting to attack the fundamental source of the problem in Korea's small to medium-sized firms by helping them develop their own niche competence and establish self-reliance. Thus, instead of the traditional umbrella-style means of universal protection, the government's support for small to medium-sized firms is now more discriminatory, more favorable toward those firms with the potential to develop technological competence.

To enhance structural adjustment, the Korean government has created various tax benefits to stabilize the transition and attract a talented labor force into prospective small-business areas. The government has also established a "think bank" to improve small and medium-sized firms' access to information about new (domestic and foreign) technologies and to engineers and scientists. The government has increased structural adjustment loans to be allocated directly by the Small and Medium Industry Promotion Corporation for technology development, automation, and data management systems. In 1991, about two hundred small to medium-sized firms received the first loans to make structural adjustments from labor-intensive businesses such as handbags, toys, and clothing to computers and electronics.[44] The Korean government planned to invest about $6.4 billion by the end of 1997 to facilitate the structural adjustment of small to medium-sized firms.

The ratio of mandatory loans by commercial banks to small to medium-sized firms has been raised from 40 to 45 percent since December 1992.[45] The Korean government has created various funds to stabilize technologically competent small and medium-sized firms that are experiencing temporary financial difficulties. The government has also started the "business incubator" system to help new ventures with potential; as of 1995, $153 million was available to support new ventures. In recent years, the Fair Trade Commission has been strictly imposing the sixty-day payment clearance law to relieve small to medium-sized firms of financial burdens. The government has also been urging the *chaebols* to improve cooperation with small to medium-sized firms so that both can strengthen their competitiveness in the global market. Large corporations are encouraged to extend financial and technological support to small to medium-sized firms by setting up joint funds, allowing loans, and cooperating on technology development.[46] In response to the government's urging, in mid-1995 Samsung announced that it had decided to use a cash payment system with its subcontractors in lieu of issuing corporate bonds to ease small to medium-sized firms' financing. Samsung's announcement also included lowering the interest rate for the loans to smaller businesses from its own insurance company, dispatching its technical personnel to smaller businesses for six to twelve months to provide technical training, allowing smaller businesses to use Samsung's foreign offices to facilitate their foreign entry and marketing, and offering free safety inspection service to smaller businesses. It was also reported that Hyundai was considering shortening its payment clearance to subcontractors from the sixty days required by law to forty. The Korean government has been encouraging large corporations to spin off their ineffi- cient businesses and build affiliated relationships with small to medium- sized firms. In 1994 alone, sixty large corporations transferred businesses— including 1,870 products—to small to medium-sized firms. As of 1990, about 70 percent of Korea's small and medium-sized firms (45,056 firms) were in buyer-supplier relationships with large corporations, and this ratio is increasing.[47]

One promising development has been the increased competitiveness of small to medium-sized firms in overseas markets. For example, Medison, founded in 1985 by a few former researchers at KAIST, has been able to overcome the barriers and become a significant global player in ultrasound diagnosing equipment. Even though Medison was not able to pay better than large corporations, talented employees were attracted to the company because of its vision and potential. Medison's persistently innovative spirit enabled the company to become the first and only producer of ultrasound testing equipment in Korea and to export its product to U.S. and European markets. Some of Korea's smaller firms, as well as the *chaebols*, that have made a dent in the U.S. market are shown in table 5-9.

In the 1990s, Korea's small to medium-sized firms are operating under the survival-of-the-fittest principle, with several dozen going under every day. The government has been attempting to enhance market competition by constraining the *chaebols'* monopoly and by liberalizing the market to foreign competitors. Survival of the structural adjustment period will take more than the government support and the goodwill of the *chaebols*. Small to medium-sized firms will have to go back to the basics; instead of being opportunistic and jumping from one business to another, they will have to rely on strong entrepreneurship and craftsmanship. The Korean government

Table 5-9 Major Korean Manufacturing Operations in the United States

U.S. Company	Parent Company	Line of Business	Korean Ownership (%)
Alabama			
Goldstar of America	LG Group	Electronics	100%
Alaska			
Suneel Alaska	Suneel Shipping	Coal mining	100
Bering Development	Korea-Alaska Development	Coal mining	50
Arizona			
Unitech Microelectronics	Unitech Systems	Semicoductors	100
Arkansas			
Outdoor Cap Company	Young An Cap	Caps	50
Pine Bluff Cutting Tools	Yangjiwon Tools	Cutting tools	100
California			
Cordata Technologies	Daewoo Electronics	Microcomputers	58
Daewon Machine	Daewon Industry	Metals	100
Mooney Aerospace	Doshin	Oil pressure equipment	50
Dong Ah America	Dong Ah Pharmaceuticals	Medicine	100
Metra Instruments	Dongyang Chemical	Equipment	11
Magnatex-USA	Magnatex-Korea	Oil chemistry	100
Baikyang USA	Baikyang	Underwear	100
Bosoung Industrial	Bosoung	Bags	100
Sammi Steel America	Sammi Steel	Stainless steel	100
Samyang USA	Samyang Foods	Snack foods	100
Genwood	Choyoung Trade	Apparel	100
Union Incorporated	Hanyang Chemical	Snack foods	100
Delaware			
Pohang Steel America	POSCO	Steel products	100
Florida			
Bultina International	Bultina	Lighters	100
Illinois			
Zenith Electronics	LG Electronics	Electronics	53
Health Protection	Dongkuk	Condoms	75
Peace Industries	Korea Staple	Staplers	100
KMC of America	Korea Machine	Equipment	100
Iowa			
PMX Industries	Poongsan	Copper products	88
Kentucky			
Sammi Sound Technology	Sammi Sound	Speakers	100
Massachusetts			
ETEX	Iljin Electric	Artificial joints	50

Table 5-9 Continued

U.S. Company	Parent Company	Line of Business	Korean Ownership (%)
Michigan			
DPI America	Daehan Paint Ink	Ink	100
Missouri			
Miho Paper	Miho Paper	Paper	100
TEKK	Taeyon Electronics	Wireless phones	51
Montana			
Mont Leather	Kumkang Leather	Leather products	100
New Jersey			
SKC America	Sunkyung	Film, tape	100
Garmy Sports	Garmy Industries	Sports equipment	100
Joint Communications	Natt	Digital phones	44
Samsung Electronics America	Samsung Electronics	Electronics	100
Princeton Biomeditech	Miwon	Medicines	51
Diadom	Sinpoong	Health foods	100
Ilkyung	Ilkyung	Clothing	100
New York			
American Tape	Seotong	Adhesive tape	100
SBS USA	SBS	Program tape	100
Windsor Toys	Choson Trade	Dolls	100
HIW America	Hoilim Machine	Sewage disposer	100
North Carolina			
Peace Textile America	Daekyung Chemical	Dyeing	100
Oregon			
Hyundai Semiconductor America	Hyundai	Semiconductors	100
Pennsylvania			
Daeyang America	Daeyang Rubber	Footwear	100
South Carolina			
Galaxy Industrial	Kunja	Sweaters	100
ACE Textile America	Korea ACE	Dyeing	100
Texas			
Namyang Aloe	Namyang Aloe	Aloe products	100
Milano Hat	Young An Cap	Hats	50
Jason Industries	Jason	Leather products	100
HDH USA	Hapdong	Leather products	100
Hyundai Furniture	Hyundai Furniture	Furniture	100
Washington			
Daewoo America Development	Daewoo	Construction	100

Source: Compiled from the *KUSEC Annual Report* (Seoul: Korea-U.S. Economic Council, 1994), 26–28.

is optimistic that once the current transformation of small to medium-sized firms into high-margin fields is complete, the nation will be able to establish balanced economic growth, possibly early in the next century, between large and small to medium-sized firms. It is believed that the economic significance of Korea's small to medium-sized firms will slowly converge to the same level of Japanese small to medium-sized firms in the beginning of the next century. Small to medium-sized firms will then be the driving force in correcting the long-standing structural and regional disequilibrium of the Korean economy.

CHAPTER SIX

Reorganizing for Globalization

In a recent meeting between corporate executives and academicians, a Samsung executive explained why Korean firms need to make themselves international: "Internationalization means reaching to the first-level companies of the developed countries, winning in world competition, and having the best management systems in the world. To achieve this internationalization, we need to have a managerial perspective that transcends borders, to utilize resources all over the world, and to develop an optimal balance of managerial insight and resource utilization."[1]

Hyundai's Chairman Chung Mong-Hun asserts: "The world is taking on a new shape. Newly emerging economic regional blocs are burying Cold War divisions. . . . As this trend continues into the twenty-first century, these economic blocs will merge to create one vast global market economy. . . . To take advantage of this trend, we must quickly adapt to these changes in the world order. We must all the more readily 'fly the flag' of globalization."[2]

The publication *Daewoo around the World* states: "With rapidly shifting global economic and political patterns beginning to emerge by the late 1980s, Daewoo perceived the advantages for rapid globalization of its efforts if it were to emerge in the coming century as a truly world-class enterprise."[3] And the *Lucky-Goldstar Annual Report 1994* pronounces: "By forming joint ventures with local partners around the world, Lucky-Goldstar is accelerating the internationalization of its operations."[4]

For many Korean firms, the globalization of business activities is at the core of their corporate strategy. Globalization is an integral part of nearly every annual report and new government program (*segyehwa*). Far from being a panacea, however, globalization of the economic sphere, at the moment centered on *chaebol* activities, carries many risks. Competing overseas brings Korean firms into direct competition with more experienced and better financed rivals from Japan, America, Europe, and elsewhere. Moreover, emerging competitors from Asia threaten Korea's foothold in its main markets. Even so, globalization is not all adverse; in fact, emerging markets in Asia and Eastern Europe provide opportunities for Korean firms to develop their international competencies. Thus, while there is agreement on the need to become international, it can be accomplished in a number of different ways. This chapter discusses Korean firms' foray into global markets and industries as they attempt to meet this challenge.

IMPERATIVES FOR GLOBALIZATION:
THE KOREAN CONTEXT

Globalization is a word in good currency. Even so, it means different things to different people. In the 1970s it was fashionable to use the term *internationalization* to distinguish activities conducted across domestic and foreign borders. The term *globalization* refers to the deepening linkages and interconnections of economic activities on a worldwide basis.[5] As these distinctions are still evolving, we will use the terms interchangeably.

Throughout Korea, globalization is a hotly debated issue, with frequent editorials on the topic appearing in national and local newspapers. Korean corporations have generally embraced globalization but have modified its meaning to suit their circumstances. Many of these firms see globalization as a means of responding to emerging trends, including (1) the increasing tendency toward open markets, (2) changes in the Korean domestic markets, and (3) the necessity of acquiring newer technologies. Consider the following:

- *Globalization and the opening of trading blocs.* As we enter the twenty-first century, annual growth of the world economy is expected to be about 3 percent, and world markets are expected to continue to liberalize as a result of the 1993 Uruguay Round agreements of GATT negotiations.[6] These growth projections are based on the expectation that world trade will increase significantly, as shown in tables 6-1 and 6-2. This is partly because there will be investment recovery in various countries owing to the reengineering of the industrial structure of developed countries and the decrease in international interest rates. Moreover, China and especially the ASEAN

Table 6-1   Predicted Changes in World and Domestic Markets

	World Markets	Domestic Markets
Positive changes	• Recovery of world economy • Greater liberalization of world markets	• Steady growth of domestic economy • Deregulation of foreign investments in domestic companies
Negative changes	• Increased competition in advanced technology • Localization of major markets • New regulations to protect the environment	• Accelerated opening of domestic markets • Unclear prospect of early recovery of national competitiveness in the world market

Source: Adapted from Chul Won Park, "Internationalization of the Samsung Trading Group" (paper presented at the Case Presentation of Internationalization of Korean Conglomerates at Han Yang University, Korea Business Association, Seoul, May 28, 1994), 5.

Table 6-2   Economic Growth Rates: Actual and Projected

	1987–1992	1992–1997	1997–2002
World in general	2.0%	3.1%	3.7%
United States	1.9	2.9	2.8
Japan	4.3	3.5	3.5
European Union	2.9	2.2	2.6
NIEs* and ASEAN	7.6	7.1	6.6
Latin America	1.9	3.7	4.7

Source: Adapted from Chul Won Park, "Internationalization of the Samsung Trading Group" (paper presented at the Case Presentation of Internationalization of Korean Conglomerates at Han Yang University, Korea Business Association, Seoul, May 28, 1994), 4.
*The NIEs cover Hong Kong, Singapore, Taiwan, and South Korea.

countries (Association of Southeast Asian Nations, which includes Indonesia, Malaysia, the Philippines, Singapore, Thailand, and Vietnam) are expected to sustain their high growth rates. Latin American countries are also expected to recover from the current recession. Finally, in view of the 1993 Uruguay Round agreements, the world economy is eventually expected to enter into a new age of borderless competition.

- *Changes in domestic markets.* Globalization entails both rights and obligations. For other countries to allow Korean firms to compete within their borders, Korea has to open up its own markets as well. This principle of reciprocity—that is, "If I sell, I must also buy"—is a key to market liberalization. Truly globalized companies must put their products in competition with first-class products manufactured by other leading companies around the world. Currently, liberalization is paced by a steady growth rate of between 6 and 7 percent in the Korean market. This growth rate should attract foreign investors at about the same time that the Korean government reduces its support for Korean domestic manufacturers. Furthermore, the Korean government is also expected to deregulate foreign investment in Korea, lifting limits on everything from the size of the investments to the markets where investments can be made. The government has also signaled that foreign businesses will be allowed to purchase land for plant construction and housing without government approval. Foreign companies investing in high-technology products will be allowed to finance plant construction with loans obtained abroad. Moreover, they will be allowed to import certain machinery from Japan that was previously banned.[7]

- *Acquiring new technologies.* Competing in the global market puts Korean firms in direct competition with firms from which they have historically licensed technologies and technological know-how. Given this history, it is expected that such firms are reluctant to pass on new technologies to Korean firms in the form of licensing agreements in the future. A more promising arrangement for Korean firms would be a joint venture, which offers both parties reciprocal sharing of complementary benefits. Development is not possible without concerted international exchanges. Therefore, more strategic alliances, mergers, and acquisitions are expected among the technologically advanced companies across the world. Moreover, more new business areas are expected to emerge from joint research and development efforts between firms of different nationalities. If Korean firms are to join the "technology club," they will have to become involved in many more such alliances.[8] While the full treatise on competing on the new technological frontier is presented in chapter 7, some of the arguments are presented here.

THE BIG FOUR: GLOBALIZATION INITIATIVES

Traditionally, the implementation of globalization has entailed four steps in which a company goes from (1) having a domestic-market orientation to (2) having an international-market orientation to (3) becoming a foreign local company to (4) becoming a global company.[9] Typically, a company oriented to the domestic market moves toward an international orientation by enlarging its production capacity and opening export offices overseas. Most major Korean companies reached this stage in the late 1970s and early 1980s. From here, successful firms gravitate toward the third phase of globalization to become a foreign local-market-oriented firm. Here, emphasis is placed on acquiring greater independence through the use of local suppliers and localized production in foreign countries. Many Korean companies reached this stage in the mid-1980s to the early 1990s. Local employees are hired to help the company understand and become integrated into the local culture. Firms that enter the final phase of globalization develop truly global organizational configurations and management systems, and they pursue manufacturing efficiencies through multifaceted production facilities around the world. Foreign employees will begin to reach the top of the organizational hierarchy—especially in corporate headquarters—and flexibility and speed become the hallmarks of organizational operations. It is this fourth and final stage that many Korean companies, such as Samsung and LG, are currently trying to enter.

In this section, we review the globalization efforts of Korea's Big Four *chaebols*, which are in many ways role models for other, somewhat smaller firms. We begin with the Samsung Group, Korea's largest conglomerate.

Samsung: A "First-Class Company" by 2000

Samsung Chairman Lee Kun-Hee's management revolution is informed by a clear message: Without understanding things that are considered "alien" to Korean culture, Samsung can never compete. "Knowing yourself and your enemies is the first prerequisite to becoming a warrior," says Lee, paraphrasing classical Chinese military theorist Sun Tzu. "My first step is getting people to this point."[10] In February 1995, Lee assembled his thirty top executives in Los Angeles. His message was clear: Samsung had to accelerate its pace of globalization. He expected his companies to be deriving 30 percent of their sales from international markets by 2000. This effort would include setting up integrated electronics facilities in China and Mexico.[11] At the time, less than 10 percent of Samsung's production took place outside Korea. The plan calls for an increase to 40 percent within the next five years, at which point all international headquarters are to be managed by host country nationals.[12]

Samsung's quest for globalization stems from the threatened status of its Samsung Trading Company. The factors that led to this crisis are summarized in figure 6-1. While the factors are largely self-explanatory, some additional information may be helpful to place Samsung's objectives in context. In its new competitive posture, Samsung no longer views domestic competitors—Hyundai, LG, and Daewoo—as its primary competitors. Rather, it targets global rivals such as Toshiba, NEC, and Sony. Yet, in many ways, Samsung finds itself still playing catch-up; its main exporter, Samsung Electronics, exports only a fraction of what Hitachi or Matsushita does. Compared with the Japanese, Korean producers still suffer from a reputation of variable quality. Korea's export revenues still come from low-margin, down-market items. Today, about 40 percent of Samsung's consumer electronics exports go to OEM customers, and Samsung's image

Figure 6-1 Recent Threats to Samsung's Long-Term Survival and Growth

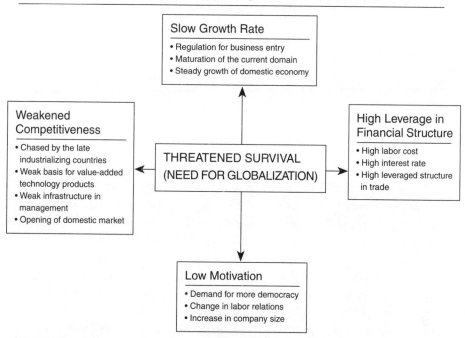

Source: Adapted from Chul Won Park, "Internationalization of the Samsung Trading Group" (paper presented at the Case Presentation of Internationalization of Korean Conglomerates in Han Yang University, Korea Business Association, Seoul, May 28, 1994), 6.

is poor outside of Asia. Only 5 percent of Samsung's electronics goods are made abroad, compared with 28 percent for Japanese firms, which have moved most of their low-end manufacturing offshore.

As with most Korean firms, Samsung's R&D budget lags behind that of its Japanese competitors. Samsung's current budget is about $650 million, up 30 percent from just two years ago. However, this sizable investment is still far short of R&D investments by Matsushita and Sony, which annually spend $2.3 billion and $1.1 billion, respectively. With the exception of semiconductors, Samsung's technology level is widely considered to be inferior to that of the leading Japanese multinational firms.

Samsung's global competition is centered in semiconductor manufacturing, where it currently holds the number one position in sales of DRAM chips. In 1983, Samsung entered the microchip business with the help of Micron Technologies, a U.S. semiconductor maker. Samsung's appearance with other *chaebols* in the one-megabit and the four-megabit market limited the Japanese ability to control prices. Samsung then entered the U.S. market in the late 1980s, benefiting greatly from the 1980 agreement between Washington and Japan that set a floor for semiconductor prices in the United States. In the second half of 1990 and early in 1991, there was a drop in demand from key semiconductor end users, but Samsung did not experience a serious drop in sales. Its strategy was to supply its consumers with a total semiconductor solution—that is, an integrated solution to consumers' problems and needs. To compete against the Japanese, Samsung has also been focusing on the thin-screen liquid-crystal-display (LCD). Samsung sees the active matrix, or collar LCD, as the most promising new technology under development.

Chairman Lee's goals are to establish Samsung as what he calls a "first-class company" by 2000. Such a company has to be stable and flexible to be competitive. To evolve into such a company, Samsung must follow three important principles, according to Lee: quality management, multifaceted integration, and globalization. Being a quality organization means being on the leading edge in terms of meeting and exceeding consumer expectations. Multifaceted integration refers to investment in information systems that are essential for analysis and simulation. Lee sees information industries as the leading high-value industries of the future. Finally, Samsung needs to globalize to build up its technological "firepower."[13] To achieve globalization, Samsung must implement what is called the STEP II movement—a program for maximizing efficiency and change that will lead the company to its "second foundation," or "rebirth."[14] The key objective is to internationalize the company by means of the following:

- *Internationalization of sales.* This effort focuses not only on enhancing international sales but also on refining the concept of the business by undergoing reengineering and by balancing the entry into foreign markets for production and marketing with appropriate management structures. This also means diversification, particularly in new domestic and foreign businesses, but with added transactions in developing nations.

- *Internationalization of management.* This effort emphasizes innovation in management and in construction of an infrastructure in information systems.

- *Maximization of employee abilities.* This effort involves encouraging employees to develop a level of expertise and requisite international business sense comparable with that of the most developed countries. A review of operations from 1990 to 1992 demonstrated the need to train employees as international experts, to manage difficulties experienced with foreign local employees, and to recruit excellent employees. There is also a need to internationalize domestic management by rotating foreign employees and by standardizing the basic tasks involving domestic and foreign management.[15]

Samsung's experience with globalization has not been trouble free. At least four kinds of problems have been identified, and they concern attitudes, human resources, management, and sales.[16] Problems in attitude stem from an independent management mindset among local branches that was not consistent with thinking at headquarters. In terms of human resources, better training was needed for international managers. As a result of not hiring enough local managers, there was a lack of knowledge of local legal systems, business traditions, and culture. Management problems involved a lack of coordination between headquarters and the local branches on matters dealing with strategic mission and the delegation of responsibility and control to the local branches. Sales problems were manifest in a need for a global information network. Moreover, Samsung still suffered from its reputation as a low- to medium-priced manufacturer. The lack of a customer-oriented marketing system—that is, after-sales service in various local markets—compounded this problem.

To redress these problems, Samsung has embarked on a program designed to foster an international attitude among its international employees. The development of an international attitude involves certain shifts in thinking, as shown in table 6-3.

Table 6-3 Developing International Attitudes at Samsung

Change Employee Attitudes from . . .	To . . .
• Company-oriented thought	• Customer-oriented thought
• Korea-centered thought (parochialism)	• World-encompassing thought
• Headquarters-oriented thought	• Delegation and autonomy
• Hardware orientation	• Software orientation
• Corporate culture based on localism	• World citizenship
• Inflexible thought	• Flexible thought (including familiarity with foreigners, adaptability to different cultures, creativity, and nonquantifying thought)

Samsung has also determined that without internationalized human resources, the implementation of its internationalization strategy and global management would be impossible. A change in organizational structure would not work well without adequate human resources support. Accordingly, Samsung defines *internationalized* as follows:

- Fluency in English or local languages to communicate and negotiate with foreign people.

- Flexible and adaptable work abilities and expertise suitable to local business environments.

- A common knowledge of and adaptability to foreign cultures so that employees can perceive and understand foreign cultures objectively.

- Attractive characteristics and manners sufficient to build friendships with foreigners in business relationships as well as in nonbusiness relationships.

In implementing its globalization program, Samsung has adopted a variety of action plans. The first is in the recruitment process. In recruiting university graduates, a priority is given to those who are fluent in foreign languages (better than third grade in TOEIC, a proficiency test emphasizing spoken English, is required). Moreover, preference is currently given to hiring Korean students who are studying at foreign universities, second-generation Koreans in foreign countries, and other people who have life experience in foreign countries, such as one whose parents worked as government officers in foreign countries. Special consideration is also given to university students who major in unpopular foreign languages. Finally, current employees are trained in foreign languages, and language ability is viewed as a requirement for promotion and transfer to foreign countries.

For new employees, there is a short foreign excursion to selected countries to acquaint them with cross-cultural issues. For first-year employees, training includes basic manners, etiquette, and the international mindset, as well as the foreign expedition.[17] For fourth-year employees, a program has been designed to develop local expertise in a special area, such as nonmetal material, grain, dairy products, fiber and fabrics, oil trading, or cotton. Additional areas include fashion, communication, international finance, and international legal systems. The training period ranges from one to three months. For positions above middle management, managers are sent to major foreign universities such as Harvard or Stanford for three to six months. Those appointed to move to foreign branches as successors to the incumbent managers are trained as part of the "21C" (twenty-first century) core-manager group.[18] This 21C leader training is for relatively senior managers (such as *chojang* and *banjang*, described in chapter 8), while the 21C chief executive officer (CEO) training is for executives. The company has also started its own MBA training for middle and junior managers in cooperation with KAIST. (This is the Korean Association of the Institute of Science and Technology, a scientific think tank sponsored by the Korean government.)

Samsung has also established an Institute of International Education to train executives in international competitiveness. Established in May 1994, the institute can accommodate 220 employees and is oriented toward training international managers in foreign languages, adaptability to foreign cultures, and specific areas of international expertise. The institute also conducts research in foreign countries. Ten different study groups have operated in Japan, the ASEAN countries, China, America, and Latin America. The objective is to provide an international information network. Information on various countries is collected for purposes of building connections with foreign data services and other institutes. The institute seeks not only to foster the internationalization of the Samsung group but also to assist other Korean companies through education, information, and consulting.

Hyundai: Straight-on Globalization

In 1970, Hyundai embarked on its first overseas assignment by taking on a Middle Eastern construction project. Not long afterward, Hyundai extended its international reach into countries like Thailand, South Vietnam,

Australia, and Singapore. Since its inception in 1947, Hyundai has been attempting to internationalize its operations. And since the incorporation of Hyundai America in 1969, Hyundai has been active in the American market. It introduced its subcompact car, Excel, to America in the 1980s. In 1990, Hyundai began a project worth $40 million to log spruce forests in the coastal mountains near the sea of Japan. Located in Svetlaya, the venture was designed to serve the mounting needs of the Japanese market. In 1992, Hyundai Engineering and Construction began a joint-venture housing project in Thailand, with an expected cost of about $3.3 billion. This marked the first of many attempts to penetrate the Thai market. Hyundai is also active in China, with a joint venture for a $100 million plant to assemble minibuses.[19]

While Hyundai's record overseas suggests mixed results, it is perhaps its entry into electronics and semiconductors that has commanded more current attention. Hyundai's entry into electronics was quite late. Other Korean *chaebols* had already been manufacturing a wide variety of electronic products, while Hyundai remained in the heavy industries. Chairman Chung Ju-Yung watched his rivals reap fortunes from electronics. His desire to challenge top-ranked Samsung as Korea's leading manufacturer of electronic products brought Hyundai to the forefront of high-technology competition.[20] Hyundai's initial foray into semiconductors came by way of an electronics plant near San Jose, California, in 1982. Designed as a research and development operation, the project encountered initial problems, ranging from personnel issues to cross-cultural difficulties to a conflict of expectations between Hyundai's corporate offices in Seoul and Hyundai employees in San Jose. The plant was shut down in 1985, with almost the same speed and decisiveness with which it was started.[21] Even so, the venture had something to show despite these difficulties: a prototype workstation complete with a microcomputer at the Hotel Lotte on October 7, 1983. After all the hasty work on the part of American designers, Hyundai Electronics demonstrated the capacity to produce four different types of computers, including one for color graphics—a symbol of Hyundai's long-awaited entrance into the electronic age.[22]

The company's recent success in semiconductors has placed it on a par with the LG Group and ahead of Daewoo. In 1989, Hyundai was selling the 1M DRAM. By 1991, it was selling 4M DRAMs. More significantly, the actual chips were designed by Hyundai, not by Japanese or American engineers—a significant accomplishment for any Korean latecomer into the industry. Just as astonishing, Hyundai began manufacturing personal computers in the fall of 1992, designing and assembling them at Hyundai

Electronics America in San Jose.[23] What is left to question is whether and how Hyundai can compete with America and Japan in the entire spectrum of semiconductors. Already, the pursuit of the ultimate semiconductor—the gigabyte, or 1024, M DRAM chip—is on the horizon. By 1992, semiconductors had become Korea's single largest export, grossing $6.8 billion in foreign sales, including $3.9 billion in sales of chips actually fabricated in Korea and another $3.9 billion from those assembled and packaged in Korea for foreign makers and re-exported.[24]

Hyundai used the same approach to the business of memory chips it had used with ships and automobiles—a brash, highly aggressive, straight-on approach. "What differentiates Hyundai from other Korean *chaebols* is its aggressiveness and 'can-do' spirit," explains one Hyundai manager.[25] By 1994, Samsung had overtaken the Japanese to become the top-ranked DRAM manufacturer in the world, while Hyundai was ranked tenth in the world of DRAMs. Beating Samsung at its own game had become Hyundai's ambition.

Hyundai's focus on semiconductors and on Samsung came about following its disappointing performance in the marketing of personal computers. In April 1992, the company decided to return to its San Jose operation, making it the focal point of both R&D and assembly operations. Hyundai quickly learned the perils of the high-technology business. Customizing to users' unique requirements was difficult, as was managing the very short product life cycles. American PC manufacturers relentlessly introduced more powerful models at lower prices. Price drops of 30 percent a year became the norm. After a full year of operation, sales had amounted to a disappointing $34 million. At the end of August 1994, Hyundai Electronics America again abandoned production of PCs in San Jose.[26] Undeterred, Hyundai sought to learn from this experience in formulating its new globalization strategy.

Hyundai's globalization strategy came of age with an emphasis on consolidating its gains in semiconductors and on building plants in the United States. The emerging motto was to "internationalize" and to hire the best native talent. After a lengthy search for an American location in which to house its next array of DRAMs, the company finally settled on its choice. On May 21, 1995, Hyundai announced plans to build its largest semiconductor plant in Eugene, Oregon: a $1.3 billion operation that would employ at least 1,000 people. It also stated that it would meet all environmental regulations, hire mostly from the local labor pool, and become a good corporate citizen.[27] Nestled in the lush Willamette Valley, and with a small population of 120,000, Eugene is home to the University of Oregon and adjoins neighboring Springfield, where a major Weyerhaeuser lumber facility is located. Just 107 miles north is Portland, Oregon's largest city and business center and home to about three hundred high-technology firms—a number that is increasing. Historically, Eugene had developed a tough stance on environmental protection, as reflected in its complex industrial zoning laws. These laws had scared away numerous Japanese and American firms contemplating locating in the area, including Hewlett-Packard, Sumitomo, and Data General. With a plentiful supply of water and relatively cheap electricity, Oregon had emerged as a natural base for high-technology industries. Its lower land costs (especially compared with California) and reputation for having a highly skilled labor force served as additional inducements. In 1994 the Eugene area managed to attract Symantec, a software company, and in April 1995 the neighboring city of Springfield built a relatively new Sony CD-ROM facility.

After the initial period of euphoria, questions emerged about both Hyundai and the process used by city planners to select it. These included concerns about environmental safety, particularly the use of toxic chemicals, Hyundai's labor record in Korea, and the wisdom of tax incentives to attract foreign firms.[28] It is doubtful whether Hyundai had anticipated this flurry of criticisms, albeit from a small vocal minority, led by the Citizens for Public Accountability—a grassroots-group opposed to the Hyundai complex—but the episode clearly illustrates some of the difficulties involved in a globalization project.[29]

Meanwhile, Hyundai continues to forge ahead on a number of fronts to compete globally. Having successfully developed the next generation of state-of-the-art 64k DRAMs in 1992, it is pushing into the 4M and 16M DRAM as well as into the development of the 1M and 4M SRAM. Hyundai is also producing a wide array of memory applications that include video RAM, mask ROM, flash memories, and various IC cards. Hyundai has strengthened its base in nonmemory semiconductors, which includes Systems ICs, various ASIC products, and other compound semiconductors. Having placed LCDs within the scope of its strategic plans for the future, Hyundai has formed a technical alliance with Image Quest Technologies for the development of the next generation of products, such as the full color TFT LCD.[30]

Daewoo: Diversification into Unexplored Markets

Daewoo's managerial strategies identify globalization as a key objective. Specifically, Daewoo seeks to expand globalization and the foreign localization of business activities by building a stronger foundation as a multinational business entity and by promoting integrated localization systems. The goals underlying globalization at Daewoo can be summarized as follows: (1) develop new markets, (2) access lower cost-factor inputs, (3) acquire new technology, and (4) overcome trade barriers.[31] Actually, Daewoo has stressed internationalization since its inception in 1967. Its goal at that time was to propel Korean exports as part of the Korean government's economic development program. In these early years, Daewoo sought to build export volumes through OEM and subcontracted manufacturing. Eventually, Daewoo expanded its range of products to include the light-industry export market. In the 1970s, Daewoo was instrumental in developing heavy and chemical industries. By the 1980s, the group had progressed into the mid- and high-technology industries, which in 1993 accounted for more than 85 percent of Daewoo's exports.

Daewoo's globalization efforts were in large part a reaction to its poor international market presence in the early years. Daewoo Electronics, for instance, had a limited technology base, negligible brand recognition overseas, and hardly any international presence. Its dependence on OEM agreements to provide it with process and product technologies and access to overseas markets was just about its only strategic option.[32] Chairman Kim Woo-Choong, with the reputation as the most traveled person in Korea, sought to improve Daewoo's position through globalization. Foremost was the need to build a quality brand name and to create consumer identification with and loyalty to Daewoo products. In the case of Daewoo Electronics, President Bae Soon Hoon has initiated an aggressive program designed to market Daewoo brands all over the world. Daewoo has also entered into brand contracts with firms in Italy, Spain, France, and Iran, and it expects to have a massive presence in Southeast Asia, especially in Singapore and Malaysia.[33] This drive has also permeated the Korean domestic market. President Bae has become something of a TV celebrity, appearing in commercials that say Daewoo Electronics' washing machines and television sets are built like tanks—sturdy, reliable, no frills. Meanwhile, Chairman Kim's goal is to sell Daewoo cars, now mainly exported to developing countries and the United States.[34]

Daewoo's globalization efforts also include a concerted drive to open new markets. Pioneering difficult markets has been a specialty of Korean firms, and no one does this better than Daewoo. In Libya, for example, Daewoo won more than $3.5 billion in contracts to build schools, roads, and a medical college between 1985 and 1992.[35] Chairman Kim has committed some $8 billion to make and sell Daewoo goods in Eastern Europe,

Central Asia, and Latin America, where Daewoo hopes to tap new consumers and cheap labor. While expanding into developing nations, most Korean *chaebols* have limited themselves to distribution networks. In contrast, Chairman Kim has relocated much of his group's industrial base to remote areas of the world; Daewoo sells television sets in Uzbekistan, cars in Iran, home appliances in St. Petersburg, and plywood in Burma.[36] Daewoo is the star in Uzbekistan, where it has a partnership with the government to build a $60 million joint-venture company to manufacture cordless phones, television sets, and vacuum cleaners for the local and overseas market. When hard currency is scarce, Daewoo accepts barter—an unconventional move. Daewoo is considering the construction of similar plants in Vietnam and Tatarstan. President Bae says that the next decade or so will be characterized by manufacturing rather than new product development and that a phased strategy into developing countries is an integral part of the plan.[37] The rationale is that Daewoo will not encounter the competition in these countries that it did in North America.[38]

Meanwhile, Daewoo has announced bold moves into other overseas markets. The Daewoo Group agreed in principle in July 1994 to establish an automotive joint venture in China. The venture, in which Daewoo will hold a 50 percent share, will include plants in four cities; production began in 1996. This is viewed as the first step toward the production of motor vehicles in China.[39] Daewoo has also entered the Australian auto market with a joint-venture sales company based in Sydney. Having established a base in Australia, Daewoo plans to extend sales to New Zealand and other areas of the South Pacific.[40] Daewoo Electronics also announced its goal to become the world's leading washing-machine manufacturer by the year 2000, with eleven new foreign production facilities in 1995.[41] Furthermore, Daewoo is expected to invest $225 million to establish thirty Daewoo Vision 2000 Car Stores for its auto sales in the United Kingdom.[42]

All in all, Daewoo's path toward globalization differs from that of the other *chaebols*. It seeks to hone in on its advantage in traditional products, but with an eye for new unexplored markets. Daewoo has traditionally been strong in shipbuilding, heavy industries, and electronics equipment and is regarded as weak in precision industries and telecommunications. In a recent interview, officials stressed their movement into automobiles and related high-technology sectors. One explained:

> *In the late 1970s, the emphasis was on shipbuilding, heavy industries, and electronics. Recently we have experienced rough times. We have reassessed our commitments, including the takeover of the GM-Daewoo joint venture. Our goals have been global*

management and technological independence. We aim to reach 2 million in automobile production, 50 percent domestic and 50 percent international. Specifically, the Espero and Sierra models should be good, considering that the Japanese are relatively weak at the low end of the car market. We aim to be more of a global player here. We have targeted a 10 percent share in home electronics, telecommunications, and VCRs.

As far as high technology, we have a research institute in Waring, New Jersey. We plan to use Chinese engineers here in Korea to offset our lack of Korean-based engineers. . . . We will have 3,500 engineers a year for the next three years. Engineers are a vital source for high-technology development. We already have one hundred persons in China for one-year training. We aim to do more.[43]

LG: Globalization through Strategic Alliances

Early in 1953, Lucky-Goldstar, now known as the LG Group, first exported plastic products. During the next four decades, the organization grew into a global business group with 39 subsidiaries, 39 joint-venture partners, and more than 130 branch offices. Currently, the group is focused on globalization, continuing to evolve into a world-class business group as it heads into the twenty-first century.

Back in 1989, however, a gloomy air pervaded the LG Group's headquarters. This largest South Korean maker of electronic appliances and consumer electronics had witnessed its market share drop in both domestic and overseas markets. Losses were mounting. However, by paying attention to changing managerial mindsets and rebuilding its innovative base, the group was able to turn around its performance in a dramatic fashion, exceeding the previous productivity record in microwave ovens set by Japan's Matsushita.[44] Yong Nam, an LG managing director, recounts the elements of this turnaround: "In 1987, we drew up the VISION-VICTORY-VALUE statement, our vision for the twenty-first century. With changes in 1989, we were losing ground in electronics and chemicals. We exposed close to 50 percent of our business. Yet, with sound management capabilities in these areas, we were able to turn this around."[45]

Part of the turnaround is explained by organizational renewal. As Yong Nam explains: "Working with McKinsey Consultants, we were continually restructuring our businesses. Now we are structured in terms of cultural units (not strategic business units). The groupings are according to similarities in businesses and cultures. This forces discipline among employees, who now take a cultural approach to business. Different cultures, different units. No recycling across departments, as we did in the past."[46]

While a number of key people were involved in the process, the transformation is credited to Lee Hun-Jo, who was recently appointed chief executive officer. Lee helped the company achieve its goal by grafting more Western management techniques onto a rigid Confucian-style leadership, with the assistance of McKinsey & Company. He was also forced to shift the management style from founding-father autocracy to professional. "You have to transform human beings," he explains. "If you can't change your people, you can't change your organization."[47] Credit is also due to Chairman Koo Cha-Kyung, who instructed his senior managers to run the show without bothering him. At present, the company is healthy and vibrant. It has regained its number one position in Korea for sales of color televisions, refrigerators, and washing machines. Globally, it has emerged as a powerful challenger in the fields of semiconductors and liquid crystal displays. It has also forged new alliances with Zenith Electronics and GE Appliances—ventures that are expected to give the LG group a presence in the United States and Europe. The group will soon make slim TV sets with large screens using Zenith's patented "flat tension mask" color picture tubes.

With its market share assured at home, the LG Group has refocused its vision overseas by shifting as much production of low-end, midrange product as possible to such countries as China and Vietnam. The company plans to increase its share of overseas production from the current 10 percent of sales to about 25 percent by 1997, a level that compares favorably with Japanese companies.[48] As part of the Zenith alliance, the LG Group will promote Zenith's digital high-definition television system, and LG's research lab in Chicago will develop videocassette recorders for Zenith's form of HDTV.

The LG Group's powerful commitment to global competitiveness is evidenced in its primary commitment to quality and cost improvement. In North America, the LG Group has reduced manufacturing costs and improved product quality by shifting TV assembly from Huntsville, Alabama, to Mexicali, Mexico. The combination thirteen-inch TV and VCR, called the TVCR, has become one of the hottest-selling items in the United States. Another product receiving high praise is its VH8 playback deck, which allows users of 8mm video to edit and transfer their home movies to a VHS format.[49]

LG's next three goals—marketing sales improvement, new market development, and new technology development—are to be achieved primarily through joint ventures with top global players. In addition to Zenith, the LG Group has invested $10 million in 3DO, headquartered in Redwood City, California, to work on the next generation of game hardware, and it is also involved with Oracle Corporation, also in Redwood City, California, in developing video-on-demand setup boxes. With U.S. companies, the group is manufacturing and marketing home appliances with GE Appliances and developing new operating software with IBM. These alliances are designed to move the LG Group away from being merely a source of cheap production to being a fully fledged partner in these ventures.[50] The group's biggest challenge is the manufacture of thin-film transistor (TFT) liquid crystal displays, the next generation of displays for laptop computers and other electronic devices. The company plans to spend $620 million to build a plant in Korea that will make these ten-inch color LCDs. Output is estimated to reach 1 million units a year by 1997, making the LG Group a player in a market dominated by Sharp Corporation and other Japanese firms. The company hopes it will be able to sustain this entry level with the assistance of the Korean government, which has strongly endorsed this technology.[51]

In semiconductors, the LG Group has succeeded against overwhelming odds. Goldstar Electron, of which Goldstar owns 62 percent, is the world's tenth largest manufacturer of DRAMs. The LG Group has partnered with Hitachi to develop and market the 1M and 4M DRAM chips. To boost further globalization efforts, the LG Group is banking on this investment in DRAMs, for which it has a 5 percent share in the world memory-chip market.[52]

Our review of the globalization activities of the Big Four reveals the strikingly different paths these organizations are taking to reach the same goal. Samsung is using its global reach and experience to leverage its efforts. It hopes to ward off Hyundai and sustain its hold on semiconductors, while challenging Hyundai on its traditional turf: automobiles. Hyundai is bent on building plants abroad through internationalization training programs and new policies of hiring native employees. The LG Group has staked its competitiveness on global alliances, while Daewoo has ventured into new, unexplored markets where it expects less intense competition. Whether each tailor-made strategy is successful for each firm remains to be seen. What is evident is that their in-practice strategies are clear, focused, and potentially deadly for the competition.

PERSPECTIVES FROM OTHER KOREAN FIRMS

While the Big Four are moving rapidly with their unique globalization strategies, the other *chaebols* are not standing still. Globalization has struck most Korean companies—big and small—and, as with the above four firms, each is seeking its own approach to the world market that is consistent with its product line, experience in the marketplace, and management philosophy. By way of example, we briefly review here the current strategies of several other firms.

KIA Motors: Globalization through High Technology

KIA Motors Corporation is the second largest automobile maker—and the leading company manufacturing compact-size commercial vehicles—in Korea. KIA is partially owned by Ford Motor Company and Mazda Motor Corporation of Japan. It currently controls about 24 percent of the commercial market. Originally a specialist in commercial vehicles, it rationalized its operations in 1986 and outpaced Daewoo in turnover from 1990 onward. KIA is capable of producing 313,779 passenger cars and 165,758 commercial cars per year.[53]

In our interviews with KIA executives, they said their response to globalization was to place more emphasis on high-technology development. A senior-ranking executive noted:

> The major challenge affecting KIA is the importation of advanced technology. After years of successful manufacturing in Korea, which provided the groundwork for our independence, it is time to face the challenge of global competition. Success in advanced technology depends on ourselves and on government policy.
>
> In the past, licensing and joint ventures worked. We learned a lot from TRW, Porsche, and others. But this might not be the case in the future. We need to develop our marketing capabilities overseas. We already have advanced high-technology centers and R&D abroad.
>
> We need to educate our manpower, send employees to prestigious engineering schools abroad, and establish "listening posts" in these countries. Government policy is also a factor. Recent policies prompted foreign companies to leave. There is need for them to stay longer so that we can learn. At home, we face the problem of mounting labor costs.[54]

Ssangyong: Growth through Human Harmony

Ssangyong started in March 1938 as a small soap maker called Samkong Fat Company. Its aggressive development and success is credited to the vision of founder Kim Sung-Kon. While the rest of the country was earning its bread and butter from textiles, Kim turned his company to the manufacture of cement. The facility at Donghae soon became the largest in the world. Eventually, Ssangyong began to diversify and entered into the construction field. Today, you can see its handiwork almost everywhere around the world. For example, one of the first sights visitors see on their arrival in Singapore is the impressive Raffles City Complex. Designed by noted architect I. M. Pei, Raffles City is to date the largest building project in Asia and includes the tallest hotel in the world, the seventy-three-story Westin Stamford. The complex also includes two towers twenty-eight stories high and a convention center for five thousand. When the site was completed in 1985—three months ahead of schedule—it was praised by *Engineering News Record* as an "engineering miracle." But this is not the only mammoth construction project successfully completed by Ssangyong in recent years.

The company is also responsible for constructing the Plaza Indonesia (the largest building complex in Indonesia), the Omariya Riyadh office complex in Saudia Arabia, the Al Shaheed Faisal College and the Shamaishani Center in Jordan, and the Maghrib Highway in Kuwait, to name just a few. Moreover, giant construction projects such as these are handled by only one of the forty-six businesses managed by the Ssangyong Group. In addition to construction, the group is involved in oil refining, cement production, engine manufacturing, truck and bus manufacturing, shipping, textiles, paper products, electronics, securities, insurance, leisure industries, and international trading.[55] And all of this emerged from a humble soap company founded in 1938.

Since 1975, Ssangyong (Korean for "twin dragons," symbolizing peace and progress) has been run by the founder's son, Kim Suk Won. Under his guidance, the company's gross sales increased twenty-nine-fold from 1975 to 1987, while total assets increased twenty-three-fold. Ssangyong's strategy has been one of diversification, remaining flexible and able to change as Korea and the world economy change. Its motto, "Integrity, Reliability, and Creativity," symbolizes its long-term drive for success. Chairman Kim often tells his employees, "Let's try to publish a book, 'Ssangyong: 100 Years.' For that we need to build a firm foundation. Ssangyong will always be in Korea no matter who is running the company."[56]

Then, beginning in the early 1990s, Ssangyong's fortunes began to change. High labor costs in its labor-intensive industries and questionable investments began to sap the company's strength. Ssangyong had to scramble to stay ahead. Further internationalization offered one key to economic survival and, it is hoped, prosperity. In our interviews, one Ssangyong official gave us these views on internationalization:

> *Our strategy is focused on developing people. A highly educated work force is the key factor in economic development. We realize the need for sacrifice, especially for the new generation. But they are more difficult to manage in that they seek more personal leisure time.*
>
> *But the key to Ssangyong is human harmony. Better treatment for workers. . . . Provide better pay. Look at Taiwan. It is noted for its small and medium-sized export-oriented companies. They learned discipline from their military traditions. Small is beautiful. . . . The relationship between big and small companies in Korea is not as articulated as in Japan.*
>
> *More financing for smaller companies is needed. Meanwhile, through joint ventures (with ARAMCO and Mercedes Benz), we will continue to learn how to compete globally. We can be quite competitive in the automobile industry. Meanwhile, we need to keep prospering.[57]*

Sunkyong: Enacting the Supex Program

The Sunkyong Group is a major producer of petrochemical products and chemicals and of textiles, as well as being an engineering specialist. It was the first company in Korea to produce synthetic fiber. The company achieved its goal of transforming oil into synthetic fibers through massive investments in R&D beginning in 1975. Its research endeavors have yet to cease. Recently, the company launched a new management campaign called Supex (for "super excellent"), with the goal of raising the group performance to that of world-renowned corporations by the year 2000. Supex is, in essence, a human capital approach to globalization (see chapter 8).[58] In a recent interview with the company, one senior executive commented on Supex and the meaning of the global imperative for his company:

> *The challenge facing Korea is to move from its export orientation to developing a competitive advantage that is not based on industriousness and low wages. Take Samsung as a good example. It is competitive in appliances and semiconductors. It leverages its financial strengths in heavy metal and shipbuilding. It is protected in refinery and basic chemicals as Chevron will not ship refined gasoline to Korea due to high transportation costs.*
>
> *For Sunkyong, our biggest opportunity is the Chinese market. It the largest national economy in five years [by 2000], growing two-and-a-half to three times*

faster than Southeast Asia. We have been in direct dealings with the Chinese government for years. This is a relationship-based business, and we are well poised to capitalize on this advantage.

We have also attained success in joint ventures. With Du Pont and 3M, we successfully acquired technologies, nurtured them, and in time developed trust with our joint venture partners. We moved from "win-lose" to "win-win" conditions.

Compared with Hyundai and Samsung, we do not have massive size and scale. Consequently, we are more dependent on human factors. This [Supex] program has received much notoriety and is a model for others. In competing abroad, hardware will be homogenized, but software will be the only source of competitive advantage.

Sunkyong is also interested in North Korea. We will help them, perhaps even give our technology for free. We will continue to spread the Chairman's motto of human development. . . . Look to Germany and Japan. There is strong support for small to medium-sized companies. Yet small Korean firms are still seeking the BIG *deal. Government support cannot last forever.*[59]

Hanwha: Focus on Globalization

Since its inception in 1952, Hanwha has enjoyed a monopolistic domestic market for explosives, bearings, and other industrial materials. As a result, the group felt the need to develop a more positive image among consumers. Ever since the arrival of Chairman Kim Seung Youn in 1981, the group has expanded into the high-technology fields of genetic engineering, integrated energy, new materials development, and ultrafine chemicals. It is also making its presence felt in the distribution and leisure industries. In 1992, the group was ranked among the top ten *chaebols* in Korea.[60] In our interview, one key executive described the company's approach to globalization:

Hanwha was traditionally the leader in industrial explosives, and not focused on exports. It now has an Economic Research Institute that reports to the government as well. The key challenges, as seen by [Hanwha's] President Ro, are as follows: (1) market liberalization, (2) rising wage costs [in oil refinery and petrochemicals, increases amount to 10–12 percent], and (3) globalization, or more attention to markets abroad.

What is unique about Hanwha? We were among the first to focus on the USSR and Eastern Europe. We already have one bank based in Greece. And we have the Economic Research Institute, which is fully supported by the government.

We see opportunities in Southeast Asia, where growth has been the highest in the world. Yet chaebols may suffer on account of government pressure to restructure.

We believe that one answer here is for the chaebols *to take the leadership in cultural projects, to go beyond the economic realm.*

Hanwha is entrenched in petrochemicals and machinery. Major competitors in petrochemicals [are] Japanese and Korean companies. In telecommunications, a field we intend to enter, we anticipate that market pressure will come from AT&T, Alcatel, and Northern Telecom.[61]

The new global initiatives defined by the Korean government and ardently pursued by Korean companies reflect several beliefs: that direct foreign investment in other countries will provide a buffer against domestic losses caused by market liberalization, will add insurance against protectionist policies (such as the suit by Advanced Micron Devices),[62] and will provide the stimulus for breaking through Korea's technological bottleneck. The eagerness of Korean companies to globalize is in marked contrast to Japanese companies' current shrinking of their overseas investment. The drive to globalize is led by the core of Korean electronics firms—Samsung Electronics, Hyundai Electronics, LG Electronics, and Daewoo Electronics. Despite their history of internationalization, the movement into high technology, with its shortened product life cycles and quickened pace of innovation, is a coming of age for these Korean *chaebols*. While the goals are similar, the primary methods of globalization can be quite distinct. Most prominent is the contrast between Hyundai's "can do" attitude and the LG Group's eagerness to form strategic alliances. In terms of market penetration, Samsung has targeted traditional large developing markets, while Daewoo is taking the uncharted course through Eastern Europe and Russia.

Each of the strategies above has potential and vulnerabilities. Hyundai's "can do" attitude sets it against the growing tide of xenophobic exposure, as evidenced by its foray into Eugene, Oregon. While the LG Group appears to have diminished this problem by making alliances with top-rated companies, it is vulnerable to the potential for opportunistic behaviors within those alliances. Samsung's global reach is impressive, but it pits the organization against larger and more experienced firms. Its human assets and financial limits will be tested. And, with Daewoo, charting new markets has staved off considerable competition for the present, but Daewoo also risks being isolated from the fast track of high-technology competition. As suggested by one observer, by the time Russia and Eastern Europe develop purchasing power, the train to product development may have left Daewoo.

As the world has become increasingly interdependent and defined by regional blocs, Korea has recognized that to remain the hermit kingdom is akin to being left behind. Globalization will present Korean firms with a serious challenge as they struggle to define their roles as competitors in the coming century. Korea's globalization initiatives also have to be interpreted in light of its geographical region—that is, where newly industrializing economies and countries, such as China and the ASEAN nations, are aspiring to improve their economic positions.

CHAPTER SEVEN

Competing on the New Technological Frontier

Park Sung Kyu, former president of Daewoo Telecom, once observed: "We are not a technological leader. We can't come up with a technology-driven product and create a new market. We look at a market and develop a product for it, watching and working quickly."[1] As a late industrializer, Korea's success has been founded on its ability to acquire and develop foreign technologies at different stages of its economic development.[2] Throughout the country's economic history, Korean firms have used a variety of methods—informal learning, turnkey plants, capital importation, licensing, joint ventures, and alliances[3]—to acquire and develop technological competencies. Their success in steel, automobiles, consumer electronics, and—quite lately—semiconductors is a testament to their abilities to learn and develop technological competencies faster than many competitors.

There is question, however, whether Korea will be able to sustain this impressive record. The year 1989 marked a turning point for the country in its shift from heavy capital-intensive to technology-oriented industries: Korean-produced electronics products and components surpassed consumer goods in value ($9.7 billion versus $9.2 billion).[4] Even so, Korea's dependence on the acquisition of foreign technologies had increased to the point where it was running a high trade deficit in most electronics fields. Its incursion into high technology (semiconductors) has prompted erstwhile partners and former suppliers to be more self-protective and less willing to license newer technologies to Korean firms. Moreover, the experience of Korean manufacturers in electronics and semiconductors unmasked a structural weakness in the economy: underdeveloped small to medium-sized firms (see chapter 4). Many observers think that taken together, these developments signal the limits of the Korean growth strategy.[5]

In this chapter, we describe how Korean firms gained access to foreign technology through a combination of informal learning, licensing, mastery of production methods, OEM arrangements, and technological alliances and what role the government played in this process. We also discuss how changes in the international market have created technological barriers for Korean companies. We end the chapter with a discussion of Korea's latest actions and strategies for coping with increasing protectionism. In our view, Korea's ability to rise to its technological challenge is inextricably linked to its ability to meet other challenges, notably, those posed by changes in industrial policy and globalization initiatives. Therefore, our assessment is broadly directed at policy issues. For a more in-depth analysis of Korea's technological development, the reader is referred to Linsu Kim's recent work *Imitation to Innovation: The Dynamics of Korea's Technological Learning.*[6]

THE EVOLUTION OF KOREA'S TECHNOLOGY STRATEGY

In this section, we describe the various methods Korean firms have employed to develop and sustain their technological competencies. Table 7-1 charts the evolution of Korea's progress in this regard since the 1960s.

Early Focus: Acquisition of Production Technologies

During the 1962–1971 takeoff period, Korean firms focused on labor-intensive industries, such as textiles, plywood, and apparel, where they had a distinct advantage in low labor costs. Foreign technologies consisted mainly of production capabilities, which were progressively updated with newer equipment.[7] Korean firms learned about these technologies through informal channels, such as the trade literature, equipment suppliers, and foreign buyers.[8] Foreign buyers, as in the case of textiles, made periodic visits and provided product designs, styling, and technical specifications to Korean firms.[9] Both government policies and actions taken by individual firms were crucial in the acquisition of technologies from advanced countries, mainly Japan and the United States. Government policies were directed at protecting targeted sectors with quotas and tariffs, as well as securing low-interest loans that were channeled for investment. Moreover, the government restricted foreign direct investment and forced foreign firms to form joint ventures with locals. In sum, compared with other newly

Table 7-1   The Evolution of Korea's Acquisition and Development of Technology, 1960s–1990s

Primary Mechanisms for Technology Acquisition and Development	Mechanisms as Applied to Korean Business	Technological Characteristics
Informed channels (trade literature, data from foreign vendors/suppliers, etc.)	1960s (Plywood, textiles, apparel)	Labor intensive
Turnkey operations, capital imports, licensing, and technical consultation	1970s (Steel, metal, machinery, ship-building)	Capital intensive
Licensing	1980s (Consumer electronics, automobiles)	Technology based
Joint ventures and alliances	1980s (Automobiles, electronics/VCRs)	Complex, technology based
	1990s (Semiconductors, automobiles)	Complex, technology based (Leapfrogging)

industrializing countries, Korea had the advantages of lower labor costs, a high-quality and highly motivated work force, and an institutional support system.[10]

Technological Acquisition through Turnkey Operations, Capital Imports, and Technical Consultation

In the 1970s, capital-intensive industries, such as steel and metal products, shipbuilding, machinery, and automobiles, replaced labor-intensive industries. As wages rose, Korean firms moved into heavy and chemical industries. In this context, turnkey plants and machinery imports were the major mechanisms for the acquisition and development of production capabilities. Unlike Korea's first exports, these industries were highly capital intensive; expertise was required not only to run them but to build and expand them.[11] Turnkey plants and machinery imports were the major vehicles for the acquisition of production capabilities. Technical consultation and licensing were also often used for relatively complicated technologies in shipbuilding and integrated steel mills.[12] However, turnkey operations and licensing appeared to be best suited to Korea's needs at the time. During the 1970s, companies fitted with low-end or mature technology could most efficiently acquire advanced technologies through simple methods like turnkey packaging and licensing.

Technological Acquisition through Licensing

In the 1980s, Korea began to enter more technologically advanced industries, such as electronics, to circumvent declining exports, rising wages, worldwide recession, increasing protectionism, and the loss of competitiveness in capital-intensive industries. Unlike steel or textiles, the products were more differentiated, which made the Japanese and the Americans reluctant to transfer advanced technologies. By the end of the 1980s, however, sales volume in electronics surpassed consumer goods, and the electronics industry emerged as the largest export industry in Korea. It grew at an unprecedented speed: total sales volume grew from $106 million in 1970 to $33.1 billion in 1991, recording a 31 percent annual growth rate. Exports also increased—from $5.5 million to $19.3 billion—for a 32 percent growth rate during the same period. In 1991, Korea's electronics industry hired more than 9 percent of the total employees in the manufacturing industry and exported 27 percent of the total manufacturing exports. The portion of value added by the electronics industry increased from 6 percent in 1975 to 11 percent in 1991. In 1991, Korea became the sixth largest producer in the global electronics industry, following the United States, Japan, Germany, France, and the United Kingdom.[13]

Statistics on foreign technology transfers to Korea reflect these trends and practices. From 1972 to 1981, there was a surge in foreign licensing, capital goods imports, and technical consultation. During the same period, there was a drop in foreign direct investment from $879 to $720 (U.S. dollars). Korea's rapid emergence as a major global competitor in electronics and semiconductors had come with a price. As technologies grew more complex, transfers became more direct and interactive, which led to a drastic increase in licensing fees in the late 1980s. Licensing fees more than tripled during 1987–1991 and were more than ten times higher in the 1980s than in the 1970s. It is also noted that technical consultation increased by about 300 percent in 1982–1986, while capital goods imports increased at a disproportionate rate. (See table 7-2.) This illustrates Korea's increasing dependence on foreign technologies as a consequence of its growth in electronics and other technology-intensive industries.

Between 1962 and 1993, the Korean government approved 8,766 cases of technology transfer for a total of $8 billion. More than half of these (52 percent of cases and 59 percent of payments) were in two technology-

Table 7-2 Foreign Technology Transfer to Korea, 1962–1991 (Millions of dollars)

	1962–66	1967–71	1972–76	1977–81	1982–86	1987–91
Foreign direct investment	47.4	219.0	879.4	720.9	1,767.6	5,636.0
Foreign licensing	0.8	16.3	96.5	451.4	1,184.9	4,359.4
Technical consultation	—	16.8	18.5	54.7	332.3	1,349.7
Capital goods imports	316.0	2,541.0	8,841.0	27,978.0	44,705.0	52,155.0

Source: Korean Ministry of Trade, Industry, and Energy, Seoul, 1994.

intensive industries: electronics and machinery. The average payment per technology transfer has grown constantly, rising from $430,000 in 1981 to $2.03 million in 1991.[14] As Korea continued its move into high-tech fields, foreign technology had also become substantially more expensive, more proprietary, and better protected. For example, more than 75 percent of imported technologies during the 1980s were patented or trademarked.[15]

A notable trend is Korea's dependence on the United States and Japan. Between 1987 and 1993, more than 75 percent of foreign technology was imported from these two countries. In 1994, both countries accounted for about 72 percent of trade with South Korea. (See table 7-3.) Until 1993, Japan was the leading source of technologies introduced to Korea, followed by the United States, Germany, England, and France. In a recent survey conducted by the Korea Industrial Promotion Association, the United States is ranked first in the transfer of technology to Korea, surpassing even Japan.[16] The survey also reports that U.S. companies are more willing to set up operations in Korea to take advantage of the market liberalization measures, while Japanese firms have opted to be conservative in their investments in Korea. While licensing continued—oftentimes laced with standstill restrictions—the disadvantages became more obvious: Korean firms were scarcely involved in the research and development process. Thus, they were allowed to learn only a small portion of the whole technology system and were given little exposure to advanced or complicated technologies.[17]

While Korea's dependence on advanced foreign technology had increased tremendously, its acquisition had become a daunting task. Because Korean firms came to be viewed as direct competitors, American and Japanese firms were more reluctant to transfer their technologies.[18] With Korean firms becoming more competitive in technology-intensive industries, American

Table 7-3 Share of Technology Imports to Korea by Country

		1962–1986 (Average)	1987	1988	1989	1990	1991	1992	1993	1994
United States	Cases	24.2	28.3	26.6	31.9	29.9	28.3	30.5	31.7	42.8
	Amount	45.2	45.8	48.9	46.8	47.3	52.6	53.2	44.2	54.4
Japan	Cases	54.2	48.2	47.1	44.9	45.1	47.5	43.5	40.3	28.8
	Amount	30.1	34.6	31.7	30.8	31.4	31.5	31.3	37.3	31.3
Germany	Cases	5.3	5.5	6.5	4.8	7.5	6.0	4.9	4.4	7.9
	Amount	4.1	3.6	3.3	5.9	5.5	5.1	3.2	5.6	2.9
England	Cases	3.5	3.3	2.7	3.0	3.8	4.3	5.6	5.1	5.1
	Amount	—	—	2.3	3.9	4.1	2.0	1.8	3.2	2.3
France	Cases	3.2	6.3	8.8	5.4	3.4	4.5	3.4	3.3	3.5
	Amount	2.9	4.8	7.1	4.5	2.8	4.1	6.6	3.4	2.1
Others	Cases	9.6	8.4	8.3	10.0	10.3	9.4	12.1	15.2	11.9
	Amount	17.7	11.2	6.7	8.1	8.9	4.7	3.9	6.3	7.0

Source: Korean Ministry of Science and Technology, Seoul, 1995.
Note: Figures are in percentages of the total imports. Before 1988, the royalty payments to other countries included England.

and Japanese firms considered working with Korea the equivalent of "raising tigers in your backyard."[19]

Learning through Strategic Alliances

With burgeoning restrictions in licensing agreements, Korean firms moved into more partnerships and alliances with foreign firms. This strategy was aided by changes in economic, competitive, and technological settings that encouraged firms to cooperate rather than compete. Alliance partners are able to enhance innovative capabilities through shared learning, transfers of technical know-how, and exchanges of resources.[20] Examples of industries that have made good use of the strategic alliance are automobiles and semiconductors.

The automobile industry

Korea entered the automobile industry as a follower, behind the Europeans, the Americans, and the Japanese. Yet it was the ability of Korean *chaebols*—Hyundai, Daewoo, Kia, and Ssangyong—to forge successful alliances that enabled them to dominate the domestic market. Furthermore, Samsung's recent entry through an alliance with Nissan is expected to fuel competition in the Korean auto industry.[21] Through alliances, Korean firms were able to overcome the effects of delayed entry and lack of technological know-how by tapping into foreign technology and expertise, by obtaining spare parts, and by using the distribution networks of foreign automakers. Korean automakers were able to learn and to introduce advanced technologies over an extended period of time, as reflected in products engineered by Mitsubishi for Hyundai, GM for Daewoo, Mercedes for Ssangyong, Mazda and Ford for Kia, and Nissan for Samsung.

Even unsuccessful alliances have provided Korean manufacturers with valuable insights on how to compete better in the future. On assurances that it would be independent, Hyundai forged an alliance with Ford during the initial growth stage of assembly production and benefited from technical support obtained from Ford in building production plants.[22] After Hyundai and Ford failed to reach an agreement regarding constraints on Hyundai's international operations, the two corporations decided to terminate the alliance in 1973.[23] In 1975, the Hyundai–Ital Design alliance provided Hyundai with comprehensive know-how and technical independence in auto design. The Hyundai-Mitsubishi alliance that was later formalized is considered a historic event in the growth of the Korean auto industry. With help from the Hyundai-Mitsubishi alliance, Hyundai was able to achieve 90 percent localization of its major components production. The

Hyundai-Mitsubishi alliance paved the way for Hyundai to export Pony Excels to America. Hyundai joined many other technological alliances in the 1980s and 1990s, thereby becoming technologically independent in automobile production. In 1995, as the most technologically advanced automaker in Korea, Hyundai broadened its cooperative relationship with Mitsubishi, which made possible cooperation across a wide spectrum of areas, from technology development to marketing.[24]

Alliances also helped two smaller *chaebols*—Kia Motors and Ssangyong. Kia benefited greatly from its alliance with Ford and Mazda; Ford offered a marketing network for 10 percent equity, and Mazda offered technology for 8 percent equity. Kia has also done business with Toyota to expand its technological base and has built alliances with TRW and Robert Bosch to improve its technological competence.[25] Since the 1990s, Ssangyong has been working closely with Mercedes-Benz to develop cars, trucks, and four-wheel-drive vehicles, harnessing Mercedes' engineering and design skills to Ssangyong's manufacturing capability. The Musso, which was introduced in 1992 and became one of the best-selling jeeps in Korea, is powered by Mercedes' four-cylinder diesel engine. In 1992, Mercedes-Benz paid $29.5 million for a 5 percent stake in Ssangyong Motors.[26] While other automakers and *chaebols* have relied heavily on Japanese capital and technology, Ssangyong's Chairman Kim Suk Won has been vocal about weaning Korean industries away from technological dependence on Japan. In an interview with *Far Eastern Economic Review*, Kim said: "If I were to tie up [Ssangyong Motors] with Nissan or Toyota, I would be building an old model that the Japanese want to sell to the Korean market. . . . I have experience with the Japanese. I know they will not give 100 percent. But it's just the technology that's the problem."[27]

Kim's preference for Western partners seems to be pragmatic. In the early 1980s, Ssangyong Heavy Industries was denied access to technology for marine-diesel engines by Daihatsu of Japan. Ssangyong then turned to Germany's BMW to acquire the technology, and it is now exporting the marine engines to Japan. The alliance with Mercedes caught the attention of most executives in Korea. Ssangyong is betting its future on the alliance with Mercedes-Benz. Ssangyong has spent about $2.5 billion on new production lines and parts and component plants for the joint-venture vehicles and related research. It is reported that Mercedes-Benz will earn 2 percent on the sale of each joint-venture vehicle, in addition to $94.5 million in licensing fees, which may amount to $2 billion by the end of the decade.[28] Ssangyong executives even dream of manufacturing a global competitor for Toyota's Lexus, drawing on Mercedes' technology and its worldwide marketing network.

The semiconductor industry

Japan and the United States were long the dominant players in the semiconductor market. The Europeans had largely ceded the market after struggling unsuccessfully to develop their own indigenous industry.[29] At the beginning of the 1980s, few considered Korea a likely contender. Capital was scarce, semiconductor design capabilities were nonexistent, and markets were overseas. It was widely assumed that the Koreans were highly ambitious but woefully unprepared. In fact, many Japanese executives felt that the Koreans "could not master the complexities of semiconductor manufacturing," echoing a sentiment of the Americans toward the Japanese just two decades earlier.[30] It has been to the surprise of many that Korea emerged as a major player in the industry in the late 1980s and today enjoys a tremendous competitive edge in memory products.

The Korean government made a decision to promote semiconductors as a strategic industry in its 1976 economic plan. Within a year, the government had created an electronics research institute, an industrial estate for semiconductor manufacture, and its own semiconductor manufacturing facility. In the fourth five-year plan (1977–1981), semiconductors became a specific target for development, with formal, quantified industrial objectives. In 1982, the government's official "Semiconductor Promotional Plan" instituted supportive measures that would improve semiconductor capability, including subsidized capital and tax benefits for semiconductor investments, increased funding for government research, and continued import protection for domestic producers.

Convinced that the only way to crack the world semiconductor market was through massive development projects, the government launched the VLSI Project, a research-and-development venture aimed at the creation of a 4M DRAM chip in 1985. The VLSI Project had an initial budget of $199 million shared by the government and participating firms. The industry portion was subsidized by government-guaranteed, low-interest loans. The visibility of the project was so pronounced that it was called the Blue House Project by Korean industry officials, a reference to the Korean president's residence. Within just four years, by 1989, Korea made its presence felt when its rapidly increasing production and aggressive export methods drove down DRAM prices worldwide.

In 1990, three of Korea's largest industrial groupings—Samsung, Hyundai, and Goldstar—declared semiconductors one of their top industrial priorities. The government had also placed strong emphasis on high-technology development. Until the past few years, these Korean firms tried to develop semiconductor technology through foreign licensing agreements, cooperative research efforts, and government-assisted reverse-engineering methods. More recently, Korean industry officials have publicly and privately expressed the need to become more independent of Japanese technology.

When Korean firms entered full-scale production of 64K DRAMS in late 1984, attempting to be cost leaders, they quickly discovered that they could not compete with the Japanese on the basis of price alone.[31] Even so, the Koreans proved to be fast learners as they dislodged the Japanese in the DRAM market, using similar pricing strategies. During the takeoff stage, Samsung acquired most of its technology from American corporations. Design specifications for the 64K and 256K DRAM came from Micron in 1983. And leading-edge MICOM and EPROM technologies came from Intel in 1985 and 1986. Once Samsung became the leading company in DRAM production, it progressed by cross-licensing with global competitors with advanced technologies. Samsung exchanged some of the 64K DRAM technology it had independently developed with Intel's MPU technology and NCR's ASIC and chip-set technology. Samsung also jointly developed the RISC CPU with Hewlett-Packard, and it cross-licensed related semiconductor patents with IBM. In 1993, Samsung initiated a large-scale joint production with Texas Instruments in Portugal to produce and market Samsung's 1M, 4M, and 16M DRAMs and Texas Instrument's high-quality Logic DRAMs throughout Europe. Samsung and Texas Instruments have also expanded the cooperative relationship further for joint development of new products.

In 1993, Samsung participated in a Korea-based joint venture with Dai Nippon Screen of Japan to build a next-generation production facility for 64M DRAMs. In the same year, it concluded a joint-venture contract with Towa Company of Japan and Hanyang Precision of Korea to produce auto-molding systems, an important part of semiconductor manufacturing facilities. Shortly thereafter, Samsung announced plans to forge a technical partnership with NEC to develop next-generation 256M DRAM chips.

In 1993, Samsung overtook Toshiba as the world's largest supplier of metal-oxide semiconductors, leading Toshiba to forge an alliance with eighth-ranked IBM and Siemens to develop 256M DRAMs. Then second-ranked Hitachi teamed up with the seventh-ranked Texas Instruments. The alliance forged by Samsung (number one) and NEC (number three) was described by executives from both companies as a reaction to the collaborative networks formed by their major rivals.[32] Figure 7-1 shows the network of technology alliances recently formed by Samsung.

Figure 7-1   Samsung's Technological Alliances in Semiconductors

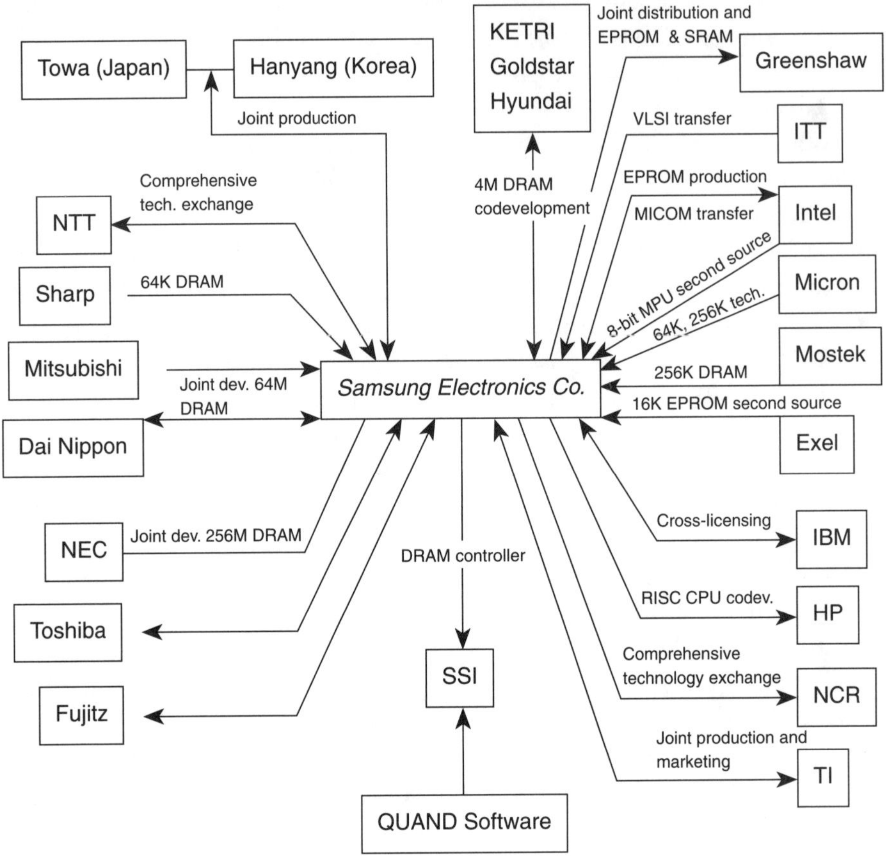

Sources: Adapted from *Topics* (Seoul: Samsung Electronics, 1994), and Y. S. Hong, *Strategic Alliances and the Globalization of Technological Innovation* (Seoul: KIET, 1994).

Since Hyundai entered the standard memory market in 1983, it has joined a series of technological alliances, mostly with American and Japanese corporations. In the 1980s, Hyundai operated under various vertically re-lated OEM contracts with Texas Instruments, General Instruments, and Intel. However, since the 1990s, Hyundai and Fujitsu have become insepara-ble business partners. In 1993, Hyundai and Fujitsu reached an agreement to start full-scale cooperation in the development, manufacturing, and mar-keting of semiconductors. The two corporations exchange various DRAM technologies. Also, Hyundai is now able to use Fujitsu's manufacturing plants in the United States to produce 4M DRAMs and other products and to market them in local markets. This helps protect the company from antidumping suits. The Hyundai-Fujitsu alliance was expanded further for cooperation on 64M DRAMs, ASIC microcontrollers, and specialized chip technologies. The alliance will help Hyundai greatly in the ASIC business and Fujitsu in the DRAM business, where it has traditionally been weak. Recently, Hyundai also participated in a domestic consortium with other rivals—Samsung and Goldstar—and the government to develop 4M DRAMs. Figure 7-2 shows Hyundai's technological alliances.

As a latecomer to the semiconductor industry, following Samsung and Hyundai, Goldstar relied heavily on technological alliances to catch up with its rivals. Since the late 1980s, Hitachi of Japan has contributed most to Goldstar's growth. Goldstar started its semiconductor business in a joint venture with AT&T, which was consolidated into Goldstar Electron in 1989 to utilize the 1M DRAM technology Hitachi offered.[33] Hitachi willingly provided Goldstar with the 1M DRAM technology because it wanted to

Figure 7-2   Hyundai's Technological Alliances in Semiconductors

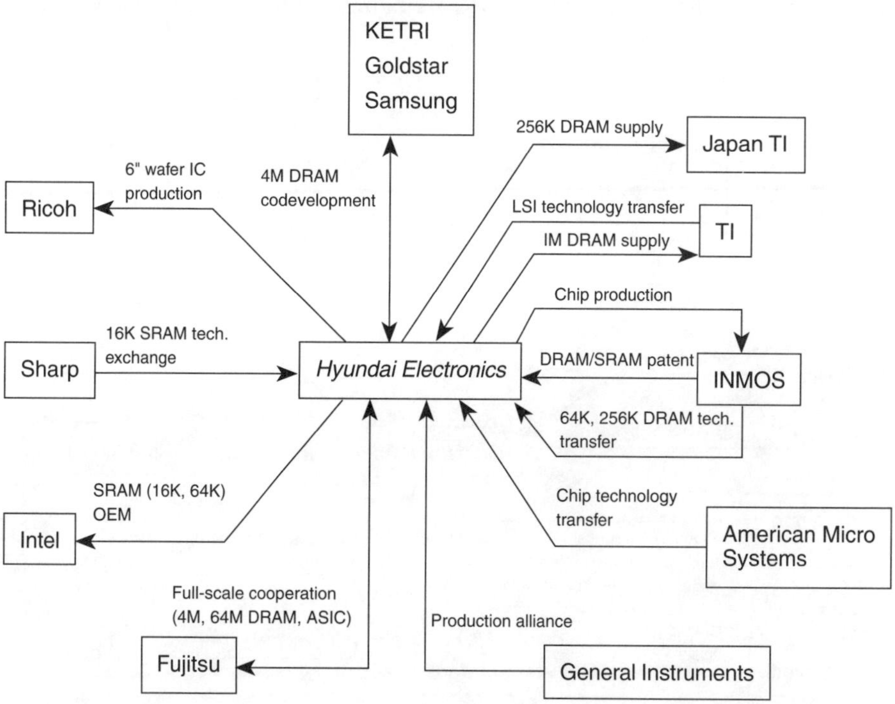

Sources: Adapted from *Topics* (Seoul: Samsung Electronics, 1994), and Y. S. Hong, *Strategic Alliances and the Globalization of Technological Innovation* (Seoul: KIET, 1994).

focus on 4M DRAM technology and catch up with its main rival, Toshiba. The Goldstar-Hitachi alliance was also expected to develop 4M and 16M DRAMs. Recently, as Goldstar became technologically more competent and Hitachi lost some competitiveness owing to the continued appreciation of the yen, the role has been reversed; Hitachi has been more anxious to open additional alliances with Goldstar. The Goldstar-Hitachi alliance has been a good marriage for both partners. Goldstar was able to narrow its technology gap with Samsung and Hyundai in a short period of time based on Hitachi's DRAM technology, while Hitachi secured a cheap supply of 1M DRAMs and was able to reinvest profits from the 1M DRAM business in the development of 4M DRAMs. Goldstar also cooperates with Hyundai and Samsung to develop 16M and 64M DRAMs. Figure 7-3 shows Goldstar's technological alliances.

PATTERNS OF TECHNOLOGY ACQUISITION: AN INTERINDUSTRY COMPARISON

Why did Korean firms succeed in acquiring and developing technologies when many other countries failed? In a penetrating study of how Korean

Figure 7-3 LG's Technological Alliances in Semiconductors

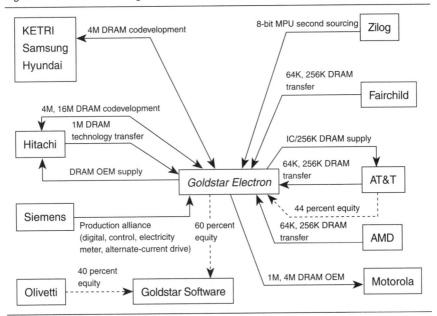

Sources: Adapted from *Topics* (Seoul: Samsung Electronics, 1994), and Y. S. Hong, *Strategic Alliances and the Globalization of Technological Innovation* (Seoul: KIET, 1994).

firms acquire technological competencies, Linsu Kim analyzed the patterns of technological acquisition on several interrelated levels: technological capability, global technological environment, public policy, institutional support, process of technological learning, and mechanism of technology transfer.[34] In comparing the nature of innovation between industrially advanced countries and late industrializers—a framework appropriate for Korea—some noteworthy patterns emerged that shed light on Korea's experience.

In industrially advanced countries, both product and process innovations give rise to particular stages of the technology trajectory that have implications for technology transfer. Firms in a new technology generally exhibit a *fluid* pattern of innovation, characterized by radical innovation, crude and expensive product technology, and flexible production systems. As market needs stabilize, alternative product technologies converge or fade away, ushering in a *transition* toward a dominant product design (often termed the "industry standard"), for which mass production methods lead to lower costs. Process improvements—not product innovations—become the benchmark. As the product becomes more mature, the production process becomes more *specific*—more automated and integrated.

For late industrializers, a different pattern of development ensues. Precisely because these firms are in the "catch-up" mode, the sequencing of product and process innovations is reversed. Local firms try to establish production operations by acquiring "packaged" foreign technology for already-developed products. Once this technology is in place, emphasis reverts to process improvements and refinement. Kim argues that firms in the catch-up mode that have successfully acquired, assimilated, and sometimes improved foreign technologies attempt to repeat the process with higher-level technologies that are still in the transitional stage in advanced countries. As these firms progress, they do not have to wait for foreign technologies to reach their specific stage. In fact, attention to process improvements, reverse engineering, tacit knowledge, and the emphasis on shop-floor operations can be leveraged in ways that allow catch-up firms to overtake or even leapfrog firms in advanced countries at the specific stage.

Within Korea, Kim also relates patterns of technological acquisition to particular firms and industries. Among large firms (called apprentices), small-batch industries relied heavily on foreign licensing as a means of assimilating technologies related to highly differentiated products. Mass production industries also used licensing, but to a far lesser extent, while continuous process industries relied heavily on turnkey plants and plant investments. Small firms (called imitators) relied more on the informal transfer of foreign technology through reverse engineering and the poaching of highly technical personnel from larger firms and from abroad. However, newly emerging technological small firms have grown using innovative, cutting-edge technologies—a practice employed by their counterparts in advanced economies. In general, Korean firms have been aggressive in acquiring foreign technologies as well as in expediting learning from technology transfers.

Following Kim's analysis, one can see how Korea's pattern of technological acquisition and development is consistent with the manner or method of technology transfer. A variety of methods can be used to transfer technology (interactive partnerships such as joint ventures, foreign direct investments, and acquisition of foreign companies), each presenting different trade-offs in terms of speed, cost, degree of interaction, and mutual dependence.[35] Informal consultation and the importation of production technology provide effective learning conditions in the transitional stages of technological development. Licensing is also effective in this stage in cases where substantial research and development costs would already have been incurred by the pioneering firm. Thus, the speed of learning and reduced developmental costs work in favor of Korean firms. Korean firms' attention to manufacturing and process improvements provides the basis for production learning (reducing costs) that accumulate as more technologies are transferred and mastered. As technology becomes more complex (in the fluid stage), the high cost of development is partially diffused through strategic alliances and research consortia. In addition, the continued sharing of these development efforts accrues and can become a competitive advantage to the extent that there is some degree of market coordination. In the cases of Korea and Japan, this is where the facilitating role of government ministries becomes consequential.

The fast pace at which Korea achieved technological success is largely the result of an understanding of these technological trajectories and cycles. One also cannot underestimate the role of government and supporting institutions. Kim lists the following explanations for Korea's success:

1. The continuous inflow of foreign technology through formal and informal mechanisms.

2. The development of highly trained workers who are willing to learn.

3. A drastic increase in R&D investment, particularly in the private sector.

4. The "can-do" entrepreneurial spirit exercised freely under restricted equity participation of multinationals.

5. The government's orchestral role in directing the *chaebols* and selectively allocating resources to them to achieve ambitious growth objectives early on.

6. The government's role in lowering corporate R&D costs and providing small firms with infrastructural support.

7. The crises imposed by the government and constructed by top management.

CHANGING TRENDS IN INTERNATIONAL TECHNOLOGY ACQUISITION

Several trends in the international technology market affect Korea's recent incursion into high technology (see figure 7-4). First, with escalating competition, there has been a growth in protectionism as commercial technology issues become more entwined with national security questions.[36] While this appears to be prevalent in semiconductor cases, there have been historical precedents. Fearful of future competition, Japan rejected POSCO's request

Figure 7-4   Factors Affecting Korea's Responses to the Changing Technological Environment

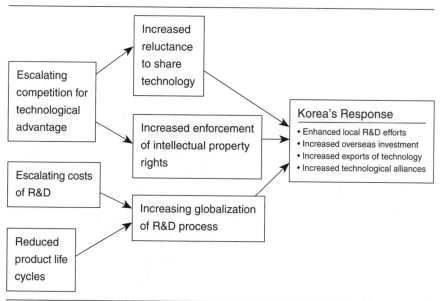

for the technology it needed for its new steel plant in the late 1970s. When Sunkyong was looking for polyester film technology to diversify into the videotape market during this period, not one Japanese firm was willing to transfer the technology. In the early 1980s, Samsung was rejected for VCR and semiconductor-related technologies, and Daihatsu rejected Ssangyong's request for marine diesel-engine technology.[37] Moreover, intellectual property rights, such as patents, trademarks, and copyrights, have all been more strictly enforced since the 1980s. Given this new protectionism, the development of indigenous technology capabilities has become not only complementary to but a prerequisite for the importation of advanced technologies under reasonable terms.[38]

A second trend, related to intensifying competition, is the "globalization" of the research and development process. Technological innovation and commercialization no longer reside in one country but are dispersed throughout the world. The implication is that traditional "first-mover" advantages, a situation in which the innovator reaps initial monopolistic rents, are not as tenable. Moreover, with the rapid globalization of technological know-how, product life cycles are compressed, forcing firms to recoup their investments in less time. For Korean manufacturers in highly competitive DRAM markets, this brings more financial and technological uncertainty when it comes to making sizable investments in plants that may be obsolete in a short period of time. This is particularly true in view of Korea's competitors, notably the ASEAN countries and China, which, because they are considered attractive alternatives to Korea's labor costs, might be given first access to new technologies from advanced countries.

Another aspect of globalization that has potentially adverse implications for Korean firms is the spiraling costs of developing and refining new technology. To compete in global markets, Korean firms have to find ways to defray the immense fixed costs arising from research (new technology) and development (production capabilities). As automation drives out variable costs of labor from production, manufacturing will increasingly become a fixed-cost activity. This rise of fixed costs has made it prohibitive to play the "one company game." Firms have to find a way to amortize fixed costs, if not develop strategies to maximize the contributions to fixed costs.

This might explain another trend involving greater use of technological tie-ups and alliances as forms of technology sharing and transfers. According to the *Wall Street Journal*, in the early 1990s more than 55 percent of fast-growing American firms were involved in an average of three alliances, and the importance of the alliance was increasing faster than ever.[39] Since Korea's entry into high-tech fields, the strategic alliance has become a necessity, oftentimes the only alternative in facilitating technology transfer from advanced nations. Korea's technological alliances have often been characterized as a one-way flow of technical competence—from the advanced nations to Korea—through OEMs or licensing. Until recent years, because Korean corporations were substantially lacking in unique technical competence, there were few technological alliances involving the cooperative research and development and the cross-licensing that call for full-scale coordination and exchange of competence. Because of this imbalance in technical competence between Korean and foreign corporations, Korean corporations were often forced to join in cross-licensing agreements that were disadvantageous and required unduly high payments.[40] Korean firms need to develop their ability to offer their alliance partners complementary benefits; they should be seeking not the previous one-way technology transfer but a broader interactive relationship.

KOREA'S TECHNOLOGY STRATEGIES FOR THE TWENTY-FIRST CENTURY

In response to some of these challenges, Korean firms have forged four interrelated strategies. Their goals are to (1) enhance local research and development, (2) increase overseas investment, (3) increase technology exports, and (4) enter into more cooperative alliances. Since the government has always played the catalytic role in Korea's technology acquisition, we also discuss recent policies that support the goal of competitiveness in high-technology industries.

Enhanced Local Research and Development

Leading *chaebols* have substantially stepped up their investments in R&D and supporting production facilities. R&D expenditures grew by 37 percent in 1994 among the top twenty-five *chaebols*.[41] Samsung's new organization and management are based on superior technology and resource reallocations that are conducive to the attainment of technological superiority in the world market.[42] Samsung's Chairman Lee Kun Hee believes that home-grown higher technology can make Samsung a peer of Sony and General Electric.[43] To meet this goal, in 1993, Samsung employed more than 13,000 researchers, invested 5 percent of its total sales in R&D, and operated twenty-seven R&D centers in Korea and twenty-six R&D-related facilities overseas. Samsung's main research lab, the Samsung Advanced Institute of Technology (SAIT), has five related centers and conducts research in high-tech fields such as electronics, computers and communications, semiconductors and telecommunications, aerospace and mechanics, and chemicals. Through the 1990s, Samsung has focused on value-added technologies in such strategic sectors as electronics (especially semiconductors), aerospace, and commercial vehicles. Samsung Electronics has been the main beneficiary of this huge investment, including $633 million invested in 1994 in new 16M-DRAM production lines. Other major investments in the mid-1990s for technology acquisition and production expansion are focused on Samsung Aerospace, the prime contractor in the Korean Fighter Project, a project to localize the production of fighter jets, and on the new commercial-vehicle-production project.

Since the early 1990s, Hyundai has also been tailoring its management plan to focus on developing advanced technology, upgrading employees' skills, and enhancing productivity, under the slogan "Hyundai of Technology, Hyundai of the World." Along with a 141 percent increase in facility investments, Hyundai expanded R&D investment to $1.5 billion in 1994—a 77 percent increase over the previous year—mainly in automobiles, petrochemicals, and electronics. One of Hyundai's projects in the mid-1990s is a $1.4 billion investment in the construction of 16M-DRAM production facilities and the establishment of a semiconductor research institute. In 1993, Hyundai employed more than 6,100 researchers (including 155 with a Ph.D. and 1,105 with a master's degree) at 26 research institutes.[44]

In the new corporate plan for the twenty-first century, the LG Group intends to build technological capabilities in electronics, electrical appliances, and petrochemicals, while venturing out into the environmental field. In 1994, Goldstar's R&D was increased to $1.3 billion, along with the expansion of production facilities for LCD and 16 M-DRAM products. In its "Vision 2000" statement, LG lays out a new managerial framework designed to lead the group into the next century and to build an innovation base that will enable it to achieve world-class quality and productivity levels in its core businesses.

Daewoo has also shown a major increase in capital investment and R&D, with special emphasis on expanding production facilities domestically and abroad in its automobile business. Leading Daewoo's technology drive is the Institute for Advanced Engineering (IAE), established in July 1992.[45] Centered around the IAE, Daewoo has built a technology network of group companies, including twenty-eight research centers in Korea and twenty centers abroad, to enhance technology-development efforts. Daewoo Electronics recently established the New Generation Production Research Center to meet market requirements for advanced products and systems in the twenty-first century. In 1996 the center began concentrating on developing various innovative auto systems and integrated audiovisual media, home appliances, display systems, and other futuristic high-tech electronic products. Daewoo's new campaign theme for growth in the coming century is "Daewoo Globalization through Daewoo Technology." On the company's twenty-sixth anniversary in March 1993, top management undertook a commitment to develop "Daewoo Technology" as the key to success in the coming century. By 2000, Daewoo plans to have employed 8,500 research personnel in auto-related research alone and to have invested about $8.3 billion, amounting to 5 percent of total revenue, in corporate R&D.[46] The *chaebols'* aggressive investment strategies reflect their commitment to developing innovative capabilities (see table 7-4).

Increased Foreign Direct Investment

Since the end of the 1980s, part of Korea's technology strategy has been to increase its overseas investments. From 1990 to 1993, total overseas projects approached 1,500; investments climbed steeply to about $2.4 billion (U.S. dollars). (See figure 7-5.) A good proportion of this overseas investment was made by small and midsized firms in labor-intensive, light industrial fields, such as garments, toys, and footwear, which were moving overseas in search of cheaper labor.[47] In terms of destination, at the end of 1994, about 25 percent of net invested cases were directed to the United States, 12 percent to China, and 25 percent to other Asian countries, such as Indonesia, China, the Philippines, and Malaysia. (See table 7-5.) Investments in China began only in 1989, but by the end of 1993 they were valued at $500 million, second only to investments in the United States. Given ever-rising wages, land prices, and the high cost of money, this move resulted from an almost desperate search to find a competitive niche for low-end light industrial goods.

Foreign direct investment by the larger *chaebols* is driven by strategic motivations different from those of small and medium-sized firms. First, overseas direct investments allow the *chaebols* to expand their market basis for end-of-cycle technologies they acquired from advanced countries. Applying their superior production capabilities in cheap labor countries, the *chaebols* are able to stretch and maintain the cost-based competitive advantage they previously held in mature industries. Second, the expanded revenue basis helps the *chaebols* quickly amortize the capital investment made in initial

Table 7-4 Investments in Production Facilities and R&D by Korea's Major
Conglomerates, 1992–1994 (Millions of dollars)

	Production Facilities			R&D		
	1992	1993	1994	1992	1993	1994
Samsung	$3,115	$3,364	$4,111	$1,308	$1,370	$1,620
Hyundai	1,645	1,713	4,111	959	847	1,495
LG	1,744	1,993	2,741	810	934	1,246
Daewoo	760	1,439	2,155	610	1,028	1,398
Sunkyong	1,620	1,445	1,906	150	162	212
Ssangyong	533	747	1,869	90	87	125
POSCO	1,723	824	1,625	116	121	131
Hanjin	1,470	1,476	1,595	81	81	87
Kia	1,370	1,059	1,744	262	274	374
Hyosung	623	480	648	81	81	100
Lotte	436	498	810	25	75	100
Han Wha	1,289	n/a	n/a	62	n/a	n/a
Doosan	436	648	424	75	81	81
Dongbu	154	201	268	7	n/a	41
Daelim	219	305	399	30	25	37
Kolon	262	324	386	32	39	46
Kumho	1,059	748	872	64	125	125

Source: Business Korea, February and July 1994.

technology acquisition; it also supports the *chaebols'* costly efforts to improve innovative capabilities and to acquire advanced technologies, which will be the foundation for global competition in the next century.

In 1993, Daewoo invested $300 million in a cement factory in China's Shandong province. The company will expand into glassware production, steel-product manufacturing, and trading company joint ventures in the future. Daewoo also has a consumer electronics plant in Burma, a tire factory in Sudan, a TV plant in Uzbekistan, and a home-appliance plant in St. Petersburg, Russia.[48] Thanks to its early move into remote areas of the

Figure 7-5 Korea's Overseas Direct Investment Trend by Invested Total Amount and Projects, 1968–1993

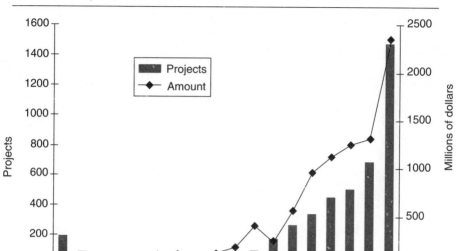

Source: Bank of Korea, *Overseas Direct Investment Statistics Yearbook 1995* (Seoul).

world, Daewoo Electronics has become a well-known name in Uzbekistan and other developing countries familiar with its consumer products, such as cordless phones, television sets, and vacuum cleaners. At home Daewoo lags behind its rivals, Goldstar and Samsung.[49]

Hyundai Motors has already set up a joint venture in China's Guangdong province to produce 6,000 minibuses annually and plans to invest $8.6 million to build a commercial-vehicle plant in Malaysia. Goldstar Telecommunications and Samsung Electronics have each established joint-venture manufacturing plants for telecommunication switching systems in Shandong province and plan to expand their manufacturing of fiber optic cable, transmission equipment, and headsets.[50] Goldstar's investment in China also goes into plants for production of color TV tubes, VCRs, and full-scale audio products.

The *chaebols'* overseas investments are also directly tied to acquiring advanced technologies. Over the years the *chaebols* have used overseas investments in advanced countries, mainly from the United States, to acquire proprietary advanced technologies that other firms were not willing to transfer. For example, the *chaebols* used research facilities in Silicon Valley,

Table 7-5 Korea's Overseas Direct Investment by Country (Thousands of dollars)

Country	Net Invested Amount (Cases)	Percentage
United States	$2,270,172 (622)	25.3
China	1,104,924 (1,477)	12.3
Indonesia	824,588 (237)	9.2
Canada	433,172 (40)	4.8
Germany	250,801 (56)	2.8
Japan	232,560 (144)	2.6
Malaysia	182,277 (116)	2.0
United Kingdom	175,590 (38)	1.9
Hong Kong	160,906 (196)	1.8
Philippines	159,889 (275)	1.7
Others	3,167,322 (1,441)	35.3
Total	8,962,201 (4,642)	100

Source: Bank of Korea, *Overseas Direct Investment Statistics Yearbook 1995* (Seoul).
Note: Based on the outstanding net investment as of the end of 1994.

employing American and Korean engineers to develop and acquire the know-how for the most advanced microelectronics products. Several Korean firms have also employed moonlighting Japanese engineers, who fly to Seoul on weekends to work in Korean labs.[51] To overcome technology protectionism and to facilitate acquisition of high technologies, several of the *chaebols* began opening research centers in advanced countries in the late 1980s. By the end of 1992, the top four *chaebols* had established seventeen overseas research centers in electronics alone: nine in the United States, five in Japan, two in Germany, and one in Ireland.[52]

The *chaebols* have used overseas investments as the means to quickly build innovative capabilities in high-tech fields. Korean conglomerates planned to spend more than $48 billion on capital investment in 1995, 57 percent more than the previous year.[53] Hyundai Electronic Industries Company's 1993 purchase of 40 percent of U.S.-based Maxtor Corporation (which holds 12 percent of the world market in hard-disk drives) is illustrative of this strategy. In addition to guaranteeing exports of Hyundai computer memory chips, the investment allows for cross-licensing of the two companies' technologies and the shared development of hard-disk-drive parts and components to boost Hyundai's global strategic advantage.[54]

The high concentration of the top four *chaebols'* overseas investments in the United States reflects efforts to acquire technology through direct investment in advanced countries. In 1995, for example, Samsung planned to spend $1.4 billion on outright acquisitions and capital infusions for equity stakes in companies based mostly in the United States and Europe.[55] "In the U.S. and Europe, there are two reasons for acquiring existing companies: technology and market," says Hwang Young-Kye, managing director and treasurer of Samsung Electronics.[56] Hwang identified multimedia software, logic semiconductors, telecommunications, and personal computers as industries in which Samsung hopes to leapfrog R&D time and effort by acquiring companies with proven technologies, existing patents, and experienced people to make them work. After losing a bid to acquire AT&T's GIS microelectronics division to rival Hyundai Electronics America, Samsung moved to acquire a major stake in personal computer maker AST Research.[57] Samsung is also on the lookout for autoelectronic parts producers in Japan to get its passenger car business off the ground in 1998.[58]

Increased Technology Exports

Korean corporations have also used technology exports through licensing, technical assistance, and project engineering to recover technology development expenses and expand their exports of parts and components in related areas. Technology exports have a relatively short history in Korea, initiated by the Technology Development Enhancement Law of 1978, but they have been used with increasing frequency in recent years.[59] The process of technology export provides a mechanism through which firms can master technological capabilities by acquiring additional capabilities and new technologies. Amsden and Kim noted that Korean corporations were able to broaden their technological capabilities by directly participating in local projects of foreign firms to facilitate technology transfers.[60] Between 1978 and 1994, there were 538 cases of technology exports, amounting to about $370 million (U.S. dollars) in payment. Of these, 107 cases (or 20 percent) were in the electric and electronics industry, next only to metals and machinery (131 cases) and petroleum and chemicals (108 cases) (see table 7-6). In the beginning, Middle Eastern countries were the primary buyers of technological capabilities from Korea, but since the early 1980s, most technology exports have gone to China and other newly developing Southeast Asian countries (see table 7-7). In 1994, China and the Philippines

Table 7-6 Trends in Korea's Technology Exports

	1978–1989	1990	1991	1992	1993	1994	Total
Food	1,273 (4)	49.5 (1)	894.9 (2)	570.0 (1)	600.0 (2)	4,320.0 (6)	7,707.7 (16)
Pulp and paper	— (1)	1,030.0 (1)	1,202.9 (—)	500.0 (1)	294.0 (2)	328.1 (1)	3,355.0 (6)
Textiles and apparel	800 (5)	2,388.5 (4)	1,413.4 (4)	1,265.0 (12)	2,145.0 (11)	794.4 (22)	8,806.3 (58)
Ceramics and cement	16,275 (3)	— (—)	30.0 (1)	333.0 (1)	991.0 (3)	10.0 (3)	17,639.0 (11)
Petroleum and chemicals	18,082 (37)	10,427.6 (13)	16,273.3 (9)	3,325.9 (12)	4,314.2 (14)	13,111.9 (23)	65,354.9 (108)
Metal and machinery	1,011 (16)	524.2 (13)	574.9 (8)	3,037.3 (30)	11,104.6 (30)	60,611.0 (34)	76,863.8 (131)
Electric and electronics	2,301 (24)	4,017.9 (12)	5,879.7 (10)	8,613.9 (17)	14,511.7 (19)	12,571.5 (25)	47,896.1 (107)
Others	85,652 (45)	3,357.8 (6)	8,894.9 (5)	14,857.5 (6)	11,142.9 (24)	19,136.0 (15)	143,220 (101)
Total	125,394 (135)	21,795.5 (50)	35,164.0 (39)	32,502.6 (80)	45,103.4 (105)	110,882.9 (129)	370,842.8 (538)

Source: Status of Technology Export 1995, Ministry of Science and Technology, Seoul, 1995.
Note: Figures are in thousands of dollars. Numbers in parentheses indicate number of cases.

Table 7-7 Korea's Technology Exports by Country

		United States	Japan	China	Indonesia	Philippines	Others	Total
1994	Cases	2	4	55	9	32	27	129
	Amount	0.7	5.8	12.8	7.6	4.0	80.0	110.9
1993	Cases	—	2	51	10	6	36	105
	Amount	1.9	2.2	10.3	4.7	0.5	25.5	45.1

Source: Status of Technology Export 1995, Ministry of Science and Technology, Seoul, 1995.
Note: "Others" inclues twenty-two countries. Amounts are in millions of dollars.

were among the top two destinations for Korea's technology exports (see table 7-7). There has also been an increasing trend in technology exports to developed countries, reflecting some degree of mutually complementary exchange of technologies.

It is widely believed that technology exports will grow much faster and play a more critical role in the future because of Korea's unique advantages compared with Japan and other developed countries in the newly developing Asian markets, such as China. Many newly developing countries regard Korea as a model for their future industrialization. Furthermore, they prefer Korean technologies to those from advanced countries, which are too sophisticated for their purposes and too expensive. The newly industrializing Asian firms also frequently choose Korea for technology transfer over Japan for political and historical reasons and over Western firms for cultural and economic reasons. Like many Asian governments, China has been keen to use Korea as a shield against undue influence by Japan, lessening its dependence on Japan for technology transfer.[61] A Western diplomat recently said: "China believes Japanese imperialism is alive and well. Beijing is always the first to express concern at Japan's growing regional influence. There are no such fears with Korea, which is the only Asian alternative for technology transfer in the heavy industries such as autos and shipbuilding."[62]

Increased Technological Alliances

One of the trends in the international technology environment that appears to work in Korea's favor is the increased use of alliances to develop technological competencies. Unlike the past, when strong rivalries between the *chaebols* deterred them from forging alliances among themselves, there is now a need to share risk and development funds. This has led not only to more alliances between *chaebols* but to still more popular alliances between the *chaebols* and small and medium-sized domestic firms. For example, Goldstar and Sunkyong joined hands in 1994 to develop a double-density video compact disk with a replay time of 148 minutes, double that of existing video CDs.[63] Goldstar also formed alliances with Haitai Electronics and Kia in 1993 to develop new visual equipment and robots, respectively, by combining each partner's technical competence.[64] In 1992, Goldstar made another agreement with Samsung for the unconditional exchange of 2,000 patents that belong to each partner in TV tubes, monitors, and LCD fields, allowing them to avoid duplication of investment and accelerate the process of technology acquisition.

Domestic alliances are also characterized by joint production and marketing, joint sourcing of parts and components, and collaborative bidding for large-scale international contracts.[65] Recently, as part of the new technology policy, the government has been playing a pivotal role in forming a large-scale, industry-wide research consortia. The Korean government recently initiated a consortium involving a government-run research center and three private corporations to develop a TDX (time-division-multiplex-exchange) system as a basis for global competitiveness in the telecommunication equipment industry. As a consequence, Korea successfully developed the requisite technology, and the resulting system has not only met domestic needs but also appears to be a promising export. HDTV technology was also successfully developed through a business-government collaboration, involving the largest competitors in the electronics industry, such as Samsung Electric, Goldstar, and Orion Electric.[66] The government and participating corporations shared the costs, which totaled $25 million, and the necessary technologies; Samsung was responsible for developing tube-related technology and Goldstar for shadow-mask technology.[67]

GOVERNMENT SUPPORT FOR HIGH-TECHNOLOGY DEVELOPMENT: THE G-7 PROJECT

On July 8, 1992, President Roh presided over a national conference on science and technology development in Taeduk Science Park that was attended by 190 representatives of government, industry, academia, and various agencies. During the meeting, Kim Jin Hyun, minister of science and technology, formally announced a new technology development plan to meet the challenges Korea faces in the global market and to lead the country into the high-technology-oriented economy. The plan for leading technology development was named the "G7 Project," its goal being the improvement of Korea's science and technology to a level comparable with that of the seven leading industrial nations by the year 2001.

Under such basic guidelines, the G7 Project is divided into two specific plans: the "Commercial Technology Development Plan" and the "Basic Technology Development Plan." The commercial plan targets the development of the essential technologies for four specific products in four different industries that will be the basis of global competition in the first decade of the twenty-first century. They must also be in areas in which Korea has the potential to be competitive. The four products are B-ISDN, a telecommunications network designed to handle video, text, voice, graphics, facsimile images, and so on; HDTV, high-definition television; new medicine and agrichemicals, and next-generation automobiles. For the first two products—B-ISDN and HDTV—the goal is to improve on Korea's current competitiveness in the global market. For new medicine and agrichemical and next-generation automobiles, the goal is to challenge the global leaders and establish national competitiveness. The Basic Technology Development Plan is designed to acquire the foundation technologies in seven high-tech fields in which commercialization is realistically impossible but which are nonetheless essential to Korea's continued economic growth and improved quality of life in the next century. The basic technologies identified in the seven fields are:

1. 256M DRAMs and other next-generation chips.

2. Advanced materials for information, electronics, and energy.

3. New capacity biological materials.

4. Advanced production systems like CIM and IMS.

5. Environmental engineering.

6. New energy sources.

7. Next-generation nuclear reactors.

In 1995, a special task force was formed to conduct a comprehensive evaluation of the research performance during the first stage (1992–1994) of the G7 Project. Achievements included the development of three new medicinal products, 256M DRAMs, digital HDTV sets, a plant for IGCC systems as a new energy source, the Ni-MH electric cell and various other key technologies for an electric car, and the completion of the design for ATM switching systems.[68] The project for HDTV involved two main research centers, various universities, and the Big Four *chaebols*. The development of 256M DRAMs, led by Samsung, was also a collaborative effort, involving four independent research centers, fifteen corporations, and nine universities. Overall, the first stage of the project involved 33,000 research personnel and about $850 million in investment ($350 million from the government and $500 million from corporations). The project succeeded in commercializing eight technologies, and it produced 2,542 patents currently pending and 545 patents registered. The 545 patents registered were heavily concentrated in two technology fields—206 patents (38 percent) in HDTV and 255 patents (47 percent) in B-ISDN.

Since 1992, the Korean government has also initiated various complementary incentive systems—tax benefits, special loans, educational innovations, and so forth—to support research and development in high-tech industries.

The Korean government is also managing a special science and technology acquisitions fund, funding up to 80 percent of private R&D budgets related to the G7 Project. Special loans are also available up to about $1.3 million per research project and $4 million per company, with a 6 percent interest rate for small and midsized companies and a 6.5 percent rate for large corporations. In a 1992 meeting, Choi Gak Kyu, minister of the Economic Planning Board, announced new tax-exemption plans to support technology acquisition efforts; a one-time amortization of up to 90 percent of the investment to commercialize new technologies, five-year carryover exemptions of technology development expenses, stepwise shortening of depreciation years for investments in science equipment, tariff exemptions for corporate investments in science equipment when they are donated to universities within five years, and progressive tax exemptions for corporate investments in technology and personnel development.

The G7 Project is complemented by two other government-initiated projects, both launched in 1992: the Large-Scale High Technology Development Project and the Electro-21 Project. The first is designed to enhance technological competence in two large-scale industries: the aviation and space industry and the nuclear industry. The Electro-21 Project is a five-year plan to improve technological capabilities in the electronics industry by developing various core technologies and by localizing component and material technologies. Despite the rapid growth of the 1980s, Korea was losing ground in intermediate technologies for electronic components and materials; the ratio of components imports in the electronics industry worsened from 47 percent in 1985 to 54 percent in 1991. Also, the payment for foreign technologies in electronics has been constantly increasing since the late 1980s. The primary goal of the Electro-21 Project is to lower Korea's dependence on foreign, particularly Japanese, technology for intermediate materials and components and to strengthen Korea's global competitiveness in the electronics industry. The Electro-21 Project specifies three objectives: (1) the development of fifty-six electronic technologies in eighteen different fields that have great potential for growth, such as electronic ceramic components, microprocessors, flat display systems; (2) the standardization of two hundred components and materials in eight fields that are generic to many related businesses, such as condensers; and (3) the localization of 1,500 technologies that are essential to improving the quality of final electronic products but that are difficult for small and midsized component suppliers to develop alone. The Korean government will fund about 50 percent of the total investment, amounting to $1 billion.[69]

In summary, Korea's movement into technology-intensive industries in the 1980s reversed the need from production mastery to design and innovation. In high-tech industries, innovative capabilities are mostly firm-specific and well protected by patents.[70] Apprenticeships and imitation—so successful in enabling Korean firms to master production processes—proved limiting when it came to acquiring innovative capabilities. A KIET study shows that Korea falls short in design, materials treatment, and testing, compared with other advanced countries. Along with weakness in design, Korea is also far behind advanced countries in basic technologies, as illustrated in the electronics industry. Korea has narrowed the gap in processing, assembly, and most industrial technologies, but it still lags in materials technology. Innovation capabilities appear to be a more fundamental issue to Korean businesses. As one observer noted: "Koreans know science and technology. They can put things together and take them apart. But they are not free thinkers. . . . You don't really see new products coming out here. Instead of aiming at just more of the same things (that others are already making) at cheaper prices, they've got to start developing really new products."[71]

As Korean firms pass the threshold of manufacturing with advanced technologies, market development will become the next challenge. Market development has been constrained by Korean manufacturers' early reliance on powerful OEM foreign buyers. It has been difficult for Korean firms to establish their own brands and discard the OEM "image." Even so, OEM arrangements gave Korean firms high-volume sales. These, in turn, allowed Korean firms the realization of scale and scope economies, that proved to be cost-effective for acquiring and developing production skills. Moreover, learning through OEM resulted in spillovers to other industries—a procedure that was facilitated by the *chaebols'* highly diversified structure. Despite such achievements, keeping pace with technological advances and enhancing market development by cultivating "world-class" images remain the key challenges for Korean firms.

CHAPTER EIGHT

Management and the New Confucianism

One of the most difficult challenges facing many Korean firms today is how to shift their organizational design and management style so that they support the firm's efforts to engage in global competition. We view this as the sixth major challenge facing contemporary Korean firms as they approach the next century. Organizational change is typically regarded as one of the most challenging tasks faced by an organization in any country, and nowhere is this more true than in tradition-bound Korea. Yet major changes are imperative if Korean firms are to succeed. In this chapter, we look inside the typical Korean firm to see how it is organized and managed and to see how organizational configuration has changed in response to the realities of the global marketplace.

Seoul National University Professor Cho Dong Sung argues that a country's international competitiveness is determined by the extent to which it "has industries with competitive advantage, . . . has them in multitude, and . . . possesses common sources of competitiveness within its boundary."[1] In examining Korean enterprise, Cho emphasizes the special role of human factors as the "drivers" of national economic development. It is often noted that certain Asian nations possess certain characteristics that their Western counterparts find difficult to attain; in particular, an ability or willingness to impose discipline on a sometimes fractious population. In some countries, such as Japan and Korea, this process has historically included heavy state involvement. In other places, such as Singapore, the government steered investment and engaged in social engineering. Many researchers suggest that what the populations of these countries have in common can be collectively referred to as Confucian values. These values, such as loyalty to the family or subservience to authority, did not create the economic vibrancy that now characterizes much of Asia, but they surely helped. According to international correspondent Joe Hawke, these values "create a better environment for accepting tough decisions," like delaying today's spending to invest in the future.[2] Hawke also notes that, unlike the multiracial mosaic that is contemporary America, most of the "Asian tigers" (the newly industrializing Asian countries) are relatively homogeneous lands of shared social norms and values.

The social changes currently sweeping Korea affect the very nature of its core values and practices. While Confucian values may have served as the stabilizing force in early economic development, there is serious question whether these traditional values will be able to sustain Korea's new efforts at globalization, especially in view of the government's new *segyehwa* movement. Employees at all levels are demanding a greater share of the benefits of the emerging economic prosperity. The new movement toward political democracy has fueled demands for workplace democracy, with greater worker autonomy and participation. Commitment to the company, once assumed, is now seen as diminishing, and workers are demanding greater input in corporate decisions. In short, Korea has reached a stage of rising entitlements, where people feel they deserve more. Such is the inevitable consequence of successful economic development.

This chapter is divided into several parts. We begin by looking inside a typical Korean firm to see how it is organized for purposes of task accomplishment and goal attainment. Following this, we describe the typical traditional Korean work environment, considering such dimensions of that environment as the centrality of work, the value of group harmony, the nature of interpersonal relationships, and the process of making decisions. We then compare Korean work environments with their Japanese and American counterparts. Next we turn to an examination of the background and current state of affairs in Korea's tumultuous labor-management relations. Finally, we focus on the recent efforts of several companies to implement significant changes in managerial style.

INSIDE THE KOREAN FIRM

A good place to begin understanding how Korean firms approach the issue of management is to consider how various employee groups are organized for purposes of management. The typical organizational hierarchy of a Korean firm is shown in figure 8-1. As can be seen, there are three principal groupings: managers and technical personnel, workers, and female employ-

Figure 8-1 Typical Organizational Hierarchy for a Korean Firm

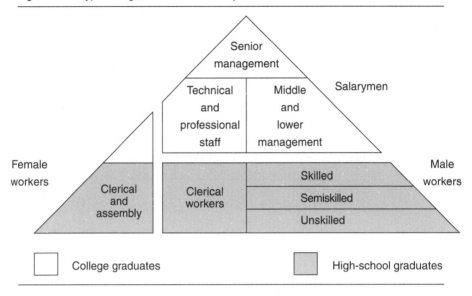

ees. As in the United States, white-collar employees can be found on one of two tracks: managerial or technical. In Korea (as in Japan), these employees are referred to as salarymen, and they invariably consist of college graduates who entered the company through a rigorous process of selection (see chapter 9).

At or near the top of the organization can be found a managerial hierarchy that resembles that in the typical Japanese firm. Korean organizational hierarchies are purposefully "tall" so that differentiation between ranks is clear. It is important that each person knows his or her place so that no one loses face in interpersonal transactions. Typical ranks at the upper levels of such firms, along with their Japanese counterparts, are as follows:

Rank	Korea	Japan
Chairman	*hwoichang*	*kaicho*
President	*sachang*	*shacho*
Executive director	*joenmu*	*senmu*
Managing director	*sangmu*	*jomu*
Director	*eesah*	*riji*
Department manager	*puchang*	*bucho*
Deputy department manager	*chachang*	*jicho*

Rank	Korea	Japan
Section chief	*kwachang*	*kacho*
Deputy section chief	*daerhee*	*dairi*
Chief clerk	*kaychang*	*kakaricho*
Regular staff members	*sawon*	*shain*

Even today, the place of women employees in corporations is perhaps best understood as consisting of a separate hierarchy, relatively distinct from and largely subservient to the male hierarchy (see figure 8-1). This situation follows from Confucian tradition and puts women in a situation in which they are typically paid less, have less job security, and are given little opportunity to contribute to the decision-making process. Women are hired most frequently as assemblers, clerks, typists, secretaries, or service workers. While female college graduates earn more and are accorded somewhat higher status and authority, they, like other women, are frequently less important to the organization than are the salarymen or other male workers and earn less than men working in similar jobs. They are often seen by their male counterparts as temporary employees whose role is to serve the (male) organization until marriage. While changes in the status of Korean women have been slow in coming, some evolution is discernible, as we will see in chapter 9.

Below the managerial levels can be found the blue-collar workers, divided—as in the United States—into skilled, semiskilled, and unskilled workers. These workers typically exhibit a level of commitment to the organization that far exceeds that of their American and European counterparts. Even during labor disputes, their commitment to the company itself is seldom challenged, even though goal conflicts are clearly evident. On the shop-floor level, we see that even after the major labor strife of the late 1980s a militaristic atmosphere frequently remains. Employees in many firms are required to cut their hair short and to wear company uniforms. Deference must be shown to supervisors. Employee rank is identified by the shape of name tags, which are attached to each worker's left breast-pocket. Supervisors frequently wear different colored uniforms, as do women employees in several companies.

A good example of this production unit organization can be seen at the Hyundai Motor Company in Ulsan.[3] As shown in figure 8-2, six to ten production workers (or *kongwon*) are supervised by a foreman (*chojang*). Twenty to forty *kongwon* with their three *chojang* report to a supervisor (*banjang*) who, along with two or three other *banjang*, reports to a technical superintendent (*kisa*). In this highly centralized arrangement, the first two

Figure 8-2 Organization Chart for a Production Unit at Hyundai Motor Compay

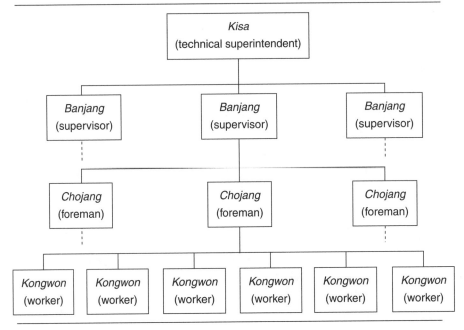

levels of supervision are almost horizontal in that their occupants work on the production line. All three levels of supervision cooperate in evaluating individual worker performance.

TRADITIONAL KOREAN CORPORATE CULTURE

Within the Korean firm's management structure lies the attitudinal and behavioral soul of the organization: its corporate culture. At the risk of overgeneralizing, it is possible to develop a composite picture of the traditional Korean work environment. A number of attitudinal and behavioral characteristics distinguish the Korean firm—especially as compared with those typical to the Japanese or American firm. (See table 8-1, which lists many of these characteristics.) These can be boiled down to seven essential categories, which express the value Korean corporate culture places on the following:

1. The centrality of work.

2. Group harmony and the social contract.

3. Personal relationships.

Table 8-1　Comparison of Korean, Japanese, and American Corporate Cultures

Feature	Korea	Japan	United States
Company loyalty	Strong	Extremely strong	Fairly weak
Importance of seniority	Very strong	Very strong	Moderately strong
Work centrality	Confucian work ethic	Confucian work ethic	Protestant work ethic
Basis of achievement	Group achievement	Group achievement	Individual achievement
Social contract	Harmony dominates	Harmony dominates	Individual justice dominates
Basis of business relationships	Personal relationships	Personal relationships	Written contract
Vertical relationships	Highly paternalistic	Highly paternalistic	Impersonal, bureaucratic
Job descriptions	General	General	Very specific
Nonverbal cues	Highly sensitive	Highly sensitive	Relatively insensitive
Individualism versus group spirit	Both equally strong	Group spirit dominates	Individualism dominates
Employment	Quasi-lifetime	Lifetime	No guarantees
Mobility	Some mobility	Immobility	Free mobility
Leadership style	Authoritarian/ paternalistic	Authoritarian/ paternalistic	Participative
Decision making	Both autocratic and consultative	By consensus	Both autocratic and consultative

4. Paternalism in superior-subordinate relationships.

5. General job descriptions.

6. Nonverbal cues.

7. The decision-making process and personal accountability.

As we'll see, most Korean corporations have created a work environment that is consistent with Korean societal norms and that is highly conducive to maximum production and maximum effort on behalf of the corporation's goals. Based on this discussion, we will turn later in this chapter to an examination of the ways in which Korean firms are attempting to modify their cultures to meet the demands of the twenty-first-century economy.

The Centrality of Work

Even after the labor struggles of the late 1980s, Koreans have continued their tradition of working extremely hard. Words frequently used by foreign observers to describe Korean workers include diligent, self-sacrificing, dedicated, and dependable. Even the Japanese frequently complain that Koreans work too hard. There is abundant evidence of this. Consider, for example, a survey taken in several countries that asked school children what quality they believed parents most wanted them to have. Results showed that "achievement" ranked first among Korean children, while it ranked sixth and eighth, respectively, among English and American children.[4] In another study, Korean managers were asked what they would do if they had enough money to live comfortably for the rest of their lives.[5] A full 96 percent responded that they would continue to work hard despite their newfound wealth. Asked if they would prefer to have more time for work or for leisure, 61 percent responded that they would prefer to have more time for work, while only 38 percent preferred more leisure time. Whether such behavior represents a strong commitment to one's employer or a national value of work centrality (that is, a belief that one must work hard regardless of one's degree of commitment to the organization) can be debated. However, from the standpoint of worker productivity and industrial competitiveness, it matters very little; Koreans simply spend more time on the job than most of their international counterparts.

Many observers feel that Koreans' attitude toward work can be traced to the Confucian value system, which permeates Korean society. Indeed, a similar hard-driving attitude can be found in all levels of Korea's educational system. The Korean term for this attitude is *eui-yok.* Roughly translated, it means "will" or "ambition." A person with *eui-yok* has an internal drive to succeed, to accomplish something important, not so much for the financial reward as for the spiritual reward. Several companies, most notably Sunkyong, consider *eui-yok* to be the "heart of the company." According to Sunkyong's Chairman Chey Jong-Hyon, the loss of *eui-yok* in employees leads to a loss of vitality that can easily destroy the capacity of the company to compete and survive.[6] It is easy to understand why he and so many other managers consider the preservation of *eui-yok* so central to good management.

It is worth comparing the nature of this achievement-oriented drive in Korea with that found in the United States. While achievement-oriented individuals exist in both countries, the basis or focus of their behavior is quite different. In Korea, reflecting a "Confucian" work ethic, an employee's work effort is primarily group oriented; hard work is done so that the group—that is, the company—will succeed. In the United States, reflecting the Western Protestant work ethic, a person's work effort is primarily focused on individual advancement and achievement. The worker generally puts himself or herself first in the striving for success.

It has also been argued that many Americans are losing their drive to work and succeed. As Daewoo's Chairman Kim observes, "The American company is not what it used to be. In the old days, Americans worked hard to challenge new frontiers. But as their economy got mature, they became more interested in nice houses, jogging, and having a good time than in doing business. How can you compete without dedication? It is not the management system that is not working in American companies, it is the people not working hard."[7]

Group Harmony and the Social Contract

The second characteristic that typifies the Korean work environment is the "social contract" upheld by employees. In Korea, the social contract is predicated on a firm belief in preserving group harmony. For many years the LG Group has had as its motto *inhwa* (Korean for "harmony"), and the importance of maintaining harmony among employees is constantly mentioned in discussions with executives and workers alike, at LG and at other companies. Like work centrality, the principle of group harmony derives from Confucian thought, which stresses smooth, constructive, and conflict-free interpersonal relations at almost any cost.

It is everyone's responsibility to maintain societal equilibrium, and this responsibility typically supersedes any conception of individual rights. In fact, in Korea and other Asian countries, one hears considerable talk about one's responsibilities to company and country and little about one's rights in either domain; in the West it is typically just the opposite. Westerners are often preoccupied with individual rights and seldom seriously consider individual responsibilities. The phrase in President John F. Kennedy's 1961 inaugural address, "Ask not what your country can do for you; ask what you can do for your country," is still remembered by Americans nearly forty years later because it does not express a typically American sentiment. In Korea, such a statement by a new leader would never receive such attention; it would be too commonplace.

Another way the social contract is played out in Korean firms is through the use of the *saboon*. A *saboon* generally consists of a phrase or slogan that embodies the company's most important values. Thus, LG has frequently used "harmony," while Daewoo uses "creativity, challenge, and sacrifice." Korean managers often frame their *saboon* and hang it in their office, sometimes noting with pride that the chairman himself painted it. What differentiates the *saboon* from Western company mottoes is its personalized nature. Many *saboons* are derived from the family motto of the company founder and represent what he believes to be important about the company.

Personal Relationships

If Koreans tend to emphasize group harmony and the West tends to emphasize individual liberties, it is not surprising that in business relationships Koreans give more credence to personal contacts and relationships while the West relies more on written contracts. In Korea, it is imperative that one be "connected," both inside and outside the corporation. Considerable time is consumed in developing and nurturing these relationships, and business deals and simple favors alike are predicated on such relationships. For most Korean businessmen, agreements between two parties change as business conditions change. Since the mutual benefit of both parties is the goal, it is frequently seen as inappropriate to hold one party to an agreement if business conditions change to his significant detriment. What is important is maintaining the personal relationship and enhancing mutual benefit. A signed contract is simply symbolic of this.

Needless to say, most managers in the West do not see it this way.[8] Contracts are the sine qua non of American business enterprise, as exemplified by the proliferation of corporate lawyers and lawsuits in the United States. As movie mogul Louis B. Mayer once observed, "A handshake is only as good as the paper it's written on." Personal relationships are often seen only as a means of securing a contract. Compared with Korea, little effort is made to nurture them. This difference becomes particularly important as more foreign businesses attempt to initiate trade or joint ventures in Korea.

Paternalism in Superior-Subordinate Relationships

In Korean firms, relationships between superiors and subordinates are characterized by a high degree of paternalism. It is expected that a supervisor or manager will assume personal responsibility for the development of his subordinates and that these subordinates will respond by showing the proper respect and obedience. These are mutual commitments and obligations. It is not uncommon for a manager to take his subordinates out drinking one night a week to discuss both business and personal matters and to continue building a harmonious atmosphere. Moreover, it is expected that a manager will take an active interest in his subordinate's personal and family life, attending funerals and birthday parties, giving gifts on certain occasions, and so forth. Like Japanese companies, Korean companies hold to the concept of the "whole person," which stresses the interconnectedness of all parts of life. Conflict or problems at home may affect work performance and, as such, must be monitored and resolved.

This practice stands in stark contrast with the Western norm that clearly separates worklife from homelife. In fact, in the United States, employers are often legally proscribed from inquiring about the employee's life outside the workplace. In the United States, superior-subordinate relationships tend to be more distant and less personal, governed largely by the responsibilities laid out in detailed job descriptions. The bureaucratic model began in Germany in the nineteenth century and spread to other Western nations as an ideal form of organization governed by rationality and merit, not favoritism or personal relationships. Emphasis was placed on a clear specification of work rules that applied universally, employment and promotion based solely on merit and qualification, and the impersonality of office (that is, authority was invested in the office, not the individual, and office holders were expected to maintain an impersonal attitude when dealing with others). Under this system, paternalistic behavior in the West has often been resented and resisted, viewed as either a form of favoritism or an invasion of one's privacy. Individuals are considered responsible for taking care of themselves. Events outside of work are no one's business. Indeed, in most Western companies, employees are actively discouraged from bringing their "personal problems" to work.

General Job Descriptions

Job descriptions in the West tend to be far longer and more specific in outlining responsibilities than those in Korea, where such descriptions serve only to define the general parameters of the job. Hence, we seldom hear an employee in Korea complain, "That's not my job!" In fact, the team atmosphere that pervades Korean companies is greatly aided by these nonspecific job descriptions, which support individual behavior that is for the good of the company.

Nonverbal Cues

Yet another facet of Korea's emphasis on interpersonal relationships is seen in the concept of *nunch'i*. *Nunch'i* translates roughly as "the look in someone's eyes." It is the nonverbal reaction of someone to a question, a directive, or a comment, and Korean businessmen pride themselves on their ability to read someone's "face." Nonverbal behavior in all forms of social interaction is far more important in the East than in the West. And in these interactions, one's ability to read *nunch'i*—that is, to silently perceive what the other party is thinking—is fundamental. In fact, there is a Korean proverb that translates "one who does not have *nunch'i* cannot succeed." Moreover, in interpersonal interactions, most Koreans will typically assume that the other party also has this capability. Thus, if an employee asks for a favor that his supervisor either cannot or will not grant, the supervisor would likely use *nunch'i* to signal his negative response, thereby avoiding the loss of face to be suffered by either party if the request were to be formally (and publicly) declined. In Korea, in contrast to the West, what is not said is often far more important than what is said, and one's ability to interpret this unspoken language accurately is essential to career or business success.

The Decision-Making Process and Personal Accountability

If significant variation can be found in the work environments of different Korean companies, it is with respect to their decision-making processes. Most international observers are familiar with the Japanese *ringi-sei* decision-making system, in which proposals work their way up from the bottom of the organization in a way that ensures widespread consensus as to the desired course of action by the time the proposal reaches top management. In theory, Korean business organizations use the same system. In Korean, it is called *pummi*, or "proposal submitted for deliberation." Indeed, *pummi* and *ringi-sei* share the same Chinese characters. In point of fact, however, the *pummi* approach is seldom followed in any systematic fashion in the big companies. Instead, the *pummi* system serves other purposes; namely, to provide documentation for all company programs and new ventures and to diffuse responsibility for implementation of the decision.

In more cases than many managers care to admit, decision making in Korean companies remains highly centralized in the hands of top executives who make decisions either unilaterally or in small groups after consultation with the various parties involved. A good example of this came up in a recent interview Daewoo President Kim Woo-Choong gave to *Fortune* magazine. The command structure at Daewoo is rather simple, he said: "I make the decisions."[9]

There are three basic approaches to employee involvement in decision making, distinguished by the amount of consultation involving subordinates: "authoritarian," in which the manager makes the decision himself, sometimes based on information provided by others; "consultative," in which the manager first consults with subordinates to learn their views and then makes a solitary decision; and "participative," in which the manager attempts to the extent possible to allow the affected group to make the decision.[10] These three styles exist on a continuum, running from authoritarian to consultative to participative. In terms of this model, the Japanese *ringi-sei* system comes closest to the group decision-making method, although exceptions can obviously be found.

Evidence suggests that most Korean companies tend to fall somewhere between the authoritarian and the participative approaches and are more top-down oriented than comparable Japanese companies. Companies that are owner-managed tend to be more authoritarian, while companies that rely more heavily on professional managers are more participative. In either case, however, we are likely to see more participative methods used as we move down the managerial hierarchy, while more authoritarian methods emerge again as we enter the ranks of blue-collar workers. Even under the so-called authoritarian approach to management, however, Confucian tradition requires the decision maker to balance the needs and harmony of the group with business demands, a phenomenon Western managers oftentimes fail to do.

As in Korea, a diverse range of decision-making styles is found in America, with some companies (such as Hewlett-Packard and Intel) known for their highly participative styles, others for more authoritarian styles. However, few firms in America or Korea approach the Japanese in terms of fostering genuine bottom-up consensus building around a proposed course of action.

One final difference concerning decision making should be noted. In the United States, a fundamental principle of "good management" rests on the idea that authority must be delegated down to the same level where responsibility to carry out the decision lies. In other words, it is believed that if someone is assigned responsibility to accomplish a certain task, that person must be given sufficient authority on matters that directly affect task accomplishment. In Korea, it is not uncommon to observe situations in which authority is centralized but responsibility is decentralized. A junior manager, for example, may be told in essence: "You didn't choose this course of action, but you must make it work." This practice can be seen in the myriad decisions made by executives to enter a new and risky business or to take over an older, failing one. Once made, it is not for subordinates to question the decision; rather, their job—and their future career—lies in making the venture successful, against any and all odds. In contrast to the typical situation in the West, such individuals are typically held personally responsible for project success, not just for giving it their best effort.

The picture that emerges from the above analysis is one of compromise. Korean management is both strong and flexible. It is rooted in Eastern traditions, yet has learned from the West. It is both collectivist and individualistic. This paradox is evident when management practices in Korea are compared with those in Japan and the United States. (See table 8-1.)

Korean management is perhaps best described as a blend of East and West with a clear Eastern bias. As we shall see below, the new realities of global competition seem to be pushing Korean firms westward along this continuum to become true global corporations instead of Korean firms doing business internationally.

MODERNIZATION OF LABOR-MANAGEMENT RELATIONS

Because industrialization in South Korea has occurred relatively recently, the country's history of formal labor-management relations is relatively brief. As in other industrialized countries, the industrial relations scene in Korea is dominated by three central players: the unions, the government, and corporate management. What follows is a brief history of the relations between the three institutions.

Early Restrictive Labor Practices

From the turn of the century through World War II, Korea was occupied by the Japanese and the economy was largely dominated by Japanese firms.[11] Korean language, culture, and customs were suppressed. As a result, the early vestiges of labor unions in Korea emerged as part of the resistance to Japanese colonialism. In fact, labor protests were often seen as patriotic and received widespread support from the Korean people.[12] By the end of World War II and the division of Korea into North and South, South Korean labor leaders were divided into two philosophical camps: capitalist and communist. For a time, both communist-oriented and capitalist-oriented unions existed in the South. In 1949, South Korean President Rhee Syungman's government threw his support behind the Federation of Korean Trade Unions, or FKTU (similar to the AFL-CIO in the United States), and helped it defeat the procommunist unions.[13] This was the beginning of strong government involvement in union activity in South Korea.

After the Korean War (1950–1953), the Trade Union Act was passed. Like the U.S. National Labor Relations Act, the Trade Union Act gave workers the right to organize, bargain collectively, and engage in collective action. One important difference between the Korean and American legislation, however, was the absence of an enforcement agency (like the National Labor Relations Board) in Korea to protect the rights of the newly created unions and their members. The lack of any enforcement mechanism made it difficult for labor to secure its rights.

Almost since its inception, the Korean government controlled the FKTU, and the enforcement of labor laws during the 1950s was minimal. Antigovernment sentiments among unionists increased, and in 1960 labor activists joined student demonstrations aimed at overthrowing the government of President Rhee. The government's response to this threat was to use its security forces to curb labor's new assertiveness. In fact, in some cases, government agents have been more aggressively antilabor than business leaders.[14] Suppressing labor activity in the 1960s and 1970s was a government strategy to control labor costs, a key ingredient of Korea's economic development plan.[15] The government took the position that strong labor unions were "conflictful, unproductive, and disruptive in the context of economic growth."[16]

Initial Reforms: Enterprise Unions and Works Councils

Government pressure on Korea's labor relations intensified during the 1970s and early 1980s under President Park Chung-Hee. In 1971, the Korean government issued the Special Act on National Security; this act mandated government approval of all labor negotiations. In 1980, the government banned industry-wide national unions altogether and replaced them with enterprise (or company) unions, following the Japanese model. Enterprise unions were managed by labor-management works councils. Korean labor laws (especially the Labor-Management Council Act as revised in 1988) required every company with more than fifty employees to create a "works council" (*nosa byeobeuiboe*, in Korean), designed much along the lines of those in Western Europe. These councils were seen by the government as a substitute for unions in handling labor-management relations.

In theory, these works councils were to provide for equal representation for labor and management. They were to serve as a means of democratizing the workplace, facilitating labor-management cooperation, and improving productivity. In actual practice, however, management typically controlled the works councils, so they never realized their potential to become real agents of change in the workplace. Management frequently influenced the selection of labor representatives, often acting on its behalf. Moreover, the councils were inexperienced in negotiating, owing in part to the Special Act on National Security. Consequently, government officials were often called in by management to settle its disputes with labor. The government policy of "growth first, distribution later," typically led to promanagement contract settlements.[17]

An example of how these works councils functioned during the 1980s can be seen in the case of Hyundai Motor Company.[18] At Hyundai, the council consisted of twelve management representatives (including the factory's chief executive officer, the personnel director, and ten members selected by the CEO) and twelve members elected annually by the workers. The council was required to meet at least once every three months but could meet more often if it wished. Agenda items that could be discussed at the council were clearly specified: (1) how to improve productivity and efficiency at work, (2) how to educate and train workers, (3) how to prevent labor-management disputes, (4) how to handle workers' grievances, (5) how to promote workers' interests, (6) how to increase safety and improve the work environment, and (7) how to increase labor-management cooperation. Regulations governing the council at Hyundai also stipulated that (1) the purpose of the council was to foster labor-management cooperation and industrial peace, (2) members of the council should not engage in any behavior that might encourage a labor-management dispute or break the industrial peace, and (3) the council could not be used for collective bargaining. In actual practice, many workers felt that these regulations put them in an impossible situation. The law governing works councils required that all worker demands be channeled through the councils, yet real collective bargaining was proscribed. Hence, all the workers at Hyundai could do was to express their grievances to management; they had no mechanism through which they could get management to agree to their demands. Even so, this system continued to function throughout most of the 1980s.

In the early 1980s, union membership hovered around 800,000. The revocation of the Special Act on National Security in 1981 revived labor rights and increased labor-organizing activities. Union membership began to increase sharply in 1985 and grew to more than 1.6 million by 1989.[19] By 1991, 2.1 million Koreans belonged to unions.

The 1987 Reforms

The rapid rise of unionism was spurred by the Korean government's Declaration of Democratization on June 29, 1987.[20] This declaration contained a pledge to reduce government intervention in labor-management relations and served to revitalize unionization rights. For example, under the reform, union shops were allowed to organize if more than two-thirds of the employees in an establishment were union members. National unions were again permitted. New amendments to the Trade Union Act identified unfair labor practices by management for the first time, including (1) dismissal of, or discrimination against, workers who join or attempt to organize a union, (2) rejection of a collective bargaining agreement, and (3) interference with workers in the formation and operation of a trade union.[21]

Workers, with their newfound rights but without bargaining experience, took their grievances concerning wages and working conditions to the public for support. As Korean companies and the country as a whole became more prosperous, workers and unions began a concerted drive to improve both wages and working conditions. The number of strikes rose from 300 in 1986 to almost 4,000 in 1987 and continued to rise in 1988 and 1989. Behind these strikes was a widespread feeling by workers that they were not sharing equally in the Korean economic miracle. Many felt that the miracle itself had occurred only as a result of the sacrifice of the Korean work force and that the time had come for a return on that investment. In fact, real wages in Korea had fallen substantially behind the nation's gross domestic product. Moreover, real wages also lagged far behind industry-wide productivity gains. Workers decided it was finally time for change.[22]

Whatever the cause, the strikes were hard fought and cost the Korean economy dearly. They resulted in major pay increases across broad segments of the work force. In 1987, the average pay increase in the industrial sector was 22 percent. This was followed in 1988 by an additional 15 percent average pay raise. Hence, in two years alone, wage rates—and labor costs—

rose 37 percent, even before considering fringe benefits.[23] Korea was no longer a cheap labor country, and Korean companies began almost at once to look for cheaper sites of production and manufacturing offshore (in China, Indonesia, Malaysia, Thailand, and, most recently, North Korea).

Despite this progress, by the early 1990s, there remained a number of ways in which labor activity continued to be constrained. For instance, unions still had no national contract, there were still no shop-steward networks, and third-party interventions were not allowed under current law.[24] Even so, the Korean government had become less involved in labor-management relations since 1987. In 1991, South Korea gained full membership in the International Labor Organization (ILO). Moreover, the number of strikes began to subside as wages and working conditions continued to improve.[25] In fact, as shown in table 8-2, strike activity declined sharply toward the mid-1990s, even as the number of trade unions increased. More unions, less labor strife. And during the same period, real wages increased an average of 15 percent per year. A new era had begun.

The 1990s and Beyond: The New Industrial Relations

In the early 1990s, another "revolution" began. Both trade unions and corporate management had come to realize that the labor strife of the previous era had been detrimental to both corporate profits and employee

Table 8-2   Trade Union Membership, Labor Disputes, and Production Loss, 1987–1994

Year	Number of Trade Unions	Union Membership	Number of Disputes	Work Days Lost
1987	2,658	1,036,000	3,749	6,947,000
1988	4,068	1,267,000	1,873	5,401,000
1989	6,142	1,707,000	1,616	6,351,000
1990	7,882	1,932,000	322	4,487,000
1991	7,698	1,887,000	234	3,258,000
1992	7,637	1,803,000	235	1,520,000
1993	7,527	1,667,000	144	1,308,000
1994	7,147	1,668,000	121	1,484,000

Source: Based on data supplied by the Economic Planning Board, Korean Ministry of Labor, Seoul, 1995.

welfare. Slowly, a fragile partnership began to develop between opposing sides and a new, albeit uneasy, labor-management consensus emerged.[26] In 1993, the Korean Employers' Federation and the Federation of Korean Trade Unions for the first time reached an historic agreement limiting wage increases to between 4 and 9 percent. Again in 1994, the two groups reached another agreement limiting wage increases to between 5 and 8 percent.

These accords led to the signing of the 1995 Declaration for Industrial Peace. This declaration calls for sincere efforts by both sides to reach wage settlements early, to avoid labor strikes, and to reduce wage gaps between large and small firms. Among the features included in this declaration are calls to increase both productivity and the quality of working life, to eliminate unfair labor practices, to increase dialog between management and labor, to improve job security efforts, to improve job training, and to facilitate more information sharing by both sides. This declaration was greeted with enthusiasm among the diverse sectors of Korea's economy, and within one month of its signing more than 1,500 companies and their workers had signed pacts of mutual cooperation. A new era of relative calm had arrived on the labor scene.

THE NEW CONFUCIANISM: FROM TRADITIONAL VALUES TO MANAGERIAL PROFESSIONALISM

Since the early 1990s, Korean firms have experienced not one, but several, revolutions. They have been leading a technological revolution in an attempt to gain preeminence over global competitors in such areas as flat panel displays and semiconductors, as we saw in previous chapters. To survive, they must become world-class players in the technology game. They have also been undergoing a revolution in the way their enterprises are funded, moving rapidly from government financial support and control to funding through private capital markets. And they have begun a revolution in the way they manage labor relations, frequently using policies and techniques borrowed from the West, as we just discussed. In addition to all of this, Korean firms are experiencing a revolution of a very different sort. They are undergoing significant changes in their fundamental approach to management. This management revolution grew out of the turmoil of the late 1980s and the recognized need to reshape organizations to allow for quicker responses to changes in the business environment. What is perhaps most interesting about this management revolution is that it represents a blend of East and West, a merger of traditional Korean and neo-Confucian cultural traits with Western ideas to form a uniquely Korean approach to management.

On the surface, the major organizational changes taking place in Korea look like the "Westernization" of the management process. The principal innovations being introduced include total quality management (TQM), increased decentralization and employee participation, development of teams, reorientation of corporate cultures to focus on organizational learning as a competitive edge, and the linking of corporate strategies to human resource management. At the heart of many of these efforts is a sincere attempt to remold the organization in a way that capitalizes on the company's human resources and prepares it for global competition. If there is to be a management revolution in Korea, this is it. Several examples should serve to illustrate this trend.

Samsung: Change Everything

Samsung was one of the first companies to signal a change. Shortly after Lee Kun-Hee became chairman following his father's death in 1987, he began sending clear signals that things were going to change. In 1993, in what company insiders called the "Frankfurt Declaration," Lee challenged his managers to ready themselves for major, sustained organizational change. Lee argued that if Samsung wished to survive to the year 2000, it would have to increase its efforts in globalization, product innovation, and quality management. Only first-class companies will survive, he said. How does a company become first class? According to Lee, by emphasizing quality over quantity, by reaching out to every corner of the globe, and by having good timing. When asked what was going to change at Samsung, Lee responded, "Just about everything."[27]

Then, in 1994, Chairman Lee announced that he intended to reduce the number of corporate subsidiaries by half and to reorganize Samsung's diverse business activities into four core sectors: electronics, machinery, chemicals, and finance and insurance.[28] The chairman of each core subgroup was given wide-ranging autonomy in running his area; he also participated in a steering committee responsible for determining broad policy issues for the entire group. Lee said such dramatic changes were necessary if the company was to compete effectively in the twenty-first century, adding, "Change everything but your wives and children."[29] Everything was to be questioned. By custom, managers typically remained at work until after 10 P.M. each evening; Lee decreed that everyone had to leave the building by 4 P.M., after only eight hours at work. Anyone found in the building after 4 o'clock risked termination. Lee also decreed that making defective parts was "a cancerous and criminal act on the part of management."[30] And above all, Lee insisted that all employees undergo what he called a "mind reformation" to become more creative and global in their thinking. If Samsung was to become a true global leader, its employees must think and act the part.

Samsung also seems serious about hiring more women into responsible managerial positions. "It will be a tremendous loss for Korea and Samsung if we do not make room for skilled women in the workplace," said Lee. "From this day forward, Samsung will devote time and effort to bring more women into the workplace. Women will be treated the same as men."[31] While such declarations are commonplace in the West, they are highly unusual in Korea.

LG: Vision for the Twenty-first Century

At LG Group, meanwhile, another revolution was taking place. As early as 1992, Chairman Koo told his key executives to run their own companies without bothering him.[32] Koo announced his "Vision for the Twenty-first Century" program, designed to make LG a world-class company by the year 2000. This plan is summarized in table 8-3, which shows the LG plans to integrate concerns for strategy, structure, systems, and people into a new global enterprise capable of competing successfully against the world's best. No longer were Samsung and Hyundai the competitors; now LG's competitors were in Japan and the United States.

LG is preparing for the twenty-first century with a four-pronged plan of attack: enhancing customer satisfaction (including a major effort at TQM), advancing into promising industries, becoming what LG calls an "insider in world markets," and fostering divisional autonomy. Divisional autonomy will be nurtured by the creation of "culture groups," autonomous management groups that will be responsible for each business unit. Reinforcing this change is a series of new training programs that serve to reinforce both the new culture groups and the redesigned organizational matrix. These programs and their place in the new matrix are shown in figure 8-3.

Hanwha: PRO-2000

At the Hanwha Group, a major manufacturer of explosives, chemicals, and machinery with twenty-one subsidiaries and annual sales approaching $6 billion, the story is much the same. Chairman Kim Seung Youn recently told his employees that past accomplishments are not as important as future

Table 8-3 Integrating Strategy, Structure, and People in LG's Vision 2000

	Items in Management	Contents
Strategy	• Business strategies	• Strengthen relationships with customers and expand the business areas strongly tied to end users. • Reinforce service areas, such as information, finance, retailing, and real estate development. • "Insiderize" in major world markets.
Structure	**D** **e** **c** **e** **n** **t** **r** **a** **l** **i** **z** **a** **t** **i** **o** **n** • Management by cultural unit (CU) • Chairman's role	• Decentralize and differentiate management according to business characteristics. • Chairman redefines his role to facilitate each company's "vision" development and realization efforts. Chairman's office also readjusts its function to "support" rather than "check and order."
System	• Delegation	• Delegate all the authorities for running each company to CU president.
Staff	• Inside development for successor, guarantee for long-term tenure • President evaluation committee/successor evaluation committee	• To ensure sustained implementation of the "vision," president's successor is internally developed and given long-term tenure. • To increase fairness and objectiveness of president's selections, these committees will be run openly.
Skill	• Management service center	• Provide know-how and support for CU's self-management.
Shared Values	• Management philosophy	• Mutual respect for employees at all levels.

Figure 8-3 New Management Programs in Support of LG's Reorganization

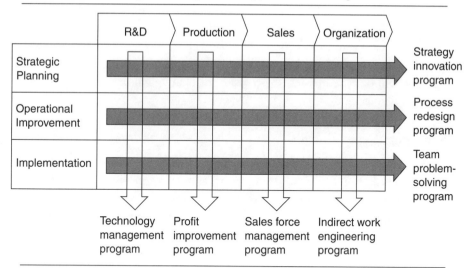

challenges. Following Hanwha's motto of "truthfulness, self-discretion, and best-effort," Kim is determined to develop his company into one of the world's major chemical enterprises, rivaling anything in Japan or America. To provide a theme for this development, Kim has led his company in two new programs. His PRO-2000 program is an effort to foster increases in managerial effectiveness and efficiency, while the ECO-2000 program is designed to heighten employee and customer awareness of Hanwha's sensitivity to environmental concerns.[33]

In a major 1994 speech to employees at all levels, Kim laid down the gauntlet. Speaking of his efforts to reform and "modernize" the company, Kim observed, "We see various signs of retreat, especially in personnel management, which has not been able to progress with the changing times. We cannot allow our group . . . to crumble due to the cynical indifference and anachronistic attitudes of many employees."[34] Instead, Kim called for a "third reform," consisting of four major parts. First, he called for significant change in employee attitudes: a new way of thinking and a willingness to change. Employee indifference or lack of commitment would no longer be tolerated. Second, Kim called for major changes in the company's human resource management system. He officially served notice that Hanwha would henceforth focus on promotion by merit instead of seniority, more delegation of authority, greater respect for professional employees, lifetime employment to valued employees, and greater use of self-managing teams.

Third, Kim called for a reorganization that would turn Hanwha into a truly global company, including a goal of achieving 50 percent of its sales outside Korea by the year 2000. Finally, Kim called for the company's corporate culture to become more people oriented and competitive. Kim's third reform has been widely circulated throughout the firm, and corporate officials are optimistic about the impact its program for change will have on corporate competitiveness.

Sunkyong: Supex Pursuit

Sunkyong Group has always been a leader in management reform, and its Chairman Chey is frequently referred to as Korea's most respected CEO. To achieve global competitiveness, Sunkyong recently introduced what it calls supex pursuit (see chapter 5). *Supex* (derived from a combination of the words *super* and *excellence*) *pursuit* is defined as the expenditure of relentless effort in the performance of a task by an individual or a group toward the goal of profit maximization; the level of "super-excellence" in the task is to be identified and pursued until it is reached.[35] In "can" (as in "can-do") meetings, employees are taught to think about adding value to their jobs by identifying the KFs, or key factors for success. Brainstorming meetings are held either before or after work to identify ways to improve quality and effectiveness. As Chairman Chey notes, "Everyone is brought into management, which makes people happier. They get together, use their minds, and see their ideas used."[36]

Initial results of the supex system seem impressive. In one plant that makes polyester raw materials, for example, the supex method is credited with enabling the plant to produce 260,000 tons of material last year, far beyond its designed capacity of 208,000 tons. Observes Chey, "The big difference comes from managing the plant so that we get brain engagement from all the workers."[37] All Sunkyong employees are expected to set and achieve a standard of performance that matches the best companies in the industry worldwide. Notes Chairman Chey, "If we merely try to be excellent, our gap with the world's top companies will remain because they keep improving. Only by seeking superexcellence can we reach their level or overtake them."[38]

Dongwon: Creating Value for Customers

Management innovation is not limited to the major conglomerates. Medium-sized firms are also experimenting with new management practices to remain competitive. One such company is the Dongwon Group. Dongwon is a major fishery firm. Kim Jae Chul, chairman of Dongwon, is regarded as one of Korea's most prominent entrepreneurs. He came from humble beginnings, starting at an agricultural high school. From a teacher, he learned that the future of Korea was in the ocean. In Pusan, he attended a special school to learn the fishing business. He pursued this goal diligently and with little regard for his immediate financial needs; he simply wanted to learn the business. In 1964, he was made a ship's captain for the Korea Deep Sea Fishing Company.[39] In 1969, he established his own firm. He borrowed industry techniques from Mitsubishi and by 1980 had gathered a fleet of fifty boats.

Known for "creating something out of nothing," Kim demonstrated considerable patience and determination. The company continued to expand over time. It diversified its product line from deep sea fishing to banking, precision instruments, tuna cans, restaurants, and social education groups. In our interviews with Dongwon, Chairman Kim described his vision of internationalization:

> *Our company is well poised to take advantage of the changing business conditions and market liberalization. Included in our business plan are details of our "vision for the year 2000," including detailed blueprints for production bases in Russia and China. Our business plan also includes three key principles for management development: (1) to serve customers, (2) respect people, and (3) create value.*
>
> *Our management system is characterized by a bottom-up approach to decision making. In fact, strategic directions are selected from those advanced by workers in various referenda. We also stress the need to link up with employees at the emotional level. Incentive systems foster creativity and hard work.[40]*

Chairman Kim believes that top managers in Korea resemble their Western counterparts but that lower-level employees are much more like the Japanese. Thus, according to Kim, "there is much [for Westerners] to learn from studying Korean corporate culture."[41]

Haitai: Welcome the Future

Another medium-sized Korean firm we can learn from is the Haitai Group. Haitai Confectionery is the flagship company of the Haitai Group, one of Korea's leading confectionery manufacturers. The company's wide range of products includes candies, biscuits, ice cream, chocolate, chewing gum, jelly, and caramel. The company has three divisions: candies and biscuits, ice cream, and other products. Haitai has attempted to diversify into high-value-added products, and it has invested heavily in its distribution channels.

In the near future, R&D efforts will be directed at developing artificial flavors and substitute imports.[42]

In our interviews, Haitai officials described their views on the anticipated market liberalization and their own prospects for internationalization.

Haitai welcomes market liberalization. Located within the food and beverages indus- tries—including ice cream, bakery, supermarkets, wines, etc.—our focus has been on food processing with some efforts in distribution. Our group looks forward to international expansion—including into North Korea—key opportunities, not risks.

In the past, companies in our industry were domestic competitors, while the United States and Japan were international competitors. Now we are looking forward to becoming a global competitor. Our bases of competition include product quality, innovative product development, access to raw materials, a broad network of distribu- tors, and brand image. We see the role of government as continuing to support us and providing low-cost loans from banks. Foreign foods are not well accepted in Korea owing to a fear of preservatives. This was validated ten years ago when a number of foreign firms entered Korea and failed.

North Korea is a key opportunity for us. Why? It can provide cheap labor and raw materials. It has a transportation advantage. Certain consumer tastes are shared by North and South Korea. And the food supply is low in North Korea. We are very optimistic about the future.

What the above firms have in common is the pursuit of excellence through technological acquisition, product innovation, and superior employees. What distinguishes their efforts from earlier ones may be the degree of fervent commitment to such techniques. The shadow of Confucianism clearly crosses the path of management change in Korea. This can be seen in the autocratic manner in which company chairmen routinely decree both the necessity of change and the means to achieve it; this is not a participative process. And it can be seen in the relentless dedication of the chairmen and their managers to implementing changes once they are announced.

From the chairman on down, work centrality is paramount. When quality control problems began to jeopardize the sales of Daewoo cars, Chairman Kim literally moved into the factory, spending most days in a borrowed office and walking through the factory at night checking on manufacturing problems. His presence sent a clear signal to workers and managers alike, and the quality control problems were quickly resolved.[43] One wonders how many Western managers would go to such extremes for quality control.

In Korea, business is still conducted in a relationship-based manner; trust and close personal ties among business partners remain the norm. Finally, respect, absolute allegiance, and, in many cases, reverence for the leader are a condition of employment; otherwise, the manager is not truly a part of the new management team. This is not American management in Seoul. This is a hybrid management model that emphasizes a new sense of professionalism among managers at all levels, yet combines it with an awareness of Korea's history, culture, and destiny as an aspiring industrial giant in East Asia. Korea is developing a distinct style of management that serves its companies well.

CHAPTER NINE

Human Resources as a Strategic Asset

The final key challenge facing contemporary Korean firms concerns how able they are to develop and manage their human resources to meet the economic and market realities of the next century. Technological innovation, quality control, manufacturing, and global marketing all depend on the quality and commitment of the managers and employees who are responsible for making the system work. In the last analysis, it will be Korea's human resources that determine the long-term viability and success of the *chaebols'* strategic initiatives. Hence, in this chapter, we will examine Korean human resource management practices. Included here is a look at several new initiatives that are designed to keep Korean firms ahead of their competitors. Throughout, our attention is focused on what Korean firms are doing to compete in terms of human talent.

KOREA'S HUMAN CAPITAL

Management practices in general tend to be influenced by the types and characteristics of the people who work in the organizations. Nowhere is this more true than with respect to human resource management practices. In the case of Korea, such practices have been built on a foundation characterized by an abundance of human resources and a scarcity of natural resources. Consider the following:

- Koreans are a highly educated people, and have been since the beginning of their history.[1] Ninety-eight percent of South Koreans can read and write, 80 percent graduate from high school, and the majority of high school graduates go on to get some sort of college or vocational training.[2]

- Korea must import most of the natural resources required to manufacture its products and exports. This general lack of natural resources has served to intensify the need to develop the country's human resources. "Manufacturing and service industries are human resource intensive," writes one observer, "and the poverty of natural resources requires, therefore, that human resources be developed in order to be able to export."[3]

- One trend that Korea is experiencing along with the rest of the industrialized world is an increase in the labor-force participation of women. While Confucian tradition has long discouraged Korean women from working, they are entering the labor force in increasing numbers. Among women fifteen years and older, 41 percent worked in 1984; today that number is 47 percent.[4] Korean women in managerial or executive positions are still quite rare, though; they typically hold low-level jobs and make roughly 90 percent of what Korean men do for the same work.[5]

- Korean firms currently face a shortage of new entrants into the labor force. Twenty-seven percent of the population is currently in school, from elementary through graduate school.[6] This shortage of workers is one factor precipitating the entrance of women into the work force. Many firms—especially small and medium-sized ones—are also now hiring foreign workers as "industrial trainees" to fill low-level jobs.[7] Most of these 120,000 workers come from Southeast Asia, and many remain in Korea as illegal immigrants after their "training" period has expired.

- Finally, it is important to remember that lifetime employment is less common in Korea than in Japan. In fact, South Korean workers are more mobile and change jobs more frequently than their Japanese counterparts (though not compared with U.S. workers).[8]

With these factors characterizing the labor market, how can Korea compete in the new global economy? One answer to this question can be found in the work of MIT economist Lester Thurow. In his 1993 book *Head-to-Head: The Coming Economic Battle among Japan, Europe, and America*, Thurow analyzes global economic trends and industrial competitiveness around the world and concludes that in the future, successful companies—and countries—will compete not on the basis of cheap labor or access to capital and raw materials but rather on a combination of superior information, technology, and human resources.[9] Given the new openness of the global marketplace, Thurow argues, capital markets are open to most anyone; they no longer represent a strategic asset. Similarly, raw materials are typically available in abundance in several parts of the world. And cheap labor is a fleeting advantage, as Korea found in the early 1990s. What will be in increasingly short supply—and hence provide comparative advantage—will be the control of information and advanced technology and access to high-quality (that is, well-trained and motivated) employees. Interestingly, this is exactly where Korean firms aim to compete. Because we have already discussed Korea's efforts to acquire and utilize information and technology, in this chapter we will focus on Korean firms' developments in the area of human capital—perhaps its richest resource for competitive advantage.

CHANGING PATTERNS IN KOREA'S HUMAN RESOURCE POLICIES

In view of the characteristics of Korea's work force, it is important to know the extent to which these characteristics are reflected in the human resource policies and practices of contemporary Korean corporations. In this section, we go beyond corporate personnel policy statements to examine the actual practices of several major companies.

Korean HR practices are primarily the result of two forces. The earliest—and perhaps still the most pronounced—influence emerges from the Confucian tradition that permeates so much of Korean society. As noted elsewhere in this book, it is in the Confucian tradition that we see the origins of corporate concern for such values as hard work, dedication, seniority, and company loyalty. Paternalistic leadership and top-down decision making remain the hallmark of many Korean businesses. This management style has until very recently extended to the management of human resources as well.

The second, more recent influence on HR practices is the contemporary push to utilize "modern" (typically Western) approaches to management and personnel development. Companies are concerned with making improvements in such practices as employee recruitment, training, and performance appraisals. This shift has been facilitated by executive decisions to make personnel policies more "scientific." Cho Nam-hong, vice chairman of the Korean Employers' Federation, refers to this new approach as a capability-based human resource management system.[10] These executive decisions, in turn, have been influenced by changes in the economic, social, technological, and political environments surrounding the corporations.

Whatever the cause, changes are indeed emerging as corporations begin moving away from the traditional Confucian-based approach to management toward a more professional approach. In this section, we review the general trends in human resource policies and practices in Korean firms.[11] Covered here are (1) recruitment and selection, (2) training and development, (3) performance appraisals, (4) reward systems, (5) the changing role of women, and (6) exits from the organization, including terminations, turnover, layoffs, and retirement.

Hiring the Best

A key strategy of most Korean firms is to hire the best possible employees possible at all levels of the organization. The methods by which they do this vary considerably, depending on such factors as company size and the positions for which they are recruiting. As one might expect, smaller companies tend to rely less on open recruitment and testing and more on personal connections in recruiting blue-collar employees. This is also true of companies located in the more rural areas of Korea. For the major corporations, however, clear trends can be identified in both white-collar and blue-collar recruitment and selection.

White-collar employees: Becoming a salaryman

For white-collar positions, applicants are frequently recruited from the better-known universities. Most applicants must pass company-sponsored examinations that typically test English-language proficiency as well as knowledge in a major field and general abilities or common sense. However, in a new trend, several companies (most notably Samsung) are beginning to substitute college grades for this examination. Good grades are important in selection. This is referred to as the *kongch'ae* system and has replaced the older practice of hiring based on personal connections. Moreover, applicants must also survive extensive personal interviews (sometimes including an interview with the company chairman) and reference checks. Personal interviews are becoming increasingly important in determining who gets hired.[12] At Hyundai, a recent survey found that 78 percent of the HR managers believe that the personal interview is the most important screening tool.[13] Hyundai has even begun to experiment with "blind interviews," in which interviewers are given no prior information on the applicants so as not to bias their judgments. In hiring decisions, new college graduates are still preferred over people with experience, and, once hired, the new employees are typically assigned to such core departments as planning, finance, or accounting after a relatively short training and indoctrination period. This contrasts with typical American recruiting practice, in which previous work experience is more valued and in which new employees are typically assigned to a functional department based on their specialty. It also contrasts somewhat with Japanese practice, in which new employees are more likely to begin their jobs in the field rather than at corporate headquarters.

One study sought to identify how the major Korean companies describe the ideal manager—that is, what are the keys to managerial success? How do companies identify these characteristics when hiring new employees?[14] Inquires at such companies as LG, Samsung, Daewoo, Doosan, Sunkyong, and Kumho yielded similar results. The ideal young candidate for most companies was both smart and highly motivated. He exhibited a strong work ethic and a positive attitude toward hard work for company and country. Personal initiative was important, as was a good character and background and a willingness to learn. Finally, the ideal candidate presented himself well and was comfortable to be around. Some companies also indicated that this candidate was a risk taker capable of making rapid and incisive decisions under pressure.

While companies are sizing up prospective new employees, applicants are sizing up prospective employers. What makes an ideal company? One study asked two thousand job applicants what they sought in an employer. In order of importance, applicants identified the following: the promise of future work (31 percent), opportunity to develop one's capabilities (16 percent), provision of worthwhile work (15 percent), and opportunity to obtain technical know-how (7 percent). When asked the most important reason for working, this same group responded: to have a better life (39 percent), to utilize my potential (29 percent), to earn a livelihood (14 percent), to support my family (5 percent), to be successful in society (5 percent), and to contribute to my country (3 percent). Interestingly, only 35 percent of the applicants surveyed believed they would end up retiring from this same company.[15]

To see how the selection and hiring process actually works, consider the example of the Samsung Group, which hires three thousand to four thousand people a year and has a selection ratio of applicants to hires of about 4:1. In examining management potential, Samsung considers native intelligence as the first prerequisite. Initial screening for this is carried out through written tests. Following are a series of interviews, in which company officials examine more interpersonal factors, such as initiative, personal responsibility, and interpersonal style. At times, two candidates are put into a debate with each other to see how they perform under pressure. Throughout the process, the company tries to select those candidates with the greatest potential to develop into long-term, committed, and useful Samsung employees.

Similarly, consider the application and screening process for "salary-men"—the term used in Korea to refer to white-collar employees—at the Sunkyong Group. Sunkyong is a diversified corporation that now ranks as the fifth largest concern in Korea. The company attributes its success to a combination of high technology and human resources. Sunkyong has been an industry leader in the development of sophisticated personnel policies that are designed to secure the best possible employees. Referred to as the Sunkyong Management System (or SKMS), Sunkyong's systematic approach to management incorporates traditional management functions with a dynamic concern for developing employees to their fullest potential. Central to this model is the notion of *eui-yok* management, which is defined as providing the conditions under which individuals and groups can draw satisfaction from and take pride in their work. (As explained in chapter 8, *eui-yok*, roughly translated, means "will" or "ambition" and refers to a person's will to achieve, financial rewards aside.)

Because it is often identified in surveys as one of Korea's most preferred employers, Sunkyong can afford to be highly selective in its new hires. In its policy manuals, the company identifies six primary criteria for selection: (1) *pae-gie*, meaning "the spirit to get the job done and win the business"; (2) business knowledge; (3) business-related knowledge, such as foreign language expertise or applied scientific knowledge; (4) appropriate social attitudes and interpersonal skills; (5) sound home management, including having a stable homelife; and (6) sound health management, including physical and mental well-being.[16] Within the company, these six criteria are referred to as the principles of "SK-manship."

When selecting new employees, information concerning these six criteria is collected from documents, personal interviews, and physical examinations. Letters of recommendation are requested from outsiders, and reviewers are asked to rate the candidate on "positive thinking," "progressive action," "responsibility," and "social attitude." Finally, applicants are asked to complete an extensive self-inventory that includes demographic data plus a self-appraisal on such variables as leadership, sociability, ambition, responsibility, and self-control. All of this information is then reviewed and assigned points by the professional personnel staff to decide who to hire. Throughout the process, the aim is to secure a small number of highly skilled and highly motivated employees likely to fit into the company's culture and willing and able to make a long-term commitment to develop and grow with the company.

Blue-collar employees: Back door and open recruitment

For blue-collar workers, corporate approaches to recruitment are quite different. It has been estimated that a large though unspecified number of blue-collar jobs are filled through what has been termed backdoor recruitment, or what in the West is called an employee referral.[17] This involves hiring someone who is recommended by a friend or relative who is already employed by the firm or, at the very least, hiring someone who heard about the job through such channels. It is often felt that such techniques lead to good employees, since the company already has someone on the payroll who will vouch for the sincerity and dedication of the candidate.

Many other jobs are filled through "open recruitment," in which prospective job candidates learn about openings through public announcements or direct inquiries. In addition, about 10 percent of blue-collar hires come from vocational school placements. Graduates of technical high schools and vocational training institutes must obtain a skill-test certificate from the National Skill Testing Agency, while graduates of other high schools usually must pass company entrance examinations or have the support of a strong connection within the company. Some of the largest corporations, such as Hyundai and Samsung, manage their own vocational training institutes to ensure a steady supply of well-trained workers.

While it is difficult to get accurate data on the relative proportions of each type of blue-collar hire, in one medium-sized company, 19 percent of all new blue-collar hires were found through open recruitment, while 73 percent were found through friends, relatives, or acquaintances.[18] Informal discussions with various managers suggest that this is probably fairly representative of the hiring procedures of small and medium-sized companies, with larger firms relying more on open recruitment, especially from technical institutions.

Developing Human Capacity

Like their Japanese counterparts, Korean companies consider human resources to be the central building block for long-term corporate success. Considerable effort goes into the development of employees at all levels.

Given the increasingly competitive business environment of the 1990s, this trend is likely to continue.

Management training and the "all-around person"

At the managerial level, the objectives and methods of corporate training and development are somewhat different from those in the West. In Korea, the focus is not so much on gaining new job-related knowledge or skills as it is on molding current and future managers to fit into the company's corporate culture. Emphasis is placed on developing positive attitudes over professional skills, under the assumption that loyalty, dedication, and team spirit are more important than current job skills. The companies' aim is to develop what is often called the all-around person. The all-around person possesses general abilities; he is not a specialist. His commitment to the company and his coworkers is unquestioned, and, above all, he fits into the group. Training is seen as one means of instilling this attitude in employees across the corporation.

To see how this process works, consider the management training methods used by the Daewoo Group. Organizationally, Daewoo has an Education and Training Department that reports directly to the Chairman's Office, in contrast to most Western companies, where reporting is much farther down in the organizational hierarchy. The executive director for Education and Training is responsible for all corporate developmental efforts. Many years ago, the company established a clear link between the development of employees and the development of the company. This can be seen in a statement of the basic principles for corporate training, in which the company expresses the belief that its business philosophy and its business spirit (summarized by the motto "creativity, challenge, and self-sacrifice") are both directly influenced by the cultivation of Daewoo personnel (see figure 9-1). The nature of this cultivation is defined by the company's six training objectives:

- To implement the Daewoo business philosophy and business spirit.
- To develop managerial techniques and improve professional knowledge and specialized ability.
- To foster adaptability to meet changing business environments.
- To maximize organizational efficiency.
- To enhance the special identity of Daewoo employees.
- To motivate self-development.[19]

Figure 9-1   Basic Training Principles at Daewoo

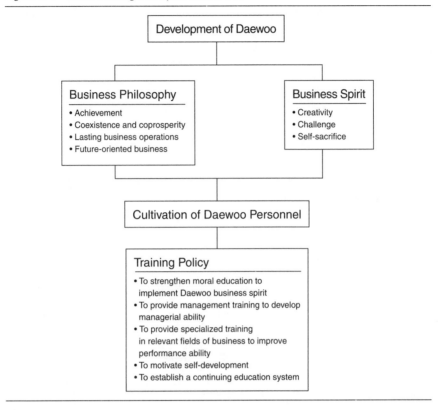

A number of specific training programs are offered at Daewoo to facilitate these objectives (see figure 9-2). We mention four here as illustrative of the variety and depth of such programs.

First, at the entry level for new employees destined for managerial positions, Daewoo offers the Newcomers' Training Program. This program lasts eleven days and nights and covers the following topics: (1) "Daewoo-manship" and the business philosophy, (2) an introduction to affiliated companies of the Daewoo Group, (3) a case study of job performance, (4) freshman's life planning, (5) a tour through affiliated companies, (6) a team demonstration, and (7) a videotaped speech by the chairman.

Second, moving up the ladder, the Middle Manager's Training Program consists of fifteen days and focuses on improving managerial abilities, especially those relating to human resource management. Emphasis is also placed on understanding corporate strategy. Third, once a manager reaches the director level, he is sent to the Advanced Management Training Pro-

Figure 9-2 Training Programs Offered by Daewoo

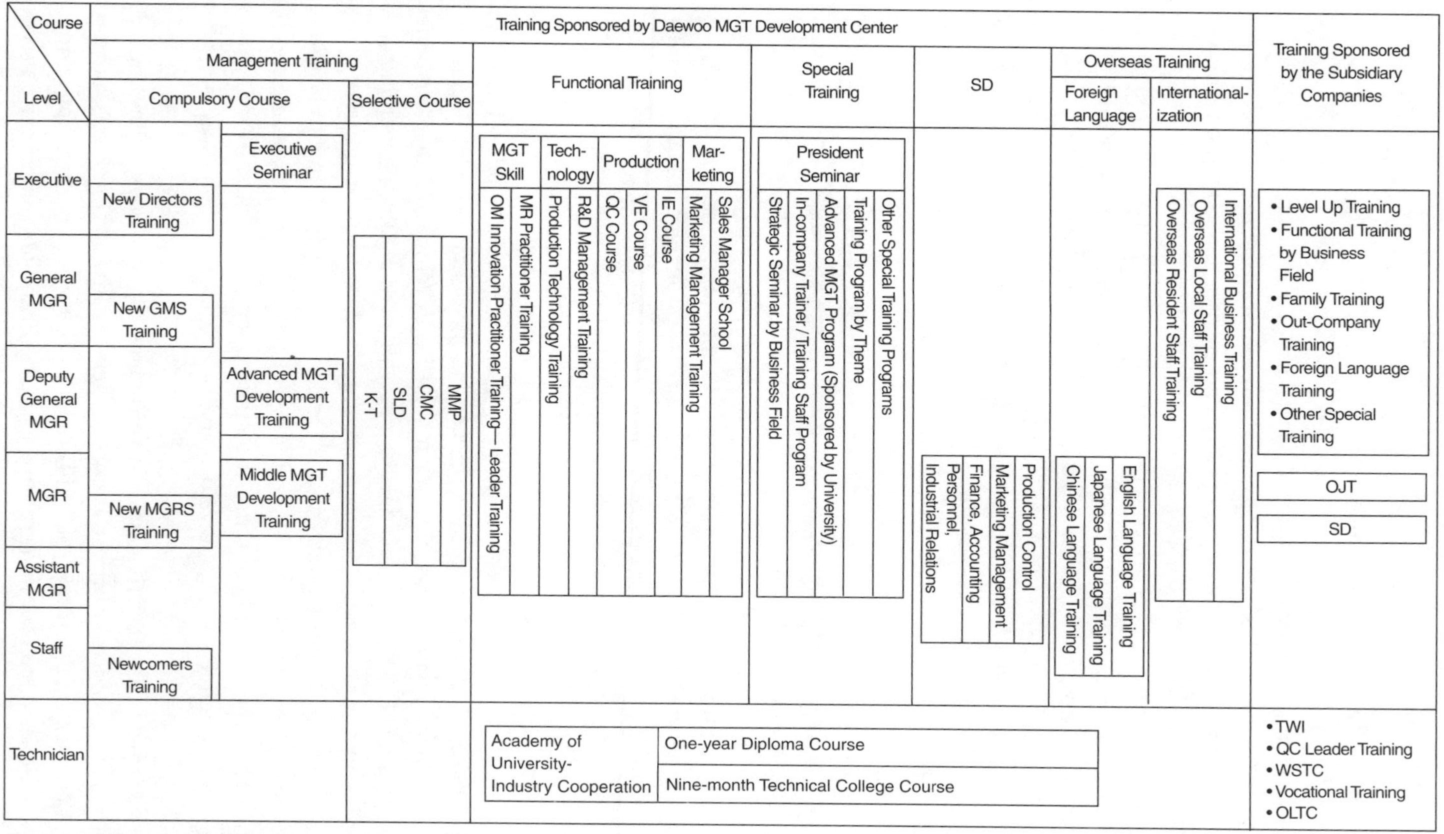

Training Sponsored by Daewoo MGT Development Center

Management Training

Compulsory Course (by Level):
- Executive — Executive Seminar; New Directors Training
- General MGR — New GMS Training
- Deputy General MGR — Advanced MGT Development Training
- MGR — New MGRS Training; Middle MGT Development Training
- Staff — Newcomers Training

Selective Course:
- MMP
- CMC
- SLD
- K-T

Functional Training

MGT Skill:
- OM Innovation Practitioner Training— Leader Training
- MR Practitioner Training

Technology:
- Production Technology Training
- R&D Management Training

Production:
- QC Course
- VE Course
- IE Course

Marketing:
- Marketing Management Training
- Sales Manager School

Special Training — President Seminar:
- Strategic Seminar by Business Field
- In-company Trainer / Training Staff Program
- Advanced MGT Program (Sponsored by University)
- Training Program by Theme
- Other Special Training Programs

SD:
- Personnel, Industrial Relations
- Finance, Accounting
- Marketing Management
- Production Control

Overseas Training

Foreign Language:
- Chinese Language Training
- Japanese Language Training
- English Language Training

Internationalization:
- Overseas Resident Staff Training
- Overseas Local Staff Training
- International Business Training

Technician — Academy of University-Industry Cooperation:
- One-year Diploma Course
- Nine-month Technical College Course

Training Sponsored by the Subsidiary Companies
- Level Up Training
- Functional Training by Business Field
- Family Training
- Out-Company Training
- Foreign Language Training
- Other Special Training
- OJT
- SD

Technician:
- TWI
- QC Leader Training
- WSTC
- Vocational Training
- OLTC

Source: Reprinted by permission from Marianne Koch, Sang H. Nam, and Richard M. Steers, "Human Resource Management in South Korea," in *Human Resource Management on the Pacific Rim*, ed. Larry Moore and Deveraux Jennings (Berlin: deGruyter, 1995), 229.

gram. This consists of four days and examines such topics as the nature of the business environment and long-range corporate strategy. In addition, this program includes talks with the chairman.

Fourth, in a move that is uncommon for a Korean company, Daewoo offers training programs for managers' wives. For directors' wives, for example, the company offers a three-day program that includes such topics as (1) Daewoo's business philosophy and spirit, (2) the relationship between office and home, (3) "economic common sense," and (4) "what makes a happy home life." The basic thrust of the wives' program is to demonstrate that the entire household—not just the husband—belongs to the Daewoo family and that the husband's success is influenced by a supportive homelife. Thus, regardless of the level, Daewoo is committed to developing its managerial personnel through a series of fairly sophisticated programs tailored to the short- and long-range goals of the company.

A similar situation can be found in the management training procedures at Hyundai. Hyundai has as a matter of policy established the goal of having each of its 13,000 managers visit the training institute a minimum of once every other year, even if only for a few days. Training is clearly important to this company.

The general philosophy that underlies much of the training effort at Hyundai involves three concepts: (1) the importance of working for the further development of Korea, (2) the importance of human resources, and (3) the importance of international relationships and a global orientation. In support of this philosophy, three training objectives have been set forth: (1) incorporating the Hyundai spirit in the manager's daily life, (2) developing managerial skills and capabilities, and (3) strengthening international competitiveness. Finally, on an operational level, three principles guide actual program design and implementation. Thus, each program includes components relating to (1) the development of managerial and technical skills; (2) the development of mental skills, including a heavy emphasis on what are termed "oriental" values, such as creativity, positive thinking, tenacity, fraternity, devotion to company, and industriousness; and (3) the development of one's physical capabilities, including mandatory physical exercise beginning at 6:30 each morning. These three implementing principles aim to develop what the company defines as the Hyundai manager.

Hyundai offers five kinds of programs for managers. They include top management executive training, midlevel managers' programs, professional courses (accounting, job skills, and so on), language training, and rather unique courses to train trainers. Courses for top and middle managers cover different topics each year, and a typical course lasts three to four days. Teaching methods are diverse and include lectures, case analyses, experiential exercises, and decision-making simulations. Instructors come from both the company staff and the more prestigious university business schools.

Training for industrial workers

By contrast, at the blue-collar level, the primary instructional methods after employment involve on-the-job training aimed at improving job-related skills and encouraging "correct" attitudes toward the company. As these employees gain experience, the focus of training shifts to the development of future first-line supervisors. At this level, the approach to training is not unlike that found in many industrialized countries, including Japan and the United States.

Evaluating Job Performance

All large Korean companies and many smaller ones use some form of an annual performance appraisal system. At the blue-collar and lower managerial levels, the primary emphasis in such evaluations is on employee development, since promotion is largely based on seniority. (For salarymen, the first promotion usually comes after three to four years of employment.) Even so, companies take these evaluations seriously because they represent a part of the human resource management process. Managers feel a special responsibility to help develop employees below them in exchange for employee loyalty to the company and its leaders. Throughout this process, evaluators look carefully at the "whole person," so that personal qualities such as sincerity, loyalty, proper attitude, and initiative receive as much attention as actual job performance in the evaluation.

At the higher levels of management, more emphasis may be placed on actual performance and contribution to the company (instead of seniority) in determining promotions. In some companies—particularly those involved in high technology—there is the emergence of the so-called star player, who moves on a fast track toward the top. Nonetheless, seniority still plays an important role in determining who gets ahead even at these higher echelons in the home office. Overseas, things seem to be changing more rapidly. For example, Samsung recently changed the promotion policy for its overseas subsidiaries so that Koreans and local managers are treated equally in promotion decisions. This is a first for a Korean company, where Korean nationals are routinely sent out to manage foreign operations. Henceforth, local managers will have equal opportunities to move up the hierarchy, including opportunities to work in managerial positions at Samsung's Seoul headquarters.[20]

One of the more comprehensive performance appraisal systems can be found at Sunkyong. Like other companies, Sunkyong's approach places heavy emphasis on employee development. The goals set forth for the evaluation process include the identification of employee inadequacies or weaknesses in need of correction, the development of managerial capabilities, and the enhancement of the company's human resource management process. Sunkyong's system begins with an extensive self-assessment by the employee. Employees are asked to complete this inventory accurately and sincerely, evaluating themselves on such factors as "SK-manship," managerial capacity, communication, ability to work with others, and their adequacy for and satisfaction with their present assignment. For each factor, employees are asked to identify anything that may be obstructing their improvement. Employees are also asked to describe the way their job performance has contributed to company well-being as well as their feelings about general company administration.

This inventory becomes input for interviews and written reports, first by one's immediate supervisor and later by the supervisor's supervisor. Peer assessments from coworkers are also sought. Through extensive discussions, efforts are made to reach agreement concerning the employee's strengths and weaknesses and a plan of action for self-improvement. Ultimately, the written materials go to the corporate HRM department for final disposition and approval. Throughout, emphasis is placed on developing the employee's long-term potential as a Sunkyong manager. To accomplish this, considerable effort is devoted to developing a trusting relationship between superiors and subordinates and to ensuring shared mutual expectations for the future of the company.

Rewarding Superior Performance

The subject of employee compensation and benefits is always a difficult one to examine. Information is often confidential, and what is public is often incomplete or misleading. Working within these limitations, we will attempt to provide a general description of the compensation and benefit policies of the largest Korean firms. As a starting point, it is interesting to note how much Korean wage rates have increased in recent years. As shown in table 9-1, from 1987 to 1994, wages increased an average of 15 percent per year, compared with 3 percent in the United States and 7 percent in Japan.[21] Productivity increased only 12 percent during this same period.[22]

Table 9-1 Wage and Productivity Changes in Korea, 1987–1994

Year	Average Wage Increase	Average Productivity Increase
1987	10.1%	10.1%
1988	15.5	14.8
1989	21.1	7.6
1990	18.7	16.4
1991	17.5	16.3
1992	15.2	9.3
1993	12.2	8.6
1994	12.7	10.9

Source: Korean Ministry of Labor, National Statistics Office, Seoul, 1995.

In fact, Daewoo recently discovered that in the electronics industry, the wages it was paying in its Korea facility were 5 percent higher than in its comparable British facility.[23] Korea is clearly no longer a source of cheap labor.

Even with the recent sizable pay raises given to Korean workers, the average Korean employee—blue-collar or white-collar—still works longer hours than his or her counterparts in most other countries, including the newly industrialized countries.[24] In exchange, the employee's compensation package generally consists of three components: (1) basic wages, (2) allowances, (3) and bonuses.

Basic wages

The basic wage is clearly the largest and most important part of the compensation package and consists of the employee's starting wage plus annual increments and cost-of-living adjustments. Starting salaries are determined largely by educational level and initial point of entry into the company. This, in turn, is influenced at least to some extent by external market rates (for example, university graduates with science or technical backgrounds generally receive a higher starting salary than those with business degrees). Currently, starting salaries for high school graduates are about 85 percent of starting salaries for college graduates; this compares with 70 percent in the United States and 80 percent in Japan.

Annual salary increases are determined largely by seniority. The concept of "pay for performance," or merit compensation, is largely avoided except at the highest managerial levels since it is felt that a seniority system contributes more to the maintenance of group harmony. Thus, over time, employee salaries tend to increase slowly for everyone as a group. The one exception to this is among production workers, who often see real pay decreases after the age of fifty, presumably owing to their reduced physical contribution to the company.

Employee allowances

The second component of the compensation package is of a set of allowances granted to employees. Allowances can take several forms. For example, the Korean Labor Standards Act requires that employers pay one-and-one-half times regular pay for each additional hour worked beyond eight hours per day.[25] For white-collar employees, an overtime allowance of two hours per day is typically automatically added to pay. One-and-one-half times the base wage is also paid to employees working from 10 P.M. to 6 A.M. Employers are also required to provide workers with eight days paid leave for one full year's service without absence; each absence is subtracted from this total. Employees also typically receive one day of paid vacation per year for each year of tenure (for example, five days annual paid vacation after five years of service). After twenty vacation days are accumulated, employees can take the extra days in wages instead of time off. In most Korean companies, as in their Japanese counterparts, few employees actually take all the vacation time to which they are entitled for fear of seeming disloyal to the company.

As noted earlier, female employees are typically paid about 90 percent of what their male counterparts receive for similar jobs. In addition, they are entitled to one day's paid leave per month and sixty days' paid leave for pregnancy. Under current law, women can extend this leave for an additional year without pay and still keep their job. And beyond what is required by law for both males and females, many companies offer allowances for such things as being assigned to a remote area, having an official skills certificate, possessing skills that are in short supply, or having a large number of dependents. Housing and car allowances are also common. In case of death, it is customary for the company to provide the family with one thousand days of wages plus funeral expenses. All told, allowances often constitute about 30 percent of the employee's pay package.

The complexity of the Korean pay system has led many companies to employ a rather unique approach to the calculation of actual compensation. This is called the Reverse Calculation System (RCS). Under RCS, the employer pays employees a fixed monthly amount based on a formulaic estimate of all the expenses associated with the employee's allowances.

This is preferred because of its simplicity over having to calculate each benefit for each employee on a monthly basis. The Korean government has generally held that such an approach is within the statutes of the Korean Labor Standards Act.

Employee bonuses

The third part of the compensation package consists of employee bonuses. While not required by law and while ostensibly based on company performance, bonuses have come to be an expected part of the compensation system. The typical large company pays annual bonuses amounting to about four to six months' gross salary (referred to as a "400 percent" or a "600 percent" bonus); smaller companies typically pay somewhat less. Bonuses are usually paid out four times a year (to coincide with New Year's Day, the beginning of summer vacation, Korean Thanksgiving Day, and Christmas). The majority of companies provide bonuses in equal amounts according to the employee's level in the hierarchy. Even those companies which give differential bonuses (that is, different bonus amounts to employees at the same level) typically give 90 percent of the employees on each level the same amount. Most managers believe that in view of the cooperative nature of work it is simply not possible to differentiate performance levels between employees with any degree of accuracy (except at the higher levels of management). It also disturbs the harmony among employees. While the amount of the bonus can vary depending on business conditions, some companies continue to pay the bonus even during difficult economic times to show goodwill and maintain harmony in the work force.

Integrating Women into the Workforce

A key factor in the economic success of many Korean firms has been the large pool of young, highly skilled and motivated—but relatively low-paid—female workers.[26] While 47 percent of women over fifteen years of age are employed in some capacity (compared with 58 percent in the United States and 50 percent in Japan), the limited range of opportunities results in an ample pool of well-qualified applicants. Most working women are young and unmarried and work as either assemblers on a production line or clerical workers in an office. The average age of employed women is twenty-four, compared with thirty-one for men, and some companies still informally pressure women to resign upon marriage or to "retire" at thirty, even if single. Still, the opportunities for women are increasing. The 1992 Equal Employment Act proscribed discrimination based on gender, and a number of companies have been fined for discriminatory practices. Many companies have begun a serious effort—albeit slowly—to hire more women into the lower ranks of management.

For the average female office worker the typical workday runs from 8:30 A.M. to 5:30 or 6:30 P.M., compared with from 8:00 A.M. to well into the evening for most men. In exchange, women tend to receive about 90 percent of the salaries of their male counterparts working on similar jobs (up from 70 percent several years ago). Annual salary increases are minimal and promotions to important positions within the company extremely rare. College graduates fare somewhat better and receive about 15 percent more salary than their high school counterparts; they also have somewhat higher status within the organization. While a small number of women are finding their way into white-collar positions, primarily in the areas of personnel or translation services, Korean tradition still prefers that they be at home. Women are typically viewed as temporary workers and are treated as such in most companies.

The role of women in Korean firms is changing. Indeed, feminism is on the rise, as are several legal aid firms specializing in discrimination.[27] As a result, the number of women hired into the white-collar ranks grew from 1 percent of all hires in 1987 to 6 percent in 1992 to 11 percent in 1995.[28] Whether this trend will continue in the face of strong Confucian tradition remains to be seen.

Managing Employee Departures

People leave companies for many reasons. We will briefly examine four such means of departure in Korean firms. First, consider the issue of voluntary employee turnover. Estimates of annual voluntary turnover in Korean firms range from 10 percent to 20 percent. Much of this turnover is attributed to women leaving the company to get married or to have children. In fact, it is estimated that more than 70 percent of all employee turnover is among women. In one study of a medium-sized company, reasons for turnover were indeed found to differ according to gender.[29] As shown in table 9-2, women typically leave as a result of marriage, illness, excessive absenteeism, or "forced resignation" (frequently meaning being forced out by the company because of age or pregnancy). Men, on the other hand, typically leave to find a better job, to open their own business, or to resolve problems of "aptitude capacity" (generally meaning failing to get along sufficiently with coworkers or supervisors). It bears mention, however, that these are

Table 9-2 Reasons for Resignation in One Korean Firm

Reasons for Resignation	Male	Female	Total
Changing jobs	12	6	18
Marriage	—	19	19
Returning to school	—	2	2
Illness	4	14	18
Absence without notification	3	16	19
Returning to hometown	1	8	9
Opening new business	9	2	11
Problems with aptitude capacity	8	9	17
Forced resignation	4	14	18
Staying home	2	5	7
Others	4	5	9

Source: Based on Chan Sup Chang and Nahn Joo Chang, *The Korean Management System* (Westport, Conn.: Quorum Books, 1994).

the results of only one study; caution should be exercised in generalizing this information to the entire working population.

Second, consider involuntary employee turnover. Under the Korean Labor Standards Act, termination of employees is legal as long as the company can show just cause. Under such circumstances, the employer must provide either thirty days' notice or one month's salary, in addition to severance pay equivalent to one month's salary for each year of continuous service. Typical reasons for dismissal include poor performance, dishonesty, strike activity, sabotage, and physical or mental disability.[30]

Third, let us look at employee layoffs. In contrast to Japan, layoffs in Korea are not uncommon, and the concept of lifetime employment is rarely seen in practice. Instead, companies typically rely on a strategy of continued corporate growth and expansion to ensure fairly stable employment. When layoffs are necessary, companies often encourage older workers or female employees of marriageable age to leave, providing extra financial incentives in the process. Given Korea's extended family system, in which the incomes of all family members are often pooled, such laid-off employees are frequently absorbed back into the family and provided for.

Finally, there is the issue of employee retirement. Retirement is mandatory for most employees at age fifty-five. According to Korea's Labor Standards Act, retiring employees typically receive a lump-sum payment equal to one month's salary for each year of service. One recent study by the Korea Employers Federation found that 59 percent of the companies they surveyed adhered to this minimum payout, while 39 percent paid above this minimum.[31] Few employees are offered part-time work or consulting work with the company after retirement, as is the case in Japan.

THE NEW HR PROFESSIONALS

One of the most profound changes in Korean management in recent years has been the development of human resource management as an area of specialization within the firm. This development has been slow to evolve and follows the recent trend toward hiring more professional managers. It also follows most firms' recognition of their need for greater levels of expertise in both HRM and labor relations as Korea moves toward a more open labor market. While few Korean HR managers have specialized degrees in HRM or labor relations, they are increasingly coming to think of themselves as specialists and to prepare themselves in ways that are bringing increasing benefits to their employers.

To examine the nature and extent of these emerging changes, Marianne Koch, Nam Sanghoon, and Richard M. Steers conducted a survey of Korean HR managers.[32] The aim of the study, published in 1995, was to replicate the 1989 study of Canadian HR managers by L. F. Moore and S. Robinson to identify differences between the two cultures with respect to the managers' perceptions of the respect and importance of their field, the extent to which the input of HR managers is sought in making key personnel decisions, and the extent to which human resource management in Korea is viewed as an identifiable profession.[33]

Three principal findings emerged from the 1995 study. First, attention was paid to how Korean HR managers saw their role within the organization. As can be seen in table 9-3, Korean HR managers tended to see their role in the organization quite differently from their Canadian counterparts. In particular, when compared with the Canadian sample, Koreans felt that they had more organizational support for their activities, provided greater leadership in hiring and promoting the best candidates, were less insular, knew more about operations than they were given credit for, actually practiced what they preached about personnel practices, and felt their primary responsibility was more to the employees as a whole than to

Table 9-3 Korean and Canadian HR Managers' Perceptions of Their Role

Perception	Percent Agreement	
	Korea	Canada
Supervisors outside the personnel office view personnel as a nuisance, not an aid	22%	35%[a]
Most personnel people keep up with recent developments in the field	67	64
Personnel people provide vigorous leadership needed to support merit principles in such actions as selection and promotion	74	58[b]
Personnel people stick together too much—speaking their own language and remaining aloof from those outside the field	21	33[a]
Personnel people usually know more about the operating programs they service than line managers give them credit for	88	68[c]
Few personnel people actually practice with their staffs what they preach to operating officials	3	43[c]
Most personnel people are prone to hide behind rules and regulations as an excuse for a lack of positive action	33	27
Most personnel programs have the respect of employees in the organizations they serve	61	55
The primary responsibility of the personnel office is to management rather than to employees	15	41[c]

Source: Based on data presented in Marianne Koch, Sanghoon Nam, and Richard M. Steers, "Human Resource Management in South Korea," in *Human Resource Management on the Pacific Rim,* ed. Larry Moore and Devereaux Jennings, 217–42 (Berlin: deGruyter, 1995). Reprinted by permission.

Note: Following the methodology of L. F. Moore and S. Robinson, percent agreement is defined as the number of respondents who either agree or strongly agree with the item on a five-point scale. Canadian data from Moore and Robinson are reported here for purposes of comparison. See L. F. Moore and S. Robinson, "Human Resource Management Present and Past: Highlights from a Western Canadian Survey of Practitioner Perceptions," in *Proceedings of the Administrative Sciences Association of Canada,* ed. A. Petit and A. V. Subbarov (Montreal: Personnel and Human Resources Division, McGill University, 1989).

N = 88 and 426, respectively, for the Korean and Canadian managers.
[a]Differences in percentages significant at .05.
[b]Differences in percentages significant at .01.
[c]Differences in percentages significant at .001.

management. Many of these findings can be explained by the Confucian tradition. For example, "good" Korean managers are expected to be a part of the entire group (not some small clique), to be role models for their subordinates (that is, to practice what they preach), and to stand up for moral principles (for example, selecting the best possible employees instead of one's friends or relatives). Moreover, the Korean practice of extensive job rotation may explain why Korean HR managers report being in possession of greater job knowledge than they are given credit for. Thus, the questionnaire results are consistent with the behavior the Korean company expects from its HR practitioners.

The second consideration of the 1995 study was the level of human resources' involvement with personnel decisions. Korean HR managers described their level of involvement in such issues as research and planning, contract negotiations, training and development, and promotions and transfers as being significantly higher than that reported by their Canadian counterparts. However, the Canadians saw their involvement in the handling of grievances, terminations, and safety as being higher than that of the Koreans. (See table 9-4.) Such differences may reflect the different emphases placed on the various HR functions in the two countries. For example, safety is a far more sensitive social—and legal—issue in Canada (and the United States) than it is in Korea, as witnessed by the plethora of health and safety regulations that exist in Canada. On the other hand, the majority of Korean companies see employee training and development as crucial to long-term competitiveness in view of the tendency toward de facto lifetime employment. Similarly, the Korean emphasis on HR planning and research and on promotion and transfer also reflects the centrality of employees as a fixed cost and a key corporate resource, compared with the Canadian (and American) view that employees are a variable cost of doing business.

Finally, the 1995 study focused on the extent to which HR managers in Korea are seen as belonging to a distinct profession. As can be seen in table 9-5, the results point to the conclusion that Korean HR managers do not see themselves as representing a distinct profession, while their Canadian counterparts do. In view of the similar nature of their respective responsibilities, this significant perceptual difference highlights not only a cultural difference in attitudes but also the temporal definition of the profession. What is seen as a distinct and identifiable profession in one culture is viewed as just one more area of managerial responsibility in another. This phenomenon is consistent with the Confucian-influenced norms of considering managers to be an integral part of the corporate family rather

Table 9-4 Korean and Canadian HR Department Involvement in Personnel Decisions
(Rank order by level of involvement)

Personnel Decisions	Percent Reporting "High Involvement"	
	Korea	Canada
Recruitment and selection	87%	79%
HR research	81	55[c]
HR planning	79	60[c]
Benefits	74	70
Contract negotiation	74	62[a]
Training and development	70	53[b]
Compensation	67	73
Human resource policy	64	71
Promotion	62	36[c]
Control/discipline	60	50
Performance appraisal	57	57
Transfer	56	36[c]
Counseling	55	56
Grievances	51	67[b]
Affirmative action/EEO	48	39
Involuntary separation	45	78[c]
Voluntary separation	40	44
Job design	37	35
Incentive payment	37	34
Safety	21	42[c]

Source: Based on data presented in Marianne Koch, Sanghoon Nam, and Richard M. Steers,
"Human Resource Management in South Korea," in *Human Resource Management on the Pacific
Rim,* ed. Larry Moore and Devereaux Jennings, 217–42 (Berlin: deGruyter, 1995). Reprinted by
permission.

Note: Data are reported in percentage agreement using the method reported in L. F. Moore and
S. Robinson. Items are rank-ordered in terms of the relative influence of the Korean HR managers
on each decision. Canadian data from Moore and Robinson are reported here for comparative
purposes. See L. F. Moore and S. Robinson, "Human Resource Management Present and Past:
Highlights from a Western Canadian Survey of Practitioner Perceptions," in *Proceedings of the
Administrative Sciences Association of Canada,* ed. A. Petit and A. V. Subbarov (Montreal:
Personnel and Human Resources Division, McGill University, 1989).
[a]Differences in percentages significant at .05.
[b]Differences in percentages significant at .01.
[c]Differences in percentages significant at .001.

Table 9-5   Perceived Extent of HR Professionalism in Korea and Canada

Professional Dimension	Percent Agreeing That Dimension Is "Highly Descriptive" of HR Managers	
	Korea	Canada
A body of specialized knowledge including standardized terminology	14%	87%[c]
Widely recognized certification based on standardized qualifications	18	31[a]
Code of ethics	31	55[c]
Members oriented toward a service objective	2	85[c]
Recognized by the general public as a profession	18	60[c]
Limited access to the field, based on acquisition of standard skills/knowledge	26	63[c]
A professional society or association that, among other things, represents and gives voice to the entire field	22	61[c]
Practitioners are licensed	15	8[a]
Collegiality among practitioners	31	73[c]

Source: Based on data presented in Marianne Koch, Sanghoon Nam, and Richard M. Steers, "Human Resource Management in South Korea," in *Human Resource Management on the Pacific Rim,* ed. Larry Moore and Devereaux Jennings, 217–42 (Berlin: deGruyter, 1995). Reprinted by permission.

Note: Results for the Korean sample were scored according to the procedure outlined in L. F. Moore and S. Robinson. Canadian data from Moore and Robinson are included for purposes of comparison. See L. F. Moore and S. Robinson, "Human Resource Management: Present and Past: Highlights from a Western Canadian Survey of Practitioner Perceptions," in *Proceedings of the Administrative Sciences Association of Canada,* ed. A. Petit and A. V. Subbarov (Montreal: Personnel and Human Resources Division, McGill University, 1989).

[a]Differences in percentages significant at .05.
[b]Differences in percentages significant at .01 (not applicable in this table).
[c]Differences in percentages significant at .001.

than members of a separate or distinct group. Family members do whatever is necessary for the family. They fit in; they do not stand out.

HR POLICIES IN INTERNATIONAL JOINT VENTURES

As we look back on the material presented in this chapter, an interesting question emerges concerning the "bottom-line" consequences of human resource policies: Do variations in Korean HR policies affect employee attitudes and corporate performance? Recent evidence from an empirical study conducted by Nam Sanghoon on the effects of HR policies in international joint ventures suggests that the answer may be yes. Specifically, the manner in which such policies are formulated may have a profound influence on important performance outcomes in such ventures. Nam studied two competing Korean banks that were operated as joint ventures. One bank, called AmKor in the study, was a joint venture with an American bank and made extensive use of American personnel policies emphasizing employee autonomy and individual rewards. The other bank, called JaKor, was a joint venture with Japanese bankers and employed a blend of Korean and Japanese group-oriented personnel policies. The basic hypothesis of the study was that the JaKor personnel policies would be more compatible with Korea's culture and employee expectations and that, as a result, performance indicators would be higher than they would be for the AmKor.

Nam found strong support for his hypothesis. Employees at JaKor exhibited significantly higher levels of commitment to the organization and generally had more positive attitudes. Moreover, JaKor also had significantly higher financial performance in each of the two subsequent years of the study as measured by return on assets, return on equity, and net profit margins. While this is only one study, it was rigorously conducted and shows that in at least one comparative case, the compatibility of HR practices with prevailing norms and culture can affect employee attitudes and performance.[34]

SEGYEHWA AND THE NEW KOREAN MANAGEMENT

Based on the discussions here and in chapter 8, it must be concluded that the organizational landscape of Korean firms is indeed changing at a rapid pace. We have provided an overview of the nature and origins of these developments as they relate to the management of organizations and human resources. The next several years will witness even more developments as Korean firms continue to try to find their place in the global marketplace. In this dynamic environment, predictions concerning the implications for management in Korea are at best problematic. However, we offer here several observations that seem to represent emergent trends in the "New Korea." As shown in table 9-6, a new style of Korean management is emerging that is consistent with Korea's drive for globalization.

- *Partnership-driven entrepreneurism.* There is a noticeable shift in the market orientation of many Korean firms toward what may be called partner-

Table 9-6 Emerging Trends in Korean Management

Changing from . . .	Toward . . .
Export-driven entrepreneurism	Partnership-driven entrepreneurism
Close business-government relations	Distant business-government relations, except in labor relations
Centralized planning and control	Decentralized planning and control
Management by family owners	Increased reliance on professional management
Paternalistic leadership	Somewhat more participative leadership
Employment based on connections and school ties	Employment based on merit and education
Rewards based on seniority and connections	Rewards based on merit and performance
Development of international managers	Development of global managers
Confrontational labor-management relations	More cooperative labor-management relations
HR managers as generalists	HR managers as professionals
Women as low-level, temporary employees	Increased opportunities for women, especially in management

ship-driven entrepreneurism; that is, entrepreneurial behavior engaged in by strategic partners from two or more countries. The future will see less export-driven entrepreneurism, in which one Korean company seeks out new markets by itself. This evolution was discussed at length in chapter 7. Such a change requires Korean managers who are skilled in dealing with foreigners.

- *A changing role for government.* Developments in Korean HRM—and Korean management in general—will depend in part on the future political landscape of Korea's government. Because of the traditionally strong links between business and government, major shifts in government policy—such as those we are currently witnessing during the regime of President Kim Young Sam—will have a direct impact on how businesses are organized and managed. Greater government support for workers' rights and ethical codes of corporate conduct are currently serving to constrain the way in which Korean firms approach employee relations. As a result, firms are having to enhance their HR expertise to reduce the threat of increased unionization and industrial action. In most other areas of business regulation, however, government controls are diminishing and firms are increasingly being allowed to chart their own futures.

- *Change in the nature of management.* As noted in chapter 8, Korean firms are undergoing an extensive revolution in the way they manage their organizations. This includes efforts to improve product design and quality, to establish a more decentralized, team-oriented approach to managing people, and to bring about closer links between corporate strategy and management practice. Throughout, Korean firms are attempting to change their corporate culture systematically. Even so, these changes are being made without losing sight of traditional Korean values. Indeed, a blend of the old and the new is emerging in what we call the New Confucianism.

- *Change in human resource management policies.* HR policies will increasingly emphasize education and merit in employee selection and reward decisions; the importance of connections and seniority will diminish greatly. The focus of management development will be on globalization—how to survive and prosper in the international business environment. While some may call these changes Westernization, the truth is that Korean firms are developing a unique blend of management that draws on both West and East in a way that serves their interests.

- *New approaches to dispute resolution.* Considering the changing social norms and values of industrial Korea, it is unclear at present how the norms espoused by traditional Confucianism will be affected by the continued rise in unionism. On the one hand, the emphasis on hard work, self-improvement, and education suggests that workers might be willing to stand up to management to improve themselves, their working conditions, and their skills. Indeed, the labor movement has made significant strides in confronting management on behalf of industrialized workers. On the other hand, the Confucian tradition favors regimentation, authoritarianism, and social harmony. Thus, Korean workers are still under great pressures to refrain from pushing too hard to improve their working conditions for fear of jeopardizing societal harmony.[35] Achieving a workable balance between these two opposing forces of change and stability represents a sizable challenge for management and labor alike. To meet the challenges of the twenty-first century, both labor and management will have to improve their skills in collective bargaining and dispute resolution. Government intervention in labor relations over the last five decades has not prevented the management and labor parties from doing so.[36] Only time and repeated interactions can teach both parties how to work through their differences by themselves.

- *Shifts in power relations and wage pressures.* A related issue in Korean industrial relations is that management will have to learn how to deal with a more vocal and powerful workforce. As a result of the growth in unionism, employee demands for better wages and working conditions have been a reality since the late 1980s. Indeed, over the past five years, wages in Korea have been among the fastest rising in the world. As worker demands continue to increase, concerns arise as to how Korean companies will be able to meet them without losing ground in the increasingly competitive global manufacturing sector.

- *The professionalization of HR managers.* The professionalization of the field of human resource management will continue to rise in importance in Korea as union activity remains high. Some have argued that proficiency in human resource management is now necessary as a means of avoiding union organizing. Indeed, some *chaebols*, like Samsung, continue to practice union avoidance by paying high wages and offering generous benefits.

- *A changing role for women employees.* Korean firms face an increasing challenge from female workers. Tradition has blocked women from achieving most positions of importance in the corporate world. However, the emergence of an organized Korean women's movement—plus the need for more skilled employees—is beginning to bring pressure to bear on Korean firms to open up its managerial ranks to female employees. This movement, if successful, will serve to bring new challenges and opportunities into the Korean HR arena and, indeed, may represent a major challenge to the fundamental Confucian traditions of the country.

In summary, current evidence suggests that the HR function in Korean firms will continue to rise in importance owing to the limited availability of highly skilled human capital. As Korea continues to be squeezed by Japan and the United States on technological frontiers, contemporary HR practices represent one avenue for Korean companies to pursue in their ongoing quest to develop their employees' capacity to contribute to the organization. It has been noted that Korea now exists as a "sandwich economy." That is, while the technological giants are increasingly reticent to share breakthrough technologies with Korean companies for fear of the competition, Korea has simultaneously lost its traditional position as a source of cheap labor. As a result, Korean firms can't move up the technology ladder as rapidly as they need to and, at the same time, can't move down the cost ladder and compete with the labor costs of China, Vietnam, and Thailand. Korean firms are thus losing ground in both technological innovation and price competitiveness, with a resulting loss of market share in several key industries. Contemporary management practices may help alleviate this squeeze by maximizing the contribution of available human resources to industrial competitiveness.

CHAPTER TEN

Toward the Twenty-first Century Korean Enterprise

In a major address to political, business, and academic leaders around the world in May 1996, President Kim reaffirmed his expectation that his *segyehwa* program would eliminate inefficiencies and regulations and raise Korea's political, economic, and cultural institutions to a world-class level. "Its ultimate objective," he said, "is to make Korea a country people all over the world would like to visit, invest and reside in. In this sense, the *segyehwa* policy is not for the sake of the development of Korea alone, but is also to help the development of the world as a whole."[1] Since some have argued that the twenty-first century will be called the "Century of the Asia-Pacific,"[2] it comes as no surprise that the theme of the 7th Annual Corporate Conference of the Asia Society was "Asia Goes Global: Korea and the Region." With the region poised to go global, it is expected that Korea will be at the forefront of change.

Korea's challenges as it strives to fulfill its goal of globalization stem from rising protectionism among its trading partners, competition from the second generation of newly industrializing economies, rising expectations among its workers, the need to sustain technological parity, and growing deficiencies within its industrial structure. To recapitulate, the seven key challenges discussed in this book are:

- *Reframing industrial policy and creating a new economic covenant.* How can Korea make a successful transition from a command economy to political and market liberalization?

- *Restructuring the* chaebols. Can the *chaebols* succeed in the world market with less support from the government and a more specialized structure?

- *Developing local entrepreneurs.* Can Korea's small to medium-sized enterprises be effective as the domestic market begins to liberalize?

- *Reorganizing for globalization.* Can the *chaebols* make the changes necessary to function in a global economy without destroying their essential strengths in the process?

- *Competing on the new technological frontier.* How well can Korean *chaebols* acquire, nurture, and develop new technologies in this changing environment?

- *Transforming the nature of management.* How can Korean enterprises transform themselves from traditional to professional organizations?

- *Developing human resources as a strategic asset.* How can Korean enterprises build and sustain a human capital base that will enable them to be strong competitors in a global economy?

While these challenges are organized and discussed sequentially in this book, they are very much interrelated in theory and in practice. Overseas competition is not independent from government policy; in fact, the success of government policy may depend on how well Korean *chaebols* can develop indigenous technologies. Building human capital is inextricably related to the implementation of new organizational structures and processes, and these new structures, in turn, foster new kinds of managerial thinking. In this chapter, we will attempt to integrate these challenges and interpret them more fundamentally in terms of overarching trends and ideologies. We also incorporate critical evaluations of Korea's so-called economic miracle and offer our own assessment of these criticisms.

TWO SCENARIOS FOR KOREA'S FUTURE

Consider two alternative scenarios for the year 2020:

Scenario 1: As envisioned by the KDI report "Vision and Development Strategy for the Korean Economy in the Twenty-first Century," Korea becomes the seventh largest economy in the world, with a per capita GDP income of $32,000. The *segyehwa* program is a major success. Government efficiency is vastly improved, the major *chaebols* are highly competitive abroad, and small to medium-sized enterprises are flourishing. While the reunification of the Korean peninsula has been accomplished with enormous costs, many of these costs are absorbed and mitigated by Korea's economic performance in a much stronger Asian continent.

Scenario 2: The Korean economy has grown slowly, clearly not in the manner depicted by the KDI. Liberalization efforts are impeded by persistent high costs and low efficiency. The effects of currency appreciation, improper liberalization, and political instability arising from the growing disparity between Asiatic economies and disharmonious reunification efforts have created significant imbalances and dislocations. While Korea is still regarded as a global force in Asia, previous talks of the "Han River Miracle" have all but faded.

Korea's swift rise to economic success has led to the development of two distinct groups of observers: admirers, who seek to know whether other aspiring countries can emulate Korea's strategy for becoming an advanced industrial state, and critics, who question Korea's ability to sustain its level of accomplishment into the twenty-first century.

For admirers, the success of the Korean enterprise has been explained in terms of many interrelated institutions: a strong, interventionist government; the Confucian legacy in a strong educational system; its investment in human capital; hard work and sacrifice; and its entrepreneurial aspirations. While some countries possess a number of these elements, we have argued in this book that Korea is unique in having combined them in a creative and purposeful manner throughout its history. Guided by a core belief that Korea had to improve and prosper, bureaucrats, businessmen, the populace, and even government critics were able to capitalize on crises and fortuitous events to fashion a disciplined strategy for fueling domestic economic growth and international competitiveness.

For critics, the sustainability of the Korean growth model is suspect, despite its success to this point. One view, espoused by Stanford economist Paul Krugman, posits that growth in Asia today is similar to that of the Soviet Union in its high-growth era of the 1960s,[3] in that it is driven by extraordinary increases in inputs such as labor and capital. He cites Singapore as the extreme example among rapidly growing Asian economies that invested heavily in education and employment. Krugman argues that Singapore's growth is limited: "Over the past generation the percentage of people employed has almost doubled; it cannot double again."[4] He asserts that the same holds for other East Asian economies—that their growth rates of the future will not equal those of the past.

At the heart of Krugman's thesis is the assumption that sustained growth in a nation's per capita income can occur only by increasing output per unit, or the *efficiency* with which these inputs are used. Growth in efficiency, also referred to as "total factor productivity," includes organizing work better and making technological improvements and innovations. As an example of sustained growth, he cites MIT Professor Robert Solow's report that technological improvements and innovations accounted for 80 percent of the long-term rise in U.S. per capita income, with increased investment in capital explaining only the remaining 20 percent.[5]

Do the Asian economies have—or could they acquire or import—the technological improvements and innovations required for sustaining high growth rates? Empirical evidence, although sparse, seems to suggest that the answer is no. Krugman cites a study by Kim and Lau that finds "no apparent convergence between the technologies" of the newly industrializing nations and those of the established industrial powers.[6] Overall, efficiency growth rates in the East Asian economies are no higher, and in some cases lower, than those in many advanced nations. Thus, Krugman believes that most of Asia is unlikely to catch up. "Unless there is convergence in total factor productivity," he asserts, "South Korea could only achieve a U.S. standard of living if every South Korean had two Ph.D.s and worked with $500,000 worth of equipment."[7]

EMERGING TRENDS AND SHIFTING IDEOLOGIES

Although there may be nothing more intriguing than trying to predict the future, the optimistic and pessimistic scenarios depicted above are not intended to be mere forecasting exercises. The two scenarios involve assumptions about emerging trends within Korean society, as well as assumptions relating to fundamental philosophies and ideologies that underlie these trends. In our view, the future direction of Korea and its enterprise system will depend largely on how well the country and its businesses respond to these changing trends and ideologies. Perhaps most significant among these trends are the following:

- From communitarianism to individualism.
- From regional competition to regional cooperation.
- From nation-states to global networks.
- From traditionalism to professional management.
- From technological imitation to technological innovation.

- From exclusion to membership in the "technology club."
- From a divided to a reunified Korean peninsula.

We close this book by considering how these trends and Korea's response to them will influence the future of the country and its enterprises—that is, whether future development will evolve toward continued high-growth and prosperity (scenario 1) or toward stagnation (scenario 2).

From Communitarianism to Individualism

The emergence of Japan as a world economic power, followed by the rapid industrialization of Korea, Hong Kong, Taiwan, and Singapore with per capita incomes that grew more than four times as fast as those in the rest of the world, challenged the traditional role of government as noninterventionist in matters pertaining to the private sector. Despite differences in origin and historical circumstance, these countries are alike in the aggressive stance their government has taken in intervening in the private sector with the expressed goal of enhancing economic development.

"Competent government" is the World Bank's term for denoting the major difference between the successful industrial policy of the East Asian economies and the failed previous policy of Latin America countries. Nevertheless, trends emerging in the 1980s and continuing through the 1990s have torn the fabric of Korea's protectionist mantle: government involvement is declining, increased political and economic liberalization limits the power of government bureaucrats, and sociopolitical democratic reforms call for a much reduced relationship between the government and the *chaebols*. Moreover, foreign governments—such as the United States and Japan, which in the past have helped Korea for geopolitical and business reasons— are much less inclined to continue their largesse as Korea begins to compete head to head with them in crucial high-technology segments of the global economy.

Beyond these trends, we argue that the shift to market liberalization reflects a more fundamental change in ideology. Korea's traditional ideological basis can best be described as "communitarian"; that is, a state in which individual interests are subordinated to those of the group, based on an authority structure of ranked status and power.[8] A universal right of benevolent rule is part of this tradition, although the leader's status is contingent on the fulfillment of that right. Even as each individual knows that he is expected to serve his superior faithfully, he is also inclined to judge his superior on moral grounds—that is, to judge if he himself is being treated fairly.[9] This coexistence of two countervailing tendencies—individual self-expression and individual subordination—has made for volatility and instability in Korean society since ancient times.[10]

Korea has long been deeply divided between those who adhere to paternalistic communitarianism and those who desire more individual self-expression. Korean businessmen have grown adept at playing both sides. On one hand, there is the frenetic competition within parameters set by the government. On the other hand, there is the close collaboration of the largest and most influential *chaebols* with the government not only on market selection but also on policies to keep wage levels in check. Korean corporate executives have attempted, privately and publicly, to influence government initiatives, particularly in matters directly related to their benefit. Yet they resent official interference into their own affairs, citing the ideals of free-market ideologies, as is seen in the case of the government's policy initiatives for greater *chaebol* specialization.[11] Moreover, Korean executives, similar to their Japanese counterparts, see themselves as benevolent, paternalistic employers who provide their employees with generous bonuses and supplementary allowances to demonstrate their sincere intent to maintain social harmony and enhance social welfare.[12]

The importation of political democracy and individualism from the West and the increasing recognition of the need for professional management have created constant tension with the established ideology. The orthodox view in the United States is that the market, not national government, is the best arbiter of which industries succeed or fail. Government intervention in the United States, for instance, is mainly for purposes of regulation. This policy is typified by antitrust legislation and the Federal Trade Commission's veto power over mergers; both represent interventions that regulate or police competitive activity rather than encourage it. By contrast, government policies designed to intervene in the private sector are deemed dysfunctional. Critics have noted that such policies can be damaging, more likely to promote inefficiencies, undue protectionism, and adverse collusion.[13] In this view, the primacy of the free-market mechanism in leading to optimal resource allocation is not disputed; competitive processes in a market minimize the cost of production and prices while they maximize economic efficiency.

It has been argued that ideology and practice follow a standard pattern over time. During particular intervals, institutions develop to support the prevailing ideology.[14] For Korean industrial policy to succeed, it has to develop a workable institutional arrangement that is democratic and pluralistic, while at the same time disciplined and consensual. Communitarian institutions have served Koreans well in the past.[15] But, as MIT economist Alice Amsden cautions, institutions are also highly unstable.[16] The manner in which restless ambitions for individual self-expression, as articulated by Korean *chaebols*, have to fit within an overarching communitarian context that now favors the welfare of small to medium-sized firms remains problematic.

The ascendancy of President Kim Young Sam signaled a changing of the guard, not only in political terms but also in terms of deep-seated beliefs about the value of redistributing income, upgrading social welfare, promoting small to medium-sized companies, and restructuring the Korean *chaebols*. The sociopolitical reforms initiated by President Kim won widespread support, particularly from those who had been discontented with the abuse of former authoritarian regimes. Naturally, there is burgeoning interest in even more reform as Koreans become aware and inspired by democratic institutions. Moreover, there is a need to organize various political groups and bureaucrats who can actively support the president's platform.

On the flip side of democratic governance, however, is the problem of how to manage dissent. President Kim's efforts to force the *chaebols* to specialize have distinguished him from his predecessors and increased his worldwide stature as an effective reformer. But his actions against Hyundai Chairman Chung Ju-Yung and the disciplinary tone he has taken with Samsung and Sunkyong for their alleged criticisms of his programs call attention to his methods of implementing government reform: the executive fiat or a highly visible initiative. Critics maintain that while the message is one of freeing markets and reducing bureaucracy, the means are still the same: the government dictates, and business must follow, or else.[17]

As a reasonably democratic regime settles in, President Kim's actions against Hyundai, Samsung, Sunkyong, and others may stall investment.[18] Should both the government and business sectors balk, a less favorable growth scenario will ensue. In our view, successful economic programs result from political liberalization and social democratization. To realize the high-growth scenario, Koreans will have to balance capitalism with democracy, align property rights with planned economic development, and promote *chaebol* competitiveness along with better social welfare for all Koreans.[19]

From Regional Competition to Regional Cooperation

Korean *chaebols* are moving at full speed to meet the globalization challenge, partly because they can no longer rely on large profit margins at home to subsidize low-priced exports, and partly because Korean wages have nearly quadrupled in the past ten years.[20] In preceding chapters, we described the incursions of various *chaebols* into a variety of international destinations. They are not alone in this endeavor, however. The success of their globalization efforts may well depend on the extent to which they are able to work with—or compete against—their Asian neighbors. There is relentless growth within the Pacific Basin economies—from Hong Kong to Singapore, Taiwan to Malaysia. Such dramatic growth has transformed a heterogeneous collection of underdeveloped countries into the highest growth region in the world. In the past twenty-five years, these Pacific Basin economies have doubled their share of world production and tripled their share of world trade. Together they account for a greater share of world trade than Japan and nearly as much as Japan and China combined.

In 1995, Asia produced one quarter of the world's output of goods and services, up from 5 percent in 1960. And if current trends continue, some experts predict 40 percent of the world's gross products will emerge from the Asian bloc within another ten years.[21] Assuming that Asia's economies grow at an annual rate of 7 percent (the annual growth rate in 1973–1993 was 7.6 percent), they will assume a collective value of $6 trillion (in 1990 dollars) by 2005, creating an economic zone larger than the United States, Canada, and Mexico combined.[22]

But what may represent success for one Asian country may spell doom for another. Of the many economies of East and Southeast Asia, Singapore, Taiwan, Hong Kong, and South Korea have been the most successful. For this they have frequently been called "Asia's Four Tigers." However, new challenges emerge from countries such as Malaysia and Thailand, where wage levels are substantially lower than in Korea and Taiwan. Looming in the background is China, with the specter of even lower wages combined with a highly motivated workforce. Already, these countries have begun to undercut Korean firms in older industries, such as textiles and shoes, and newer ones, such as petrochemicals and steel. Some regions in Korea, notably around Pusan, where traditional manufacturing industries are concentrated, have been hit especially hard.

Yet weakness can be transformed into strength. The impact of competition from the emerging economies has been offset by the rapid growth of regional markets. Already, Southeast Asia has replaced the United States as Japan's leading trading partner. As these countries become more affluent, their ability and willingness to procure Korean products may become a significant factor. Indeed, Korean firms are already assuming the role of the multinational, rapidly building factories in fast-growing Southeast Asian markets, with their relatively cheap labor.[23]

Whether the growth of Asian markets becomes a threat or an opportunity for South Korea depends on how Korean firms craft their strategies for leveraging their strengths in these markets. The ambitions of Korean firms, notably their "can do" spirit, has made Korea the world's largest shipbuilder, a major producer of steel and cars, and the world's largest manufacturer of DRAM chips. Yet, even with stringent attention to product quality, successful Korean firms such as Samsung and Hyundai will still have to discard the image their products have as second-best alternatives to Japanese products. This will be a particular challenge in East and Southeast Asia, where status is important. The question for Korean firms, then, is how they will meet the threats and opportunities from Asia's other tigers, the late developing industrializers. Cutthroat competition will erode Korea's advantages and slow down its growth; creative collaboration will only enhance it.

From Nation-States to Global Networks

Because many important developments are still unfolding, the prospect of assessing Korea's impact on the rest of Asia (and vice versa) is daunting. On the surface, the region reflects deep-seated geographical demarcations defined as nation-states. However, a closer examination reveals emerging patterns that are shaped by the relationships between countries, including major flows of people, goods, and ideas. Thus, the relative position of countries is fundamentally affected by prevailing economic, trade, and political trends, if not the distribution of social capital.[24]

Perhaps the most prominent among the emerging region states is the Hong Kong–Shenzhen connection, but with linkages to Zhuhai, Amoy, and Guangzhou. Hong Kong, with a per capita GNP of roughly $12,000, is the driving force in this region. GNP per capita in Shenzhen reached $5,695 in 1995 compared with China's as a whole, at $317. By the year 2000, this cross-border region state is expected to raise the standard of living of more than 11 million people to more than $5,000.[25] If one considers the Republic of Southern China Guangdong, the Fujian Province, Hong Kong/Taiwan, then this region has a combined GDP of $310 billion.[26] Guangdong does not suffer from limitations of labor and land, and its geographic proximity to Hong Kong supports the Cantonese language and historical traditions—an advantage over the dominant Mandarin language that is primarily associated with Beijing.[27]

The growth of this region attests to shared economic interests on the part of Hong Kong and the coastal regions of China. Historically, Hong

Kong has enjoyed economic success out of proportion to its small land base and population. In Guangdong, Hong Kong is able to leverage its economic strengths, while building a more secure land and labor base. For Guangdong, Hong Kong is a natural partner, given its economic prominence and future ties to the mainland. It has been suggested that with enhanced ties between the two, it is actually Hong Kong that has taken over China's coastal province, rather than China taking over Hong Kong.[28]

Not unlike the Hong Kong–Guangdong connection, the relationship between Taiwan and Fujian is complementary in nature. For the past decade, Taiwan has been beset by rising costs and labor shortages. Manufacturing costs have already risen to five to six times the level of those in Fujian. Taiwan's trade surpluses and the resulting monumental capital reserves prompted a 40 percent appreciation of the currency in 1985.

These two Chinese-based regional economies have flourished together. In economic terms, the combined entities of Guangdong, Fujian, Hong Kong, and Taiwan would form a population base of 120 million, roughly equal that of Japan. Their combined GNP is equal to the size of the five ASEAN economies. And real growth in this expanded region averages around 10 percent a year, seven to eight times that of China.[29]

A third region is emerging within the Singapore basin, incorporating the Rian islands of Indonesia, Johor (the largest state of peninsular Malaysia), and the adjoining developments in Thailand, Vietnam, and the Philippines. To date, development has focused on the island of Batan. The population of ASEAN (Singapore, Indonesia, Malaysia, the Philippines, Thailand, and the principality of Brunei, with Vietnam and Laos moving to become full members) is more than 300 million, or about that of the European community. Yet the total GNP of the five established member nations totals only a little more than $300 billion, not much more than that of Australia. Thus, the region is still characterized by uneven growth and wealth.[30]

The discussion of regional connections serves as a reminder that geographical boundaries are not impermeable but rather defined by the economic, political, and trade flows between them. In Asia, the three emerging blocs—Hong Kong–Guangdong, Fujian-Taiwan, and the Singapore-ASEAN—will be of consequence to South Korea. Korea's eventual response will help determine which of the two growth scenarios described above emerges. On the surface, each region has the potential to boost its competitiveness in ways that can undermine Korea's strategies. The movement of footwear, for example, from Taiwan to Fujian resulted in a combination of excellent design, quick response, and low labor costs that significantly limited Korea's expansion in this sector.

Yet Korea can also compete through cooperation, or through global networking. The significant presence of Koreans in the Shandong province, for example, suggests a strong overture from China. China seeks the kind of investment in Shandong and the northeast provinces that only Korea (or Japan) can provide. Should Korea elect this path, it can strengthen its globalization efforts in the rest of the world, using the natural synergies between itself and these countries in ways that have bolstered the economic stock of Taiwan and Hong Kong.

From Traditionalism to Professional Management

Regarded as an understated asset, Korea's human resources may well be the engine of economic development and vitality. While it is generally assumed that Korea's early competitive advantage was its lower labor costs, what is understated is the quality of work relative to its cost. Koreans have a worldwide reputation as a hardworking, tenacious people with the proven capability to produce high-quality goods and services.

In large part, this is attributed to Korea's Confucian past, although it has been claimed that Confucianism was invoked only after the Western world became interested in the East Asian "miracle." A number of Confucian values have played a role in Korean economic development. These include the great stock put in education—an important prerequisite to technological learning. The Korean work ethic also stems from the perseverance the people showed during the times of hardship and turmoil brought on by foreign invasions and occupations. Other cultural values stress the importance of harmonious interpersonal relationships, a respect for elders, group solidarity, and discipline. Moreover, family and clan loyalty are regarded as a supreme duty, and Korean society emphasizes the virtues of self-discipline, hard work, diligence, and frugality.

Professor Rhee Song Ni notes, however, that Confucian values, as a whole, do not necessarily correlate with economic progress. In fact, many facets of Confucianism, such as its rigid ethical codes and disdain for democracy and equality, might be regarded as retarding economic progress.[31] It is the combination of traditional Confucian values and new pragmatic ethics—including scientific and technological know-how, educated workers, elite technocrats, and entrepreneurial leaders—that turned Korea and Japan into industrial powers.

In the context of modern enterprise, the challenge for Koreans is how to blend the family or collectivist values of the East with the more pragmatic or professional values of the West. Among the many critics of this program is Francis Fukuyama, who sees Korea—like China—as a "low trust" society.[32] Fukuyama asserts that the Japanese concept of "household" (*ie* in Japanese) typically corresponds with the biological family. For the Japanese, it is the continuity of the *ie* that must be preserved, and no stigma is attached to adopting children (especially male children) outside the kinship group (see discussion in chapter 2). This differs considerably from the practices of the Chinese and the Koreans, where trust resides principally within kinship (or blood) ties.[33] In the context of the modern economic enterprise, it is much more difficult for the Chinese and Koreans to bring outside professional managers into their organizations—a finding that is reflected in the management structure of many *chaebols.*

Even so, Korean firms are moving resolutely forward with the professionalization of their management structures. They are committed to becoming truly global corporations and will require managers who can facilitate this process. Each year, companies like Samsung, LG, and Daewoo send hundreds of managers to the United States for advanced managerial training. Daewoo, for instance, has established a company-sponsored MBA program with the University of Michigan. LG has worked for several years with McKinsey & Company on a major overhaul of its entire organization structure aimed at sharpening its strategic focus in the marketplace. And when Hyundai established its new $1.3 billion semiconductor facility in Eugene, Oregon, it selected as its new president an American manager who was hired away from a Japanese competitor. There is no question that Korean organizations are changing significantly. The question is whether they are changing with sufficient speed to catch up with—or even surpass—their Japanese and American rivals.

From Technological Imitation to Technological Innovation

Clearly one of Korea's most significant challenges lies in its ability to maintain its technological edge, particularly since Korean firms have decided to directly challenge more advanced economies, such as the United States and Japan, in important high-technology sectors. A critique by Professor Dieter Ernst, project director for the Berkeley Roundtable on the International Economy, directly addresses the limitations of the Korean model.[34] Ernst argues that most of the current problems faced by Korean electronics manufacturers can be traced to policies that focused on rapid export expansion based on imported technology and on the "octopus-like" diversification strategies of the *chaebols.*[35] Specifically, this growth pattern has limited the formation of broader domestic technological policies that are oriented to systems design, research innovation, and market development. In effect, the emphasis on standard/mass production and OEM manufacturing and a catch-up mentality have precluded the development of new capabilities that are crucial in the emerging international technology environment.

The extraordinary speed with which Korean electronics manufacturers achieved technological parity has not been matched by a sufficient degree of industrial deepening, defined as sufficiently strong backward and forward linkages both within and between the electronics industry and other related sectors. To keep up with the challenges imposed by this new environment, Ernst argues, Korea will need to fundamentally change some government policies, shift to a process of technological deepening that involves synchronous development of related industries with strong product innovation, strengthen the competitiveness of small to medium-sized companies, pursue selective liberalization aimed at gaining access to generic technologies, and globalize its marketing and production operations throughout the world.[36]

These criticisms highlight two elements of Korea's technological policies. The first is the sufficiency of these policies vis-à-vis Korea's global competitors. Given the levels of investment made by Japanese, American, and some European firms, it is not likely that Korea can overtake their lead. The second element is the direction of technological development. This calls into question the nature of technology that leads to patterns of market development, whether this be diminishing growth, as suggested by Krugman, as assumed by Ernst, or alternative models of technological growth. Ultimately, the fate of the Korean electronics industry will depend not only on the sufficiency of resources applied toward technological development but also on the limits of technological development of the industries in which they are engaged.

Krugman's criticism that East Asian economies have grown primarily from inputs rather than total productivity raises several questions: Are the resources currently invested in Korea's technological development sufficient to maintain parity with its competitors? Will Korea's future growth continue to come from additional input factors or from total productivity? Krugman's point that the high growth rates exhibited by a number of East Asian "tigers" cannot continue indefinitely is well taken. Following the cases of Japan and Korea, high growth appears to be leveling off. Even so, there is some question whether his second assertion—that East Asian economies are not likely to grow significantly in terms of total factor productivity—is a necessary given.

First, Krugman restricts his arguments to nation-states (Singapore, Japan, and the like), not regional developments in Asia. Taiwan was once depicted as bordering on a precipitously dangerous "limited growth" scenario: compressed land area, burgeoning population, and so forth. Yet the emerging Taiwan-Fujian connection has resuscitated high growth in Taiwan and paved the way for renewed economic and technological development. Framed in the context of regional developments, as opposed exclusively to nation-states, one might qualify Krugman's hypothesis as to the source and magnitude of input growth. Because Korean businesses have strong connections in China and Southeast Asia and are in the process of developing even broader networks, the prospects for high growth may indeed be reasonably good. The movement of Korean firms into Southeast Asia suggests that input-driven growth is not a domestic "win-lose" situation but one that might extend to these areas as well.

Second, growth through factor productivity comes from both factor inputs and intangible variables, which include synergies from technological alliances. We have described Korea's strategies for broadening its technological alliances and argue that Korea's future growth hinges on the learning that ensues from such alliances.

In sum, while there are clear limits to input-driven growth, future growth might be driven by other sources, such as the development of regional connections and global networks in Asia, the proliferation of technological alliances, and the growing sophistication of institutions and infrastructures in Korea. In one study of Korea's potential growth during the 2000–2010 period (estimated at 5.5 percent), it was predicted that about 50 percent of Korea's future growth will come from total factor productivity improvement. Typically, this comprises about a quarter of the growth in output in major capitalist economies.[37]

From Exclusion to Membership in the "Technology Club"

A related consideration in analyzing Korea's competitiveness in technology-intensive industries is the pattern of technological growth and diffusion. One depiction of technology is that, similar to inputs, it is subject to diminishing returns to scale, which implies a single equilibrium point.[38] Economic actions trigger feedback that stabilizes the economy and leads to a predictable equilibrium for prices and market shares. Equilibrium marks the "best" outcome regarding the most efficient use of resources. Fifty years ago, economist J. A. Schumpeter argued that technological innovation was the most powerful form of competition.[39] In the Schumpeterian system, profitable companies and technologically progressive industries are characterized by strong research and development, where innovative know-how is both preserved and enhanced.

In such a perspective, technologies have limited life spans, and the migration of technologies from one country to another presents significant risk. For example, investment in electronics and semiconductors, which has been the driving force behind Korea's surge in high technology, becomes vulnerable to high-end innovations on the one hand and to low-cost adaptations on the other. Korean firms are sandwiched between low-and high-end competitors. At the low end, newly industrializing countries see Japan and Korea as their models and fashion their industrial policies and institutions to compete as low-cost manufacturers in selected market niches. As the gap in wage rates between Korea and these newly industrializing countries increases, Korea, its officials realize, will not be able to sustain its market presence in these increasingly saturated, lower-end markets. Yet competing at the high end of the technological spectrum also entails risk. The technological gap between Korea's level of sophistication and that of Japan and America can widen considerably, given available financial resources, technological experience, and competitive resolve. Thus, Korean firms are seen as vulnerable to attacks from low-wage competitors that can undercut them in price and to competition from their more technologically advanced rivals that can outperform them in product development and differentiation.

An alternative view of technology transfers depicts widespread transfers of technology between highly industrialized and newly industrializing countries, resulting in the proliferation of technology capabilities across different countries.[40] These result from continuous advances in technology that create new systems applications and new markets. In this scenario, Japanese and American high-technology firms are expected to stay at the forefront of new technology, entering higher-value-added, emerging sectors. Because it is not lucrative to compete in every market segment, these firms will be willing to transfer older technologies to developing countries as they enter higher-value-added markets. While investing proportionately higher amounts in research and development, Korean firms need not keep pace with the Americans and Japanese in pioneering new segments because they stand a better chance when competing in segments representing older technologies. Korean firms can also master the next level of technological sophistication at each iteration, thereby reducing their technological dependence on market leaders. Far from being uncomfortably squeezed, Korean firms become members of technology's inner circle by filling market segments at a pace consistent with their technological stage of development.

This scenario, however, is based on a conception of technology that is more consistent with increasing returns to scale as opposed to the more popular diminishing returns concept that supports more pessimistic appraisals of Korea's technology prospects.[41]

The characteristics of the new technological environment permit the gradual phasing in of newer technological and market sectors. New technological advances lead to the proliferation of market niches that are attractive to market leaders. As market leaders retreat from market segments with each transition from old to new technology, niches are made available to Korean firms. They can reap economic rents, while learning new technological skills at each iteration. Utilizing a niche strategy, Korea can acquire further advanced, innovative know-how at a reasonable price through more extensive technological alliances. In doing so over a sustained period of time, Korean corporations will be able to gain membership into what Samsung's Park Ungsuh refers as the "technology club"—a loose coalition of worldwide companies that have achieved a level of technological sophistication that enables them to simultaneously cooperate and compete in an industry.[42] However, membership in the club requires the ability to make a contribution to current members, that is, the technology system, as a global player. Professor Frank Contractor points out, "with money and expertise, doors open and admission is cheaper."[43]

Sunkyong learned the value of being a member in the club early when it attempted to develop videotape technologies. When technology protection was prevalent in the global market in the late 1970s, Sunkyong was looking for technologies to diversify into a new field. Japanese and Western firms either rejected Sunkyong's request or demanded what the company felt was unreasonable compensation and royalties. Sunkyong had to internally develop the technology with the cooperation from the government-funded research center KAIST. Once Sunkyong succeeded in developing the crude technology, it could easily access other advanced technologies to improve quality and manufacturing efficiency. For members of the club, advanced technologies are exchanged with their own complementary asset or they are willingly given by other members as a preemptive gesture to avoid a new competitor.

The semiconductor industry provides additional insights into Korea's ability to overcome its technological weaknesses and compete with advanced nations.[44] In this industry, American companies pioneered the technologies but eventually ceded them to the Japanese firms that succeeded in developing both the technology and the markets. A variant of this strategy, pursued by the Koreans, was to fill niches vacated by the market leaders, or to directly challenge them in segments where they had weak competitive position. Deriving competencies from their own institutions, Korean firms have succeeded in entering market niches that had been dominated by other competitors. The patterns of entry and exit by American, Japanese, and Korean firms also denote a technology growth trajectory that differs substantially from one characterized by diminishing returns, as well as from the "first-mover" advantages previously associated with Schumpeterian theories.

From a Divided to a Reunified Korean Peninsula

Korea remains the only culturally homogeneous, firmly divided nation in the world today. Relations between China and Taiwan, while occasionally feverish, have begun to thaw. The end of the Cold War and the fact of German unification have provided hope for peaceful reunification in Korea, although the economic and political condition on the peninsula have become less stable.[45] While deterrence measures have served the two Koreas well in the past, recent economic and political shifts perhaps call for a different strategy.[46]

Economically, North Korea has lost its chief sponsor and ally—the Soviet Union. With Russia and China ending aid programs to North Korea, its economy has commenced a deep slide and has dramatically expanded the already wide gap between itself and South Korea. Politically, a destabilizing factor was the revelation in 1996 that North Korea was on the brink of developing a nuclear weapons capability—a development with serious security consequences for the Northeast Asian region and beyond. The death of *suryong* (the great leader Kim Il Sung) in 1995 was also unsettling. In the North, Kim and his son had been viewed as a central deterrent to the possible revival of factionalism and interference from neighboring powers.[47]

These destabilizing events have provoked the development of a new strategy on the part of Japan and the United States that transcends deterrence. "It is not in our interests for the DPRK (Democratic People's Republic of Korea) to lash out militarily, or to collapse into chaos," said U.S. Ambassador to Korea James Laney. "Everyone's interests are served by economic assistance to the North, reduction of tensions, and comprehensive North-South engagements."[48] In 1995, this new strategy took the form of a continued three-way consultation, between Seoul, Tokyo, and Washington, from which additional economic assistance to North Korea is expected.

With no tradition of a reform movement in North Korea, such talks are fraught with uncertainty. Current optimism, however, is based on the perception that North Korea is shifting from a revolutionary diplomacy based on ideology to one based on a pragmatic assessment of its poor economic position, from outright nuclear blackmail to nuclear bargaining, and from undesirable military confrontation to peaceful coexistence.[49] Should the North Korean regime collapse, great confusion is bound to follow. If the North Korean regime persists, the two economies can be integrated with increased bilateral trade and cross-border projects.[50] By 2000, it can be reasonably assumed that the South Korean economy will be twenty times the size of the North Korean economy. At such time, a 5 percent share of South Korea's GNP will correspond to the entire North Korean GNP. An investment by South Korea of about 5 percent of its GNP could provide a tremendous boost to the North.[51] Therefore, unless political chaos develops, opportunities for greater economic integration appear good—with or without reunification.

SOME FINAL THOUGHTS

The study of Korea reveals important insights into the dynamics of late industrialization and the problems of making the transition from newly industrializing country to advanced economy. In describing the movement of countries up the "ladder of development," Kenichi Ohmae argues that the transition from a $5,000 to a $10,000 per capita GNP economy—as in Korea—is characterized not only by expansion of global linkages but also by some rigidities in opening up the "softer" aspects of the economy (for example, currency, financial services, communications).[52] Korea's transitional problems are well illustrated by Rha Woong-Bae, Korea's deputy prime minister and finance minister, who recently asked: "How can Korea adopt capital/market liberalization without significant macroeconomic dislocations and without undermining the competitiveness of Korean industries?"[53]

The advanced countries in the Western world would like to see a more rapid pace of market liberalization in Asia. These Asian countries, including Korea, contend that they have to manage the pace of liberalization in ways that will not create macroeconomic or societal imbalances. Despite these different views of what may be the best pace of change, the prominence of the Korean economy as a power to be reckoned with in the dawn of the twenty-first century is indisputable. In economic terms, Korea will be a major global force in East Asia, with the ability to deal equally well with the developed economy of Japan and the developing economy of China.

Within the rest of Asia, Korea has established commercial roots that will be deepened as the region establishes a stronger competitive position. Through its recent policies, the Korean government has exhibited serious intentions to open its financial markets. This will present tremendous opportunities for American (and other) institutions and investors.

With Korea providing us with a macrocosm of an economy in transition, it is tempting to use it to prescribe some lessons for other economies, if not for the practicing manager. Korea's strong performance was the consequence of sound macroeconomic policies, favorable interventionist policies, the role of the *chaebols*, hard work, and entrepreneurial aspirations. But it is also clear that Korea's success was assured by market access opportunities made possible by an open and liberal trading system. Having reaped these benefits, Korea will be asked to provide greater leadership in the future. Domestically, it needs to manage structural adjustments as well as meet societal expectations for greater equity, harmony, and balance. Internationally, it needs to become a full partner in the evolution of the new multilateral trading system that includes the attendant issues of the environment, regionalism, and labor standards. In an era of liberalization and globalization, the efforts of government and business will not be sufficient to achieve worldwide competitiveness. With greater economic liberalization, the active participation of the Korean people will become a defining variable. Changing attitudes and greater awareness of what it means to be global are prerequisites for a fully realized *segyehwa* policy. Through these efforts, it is not difficult to see Korea taking its place among the world's most advanced countries in the coming Asia-Pacific Millennium.

Notes

Chapter 1

1. Leslie Helm, "The Koreans Are Coming: South Korea Bets Its Future on an Export Drive Aimed at the U.S.," *Business Week*, December 23, 1985, 46–52.
2. William Holstein and Laxmi Nakarmi, "Korea: Headed for High Tech's Top Tier," *Business Week*, July 31, 1995, 56–64.
3. Robert Warne, "Korea: A Model of Growth and Stability," *U.S. News and World Report*, August 19, 1995, 23.
4. Ibid.
5. Lee Hamilton, "The U.S. and South Korea: A Successful Partnership," *Korea Economic Update*, September 1995, 3.
6. *KUSEC Newsletter*, August 31, 1995, 9.
7. Warne, "Korea: A Model," 23.
8. Hamilton, "U.S. and South Korea," 3; Warne, "Korea: A Model," 23.
9. Ibid.
10. While *globalization* is not precisely defined, it generally means the deepening of all economic sectors across country borders. See Michael E. Porter, *The Competitive Advantage of Nations* (New York: Free Press, 1990); George Yip, *Total Global Strategy* (Englewood Cliffs, N.J.: Prentice Hall, 1995); and Kenichi Ohmae, *The Borderless World* (New York: HarperCollins, 1990).
11. *The 1994–95 Korea Company Handbook* (Seoul: Business Korea Co., 1995), III-11.
12. As the reader will discover, the so-called Miracle on the Han River that we have heard so much about was sparked by necessity, not desire.
13. *Korea Business: The Portable Encyclopedia for Doing Business with South Korea* (San Rafael, Calif.: World Trade Press, 1994), 22.

14. Ibid., 26.
15. See *Korea in the Twenty-first Century*, prepared by the Presidential Commission on the Twenty-first Century (Seoul: Seoul Press, 1995).
16. Quoted in *Korea Business*, 27.
17. *Korea Business*, 22–23. The examples that follow are taken from this source.
18. *Korea Business*, 24.
19. Former President Roh was accused of having taken 235.9 billion won ($310 million) in bribes from thirty businesses in return for awarding them lucrative government contracts including government infrastructure and military procurement programs. Former President Chun was held to answer for his alleged role in the Kwangju scandal.
20. Choi Shi-yong, "Kim Vows to Achieve Clean Politics," *Korea Herald*, November 18, 1995.
21. These figures are taken from numerous sources including *The 1993–94 Business Korea Yearbook on the Korean Economy and Business* (Seoul: Business Korea Co. 1994) and *Korea Business*.
22. *The 1993–94 Business Korea Yearbook*, 14–15.
23. *Korea Business*, 14.
24. *Asia 1995 Yearbook* (Hong Kong: Review Publishing Company, 1995), 155.
25. An editorial column in the *Korea Times*, May 10, 1996, in particular, noted that the KDI projections took into account neither the possibility of Korean unification, which would be very costly, or the way in which growth would be financed.
26. *Korea in the Twenty-first Century*, 90.
27. Speech given at the Asia Society, Seoul, Korea, May 11, 1996.
28. See *Asia 1995 Yearbook*, 155.
29. Han S. Park, *North Korea: Ideology, Politics, and Economy* (Englewood Cliffs, N.J.: Prentice Hall, 1996).
30. Alice Amsden, *Asia's Next Giant: South Korea and Late Industrialization* (New York: Oxford University Press, 1989).
31. *Korea Business*, 15.
32. Amsden, *Asia's Next Giant*. See also Yoo Seong-Min, "Korean Business Conglomerates: Misconceptions, Realities, and Policies," in *Korea's Economy 1995*, 12–20 (Washington, D.C.: Korea Economic Institute of America, 1995).
33. Yoo Seong-Min, "Korean Business Conglomerates," 12.
34. Michael E. Porter, "Korea," in *Competitive Advantage of Nations*, 272–293.
35. Ibid., 274.
36. Mark Clifford, *The Troubled Tiger: Businessmen, Bureaucrats, and Generals in South Korea* (New York: M. E. Sharpe Publishers, 1995).
37. *Collaborative Ventures: An Emerging Phenomenon in Information Technology* (New York: Coopers and Lybrand, 1986).
38. See two works by K. R. Harrigan: *Strategies for Joint Ventures* (Lexington, Mass.: Lexington Books, 1985), and "Strategic Alliances and Partner Asymmetries,"

in *Cooperative Strategies in International Business,* ed. F. J. Contractor and P. Lorange (Lexington, Mass.: Lexington Books, 1988).

39. S. H. Park and M. Russo, "When Cooperation Eclipses Competition: An Event History Analysis of Joint Venture Failures," *Management Science* 42, no. 6 (1996): 875–890.

Chapter 2

1. Holstein and Nakarmi, "Korea: Headed for High Tech's Top Tier," 56.
2. Louis Kraar, "Korea's Tigers Keep Roaring," *Fortune,* April 12, 1995, 62.
3. Sangjin Yoo and Sang Lee, "Management Style and Practice in Korean Chaebols," *California Management Review,* Summer 1987, 95–110.
4. Amsden, *Asia's Next Giant.*
5. Clifford, *The Troubled Tiger.*
6. Amsden, *Asia's Next Giant,* 262–265.
7. Ibid., 264.
8. Alfred D. Chandler, Jr., *Scale and Scope: The Dynamics of Industrial Capitalism* (Cambridge, Mass.: Belknap Press of the Harvard University Press, 1990).
9. Amsden, *Asia's Next Giant.*
10. Ibid.
11. *Business Korea,* December 1987, 47.
12. *Business Korea,* March 1988.
13. Laxmi Nakarmi, "Look Out, World—Samsung Is Coming," *Business Week,* July 10, 1995, 52–53.
14. Ibid.
15. *Business Korea,* October 1988.
16. "Korean Cars Regain Popularity in U.S.," *Korea Times,* November 12, 1994, 16.
17. Kwon Moon-Koo, personal communication, 1989. See also Michael Byungnam Lee and Yong-Hee Chee, "Business Strategy Participative Human Resource Management, and Organizational Performance: The Case of South Korea," *Asia-Pacific Journal of Human Resources* 34 (1996): 77–94.
18. Koo Cha-Hak, personal communication.
19. Laxmi Nakarmi, "Goldstar Is Burning Bright," *Business Week,* September 26, 1994, 129–130.
20. *Lucky-Goldstar: 1987,* 19.
21. David Dishneau, "Zenith Acquisition End of an Era," *Register-Guard,* July 18, 1995, B1–B2.
22. Roy Barun, "Daewoo's Kim Woo-Choong: The Sky Is the Limit in Perfection," *Asia Finance,* November 15, 1985, 63–65.
23. Clifford, *Troubled Tiger.*
24. Ronald Yates, "How Daewoo Became a Giant in Just 17 Years," *Chicago Tribune,* October 20, 1985, 25; Simon Caulkin, "Why Daewoo Works Harder," *Management Today,* July 1986, 62–67.

25. Kim Woo-Choong, "Daewoo's Story: The Revitalization of Entrepreneurship" (speech delivered at the Fifth Annual ACE-TEO International Conference, Washington, D.C., March 5, 1988), 8.
26. R. M. Steers, Y. K. Shin, and G. R. Ungson, *The Chaebol: Korea's New Industrial Might* (New York: Harper & Row, 1989), 66.
27. Ibid., 4.
28. Ibid., 4–5.
29. Louis Kraar, "Kim Woo-Choong: Korea's Export King," *Fortune*, January 5, 1987, 74.
30. Kim Woo-Choong, "Daewoo's Story," 5.
31. Kim Woo-Choong, *Every Street Is Paved with Gold* (New York: Morrow, 1992).
32. The family structure in Korea resembles that in China in that it is strictly patrilineal: inheritance flows through males only and is shared equally by all of the father's sons. Although it is possible to adopt a son into the family, primarily through his marriage to one's daughter, this is not the preferred way. In Korea, therefore, family members typically own a larger share of the company because fewer people are considered family members. Hence, we see a greater concentration of wealth or assets in fewer hands. In the Japanese household, by contrast, the roles of the father and the eldest son need not be played by blood relations. Korea has no equivalent of the Japanese *mukoyoshi*, or a nonbiologically related adopted son. See Francis Fukuyama, *Trust: The Social Virtues and the Creation of Prosperity* (New York: Free Press, 1995), 88–89 and 130.

Chapter 3

1. S. M. Lipset, "Some Social Requisites of Democracy: Economic Development and Political Legitimacy," *American Political Science Review* 53 (1959).
2. Yoo Seong Min, "Korean Business Conglomerates: Misconceptions, Realities, and Policies," in *Korea's Economy 1995*, 12–19 (Washington, D.C.: Korea Economic Institute of America, 1995).
3. Several books examine Korea's industrial policies in depth: Amsden, *Asia's Next Giant*; Shin Doh-Chull, Myeong-han Zoh, and Myung Chey, *Korea in the Global Wave of Democratization* (Seoul: Seoul National University Press, 1994); Park Tae-Kyu and Roy Wilkinson, *Industrial Policy in Korea and the EU* (Korea: Institute of East and West Studies, 1995); Cho Soon, *The Dynamics of Korean Economic Development* (Washington, D.C.: Institute for International Economics, 1994); Il Sakong, *Korea in the World Economy* (Washington, D.C.: Institute for International Economics, 1993); and Kim Eun Mee, *Big Business—Strong State: Collusion and Conflict in Korean Development, 1960–90* (Berkeley: University of California Press, forthcoming).

4. Lee Hong-kyu, "Industrial Success and Business Concentration" (speech to the University of Oregon MBA class, Eugene, Oregon, May 22, 1995, 4).

5. This section on Korea's reconstruction phase (1953–61) is summarized from *The 1993–94 Business Korea Yearbook,* I-1 to I-2.

6. Clifford, *Troubled Tiger,* 43.

7. Attributed to General Charles Helmick, who made the statement in February 1948. Cited in Clifford, *Troubled Tiger,* 29.

8. *The 1993–94 Business Korea Yearbook,* I-2.

9. Ibid.

10. Ibid., I-1.

11. The government package of reform between 1964 and 1967 included the devaluation of the won from 130 won to 225 won per U.S. dollar in 1964. A unitary floating exchange rate was adopted in March 1965. The government also doubled interest rates on bank deposits and loans in 1965 to increase voluntary savings. *The 1993–94 Business Korea Yearbook,* I-1 to I-2.

12. *The 1993–94 Business Korea Yearbook,* I-2 to I-3.

13. Yang Soo Rhee, B. Ross Larsen, and Garry Pursell, *Korea's Competitive Edge* (Baltimore: Johns Hopkins University Press, 1984).

14. Lee Hong-kyu, personal correspondence, December 4, 1995.

15. Clifford, *Troubled Tiger,* 115.

16. Ibid., 46.

17. Park Chung Hee, *Our Nation's Path* (Seoul: Dong-A Publishing, 1962), 204.

18. Clifford, *Troubled Tiger,* 46.

19. Rhee et al., *Korea's Competitive Edge.*

20. *The 1993–94 Business Korea Yearbook,* I-1 to I-2.

21. Lee Hong-kyu, "Industrial Success and Business Concentration," 11.

22. Clifford, *Troubled Tiger,* 132–133.

23. This entire section is summarized from two key sources: Lee Hong-kyu, "Industrial Success and Business Concentration," and *The 1993–94 Business Korea Yearbook,* I-1 to I-25.

24. *Korea Business,* 21.

25. "Trade Policy and Tariff System," in *The 1994–95 Korea Company Handbook,* III-1. Moreover, between 1987 and 1992, wages rose at an average annual rate of 18 percent and a total of 109 percent. Employers estimate this to be even higher because of benefits and work rules. Meanwhile, productivity rose by only about 50 percent. *Korea Business,* 9.

26. *The 1993–94 Business Korea Yearbook,* I-1 to I-2.

27. *Korea Business,* 9.

28. In 1992, the average weekly wage in South Korea was $254.44, plus mandated benefits of 19.9 percent, or $50.63. This was roughly 20 percent higher than the average weekly wage in Taiwan (U.S. $244) and 15 percent higher than in Singapore (U.S. $261). In contrast, the average weekly wage, including

benefits, was $705 in Japan and $7.37 in China. The figure for Korea leaves out additional compensation such as bonuses, allowances, and overtime, which routinely account for 40 percent of the total compensation package. This makes Korea even less competitive. *Korea Business,* 9.

29. *Korea Business,* 10.

30. Ibid., 7–13.

31. Paul Krugman, "The Myth of Asia's Miracle," *Foreign Affairs* 73, no. 6 (November–December 1994): 62–78.

32. See the critique by Chalmers Johnson, *MITI and the Japanese Miracle* (Stanford, Calif.: Stanford University Press, 1982).

33. See G. Ungson, A. Bird, and R. Steers, "Institutional Foundations of Japanese and Korean Industrial Policies" (working paper, Lundquist College of Business, University of Oregon, January 1996).

34. Paul Krugman, "Is Free Trade Passé?" *Economic Perspectives* 1, no. 2 (Fall 1987): 136.

35. Paul Krugman, *Strategic Trade Policy and the New International Economics* (Cambridge, Mass.: MIT Press, 1986).

36. We are grateful to an anonymous reviewer for pointing this out; it is also suggested in the *State and Markets Teaching Note,* Harvard Business School, 5-389-049, 1988, 8.

37. Michael Borrus, Ronald Millstein, and John Zysman, *The Effect of Government Targeting* (Berkeley, Calif.: SIA Publications, 1993).

38. Amsden, *Asia's Next Giant.*

39. A virtual organization resembles a temporary project team with a specific task. Intelligence is its prime asset. See Charles Handy, *The Age of Paradox* (Boston, Mass.: Harvard Business School Press, 1994), 35.

40. See Borrus, Millstein, and Zysman, *Effect of Government Targeting,* and see in particular John Zysman, *Governments, Markets, and Growth* (Ithaca, N.Y.: Cornell University Press, 1983), who directly relates industrial policy to capital structures. For a recent treatise that compares the United States and Japan in this aspect, see Michael E. Porter, "Capital Disadvantage: America's Failing Capital Investment System," *Harvard Business Review* 70, no. 1 (September–October 1992): 65–83.

41. Clifford, *Troubled Tiger.*

42. Ibid.

43. Amsden, *Asia's Next Giant.*

44. Chandler, *Scale and Scope.*

45. Amsden, *Asia's Next Giant.*

46. Ibid.

47. Ibid.

48. Ibid., 143–144.

49. Ibid., 173–174.

50. Shortly after the reorganization of the former Soviet Union and the opening of the Eastern Bloc, there emerged 634 trade bills in the United States, 99 of which are directly protectionist, and 77 being indirectly protectionist in that they would make quasi-judicial trade relief easier to obtain. Omnibus trade bills, such as S.1860 sponsored by Danforth, do not restrict tariffs directly but make it easier for firms to claim import relief, with measures to make it difficult for the White House to deny it to them.
51. The Uruguay Round, conceived in 1986, was an attempt to revitalize the General Agreement on Tariffs and Trade (GATT), which is the principal multilateral agreement covering world trade. The objective of GATT is to foster unrestricted multilateral trade by binding participating nations to negotiate trade rules and by penalizing deviations from these obligations. In the 1993 Uruguay Round agreements, it was agreed that the World Trade Organization would be formed.
52. Having a trade deficit with the United States, Korea was not as contentious as Japan, although it was considered to be among the nations listed as violating H-308 Law (identified nations with questionable trading practices) in 1991.
53. Lee Hong-kyu, "Industrial Success and Business Concentration."
54. Ibid., 14.
55. Ibid.
56. Ibid.
57. Ibid.
58. Ibid., 17.

Chapter 4

1. K. Matsumoto, "The Chaebol: Dynamic Management," *Journal of Japanese Trade and Industry* 2 (March–April 1986): 21.
2. Former President Park of Kumho Group, personal communication, November 1988.
3. Dr. Ungsun Park, personal communication, June 1989.
4. Matsumoto, "The Chaebol," 23.
5. Lee Byung-Chullm, "The Three Crises of Samsung: A Founder's Tale," *Executive Digest*, May 1987, 38–56.
6. Ibid.
7. Steve Glain, "For South Korean Firms, Speaking Too Freely May Carry Steep Price," *Wall Street Journal*, August 18, 1995, 1.
8. Joe Kidd, "Hyundai's Past Haunts Future Plans," *Register-Guard*, July 22, 1995, 1A, 15A.
9. Yoo and Lee, "Management Style and Practice of Korean Chaebols," 95–110.
10. *Business Korea*, December 1988, 30.
11. Steers, Shin, and Ungson, *The Chaebol*.

12. Amsden, *Asia's Next Giant.*
13. Yoo Seong-Min, "Korean Business Conglomerates."
14. Ibid.
15. Amsden, *Asia's Next Giant.*
16. Lee Hong-kyu, "Industrial Success and Business Concentration," 12.
17. Yoo Seong-Min, "Korean Business Conglomerates," 13.
18. *Korea Business,* 6.
19. K. U. Lee and J. H. Lee, *Business Groups and Small to Medium-sized Firms,* Korea Development Institute Report (Seoul, 1990), 15.
20. Steers, Shin, and Ungson, *The Chaebol.*
21. Yoo Seong-Min, "Korean Business Conglomerates."
22. Hong Lee, personal communication, 1996.
23. Michael L. Gerlach, *Alliance Capitalism: The Social Organization of Japanese Business* (Berkeley: University of California Press, 1992).
24. Amsden, *Asia's Next Giant.*
25. Yoo Seong-Min, "Korean Business Conglomerates," 15.
26. Ibid., 19.
27. Ibid.
28. As of May 1996, the Korean government directed the major *chaebols* not to divert corporate funds without providing convincing reasons. It also asked the thirty *chaebols* to reduce cross-payments to subsidiaries below 100 percent of their capital by 1998, stating that the *chaebols* might have to terminate cross-payment-guarantee amounts by 2001. Existing tax laws will also be tightened to prevent family-oriented *chaebols* from transferring wealth to sons and grandsons. The top ten business groups, including Hyundai and Samsung, will be denied free access to bank loans and payment guarantees.
29. Since May 1996, many economists have called the measures to slim down the *chaebols* a failure. New measures call for a ban on cross-debt repayment guarantees, which would lead to additional financing of up to 3 percent. President Kim has also called for a crackdown on intragroup transactions, a practice he claims has sustained inefficient subsidiaries while suffocating healthy firms outside the group. See Amson Park, "New Industrial Policy Faces Stiff Opposition from Firms," *Asian Times,* May 17–23, 1996, 9.
30. "South Korea Looks Outward," *Asian Business* 31, no. 6 (June 1995): 28–37.
31. Alfred Chandler critiques American diversified firms as follows: "More serious to the long term health of American companies and industries was the diversification movement of the 1960s—and the chain of events it helped to set off. When senior managers chose to grow through diversification—to acquire businesses in which they have a few if any organizational capabilities to give them a competitive edge—they ignored the logic of managerial enterprise. Under these circumstances, bigger was worse, not better" (*Scale and Scope,* 302).
32. Ungsuh Park, personal communication, May 1994.

33. See Lee Chang-sup, "Debate Looms Large over Korean Corporate Shape," *Korea Times*, May 12, 1996, 8.
34. Ibid.

Chapter 5

1. "It Is Not Easy Being Small," *Business Korea*, January 1993, 14.
2. Ibid.
3. This story was paraphrased from reports in "It Is Not Easy Being Small," and Sohn Jie-Ae and Lee Yoo-Lim, "Too Weak to Survive," *Business Korea*, February 1993, 24–30.
4. Jie-Ae and Yoo-Lim, "Too Weak to Survive."
5. Ibid.
6. Amsden, *Asia's Next Giant.*
7. N. K. Baik, H. B. Yang, D. H. Cho, and C. Cho, *Growth Patterns for Small and Medium-sized Firms for the Year 2000,* KIET Seminar Series (# 91-19) (Seoul, 1991).
8. The year 1973 is used as the comparison year because the range of small to medium-sized firms in employment was changed in 1974 from 5–199 to 5–299.
9. Further details are presented in chapters 8 and 9.
10. D. S. Cho, "Problems and Policies in Industry Restructuring for Small and Medium-sized Firms," in *Korea's Small and Medium-sized Firms* (Seoul: Industrial Bank of Korea, 1992), 277–298.
11. National Statistical Office, *Korea Statistical Yearbook 1994* (Seoul).
12. Ibid.
13. Korea Federation of Small Businesses, *1995 Major Statistics of Small and Medium Industries* (Seoul).
14. Amsden, *Asia's Next Giant,* 181.
15. Ibid.
16. C. T. Lim, "The Current Status of Foreign Direct Investment by Korea's Small to Medium-sized Firms," in *Korea's Small and Medium-sized Firms,* 5–72.
17. N. K. Baik, H. Joo, and C. Cho, *Causes and Responses for the Recent Problems in Small and Medium-sized Firms,* KIET Seminar Series (# 92-72) (Seoul, 1992).
18. The cutoff point for normal operation is an 80 percent capacity rate.
19. Jie-Ae and Yoo-Lim, "Too Weak to Survive," 25.
20. Korea Federation of Small Businesses, *1995 Major Statistics of Small and Medium Industries.*
21. Baik, Joo, and Cho, *Causes and Responses.*
22. Jie-Ae and Yoo-Lim, "Too Weak to Survive," 25.
23. *Business Korea,* April 1995, 12.
24. Baik, Joo, and Cho, *Causes and Responses.*
25. Cho, "Problems and Policies in Industry Restructuring," 277.
26. Baik, Joo, and Cho, *Causes and Responses.*

27. Jie-Ae and Yoo-Lim, "Too Weak to Survive," 26.

28. Amsden, *Asia's Next Giant*.

29. Jie-Ae and Yoo-Lim, "Too Weak to Survive," 26.

30. Other sources of the balance of loans for small and medium-sized firms are other financial institutions (11.9 percent), bonds payable (6.8 percent), and private curb loans (1.8 percent). Source: Citizens National Bank.

31. "It Is Not Easy Being Small," 14.

32. Ibid.

33. *Han-kuk Ilbo*, September 14, 1995.

34. Ibid.

35. Shortage rate = insufficient employees/total employees. From Baik, Yang, Cho, and Cho, *Growth Patterns for Small and Medium-sized Firms*.

36. K. W. Lee, "Current Status and Responses to Labor Shortage in Small and Medium-sized Firms," in *Korea's Small and Medium-sized Firms*, 123–164.

37. D. S. Cho, "Problems and Policies in Industry Restructuring."

38. Interview with Paul Chung, November 17, 1994, in Seoul.

39. D. S. Cho, "Problems and Policies in Industry Restructuring."

40. Interview, November 1994.

41. Paraphrased from the story by Jie-Ae and Yoo-Lim, "Too Weak to Survive."

42. Baik, Yang, Cho, and Cho, *Growth Patterns for Small and Medium-sized Firms*.

43. Ibid.

44. N. K. Baik, H. B. Yang, and D. H. Cho, *The Strategy and Policy for Structural Adjustment of Small and Medium-sized Firms*, KIET Seminar Series (# 92-22) (Seoul, 1992).

45. The ratio is 70 percent for local banks and 35 percent for foreign banks.

46. "Suffering Small and Medium-Sized Firms," *Hankuk Ilbo*, December 20, 1995, 2.

47. Baik, Yang, and Cho, *Strategy and Policy for Structural Adjustment of Small and Medium-sized Firms*.

Chapter 6

1. Park Cheol-Won, Senior Executive Director, Samsung Trading Company (case presentation at the Korea Business Association, Seoul, May 28, 1994).

2. Chung Mong-Hun, *My Perspective* (Seoul: Hyundai Electronics Industries, 1994).

3. *Daewoo Around the World* (Seoul: International PR Department, 1994).

4. *Lucky-Goldstar Annual Report 1994*.

5. See Porter, *Competitive Advantage of Nations*; Yip, *Total Global Strategy*; and Ohmae, *Borderless World*.

6. Park Cheol-Won, case presentation at the Korea Business Association.

7. "With Open Arms," *Business Korea*, December 1993.

8. Interview with Ungsuh Park, Samsung Petrochemicals, November 17, 1994.

9. Adapted from Park Cheol-Won, case presentation at the Korea Business Association.

10. "Samsung—A Management Revolution," *International Business Week*, February 28, 1994, 2.

11. "Bold Directives to Globalize," *Business Week*, February 1995, 35.

12. Interview, Ungsuh Park, President, Samsung Petrochemicals, May 22, 1995.

13. *Samsung's New Management*, Office of the Executive Staff of the Samsung Group (Seoul, May 1994).

14. Specific content was not provided.

15. This list was paraphrased from a translation of *Internationalization of the Samsung Trading Group* (1995).

16. Ibid.

17. *Single* means the person who is not yet married.

18. The term 21 C generally refers to managers targeted for the twenty-first century (see chapter 8).

19. This information is summarized from Chang Young-Chul, "Hyundai Group" (unpublished case, Department of Organizational Behavior, National University of Singapore, undated).

20. An account of Hyundai's late entry into electronics is discussed at length by Donald Kirk, *Korean Dynasty: Hyundai and Chung Ju Yung* (New York: M. E. Sharpe, 1994), 178–195.

21. Kirk, *Korean Dynasty*, 190.

22. Ibid., 187.

23. Ibid., 206.

24. Ibid., 206–207.

25. Interview with D. S. Shin (assistant manager), J. I. Hoh (executive managing director), and S. W. Hong (executive managing director) on November 19, 1994.

26. Kirk, *Korean Dynasty*, 210–216.

27. Joe Kidd, "Hyundai Comes to Town," *Register-Guard*, May 22, 1995.

28. The concerns were addressed in at least two public forums on Hyundai's plant announcement.

29. Hyundai was finally given approval after months of sometimes contentious debate. See Joe Kidd, "Hyundai Given a Green Light," *Register-Guard*, December 21, 1995.

30. Chung Mong-Hun, *My Perspective*.

31. Chang Young-Chul, "Management Philosophy and Strategic Orientations of a Korean Company: A Case of Daewoo Electronics" (unpublished case, Department of Organizational Behavior, National University of Singapore, undated).

32. Ibid.

33. Ibid.

34. Louis Kraar, "Korea Goes for Quality," *Fortune*, April 18, 1994.

35. Kraar, "Korea's Tigers Keep Roaring."

36. "Korea's Daewoo Places Bet on Selling to Third World," *Asian Wall Street Journal,* October 12, 1993.
37. Ibid.
38. "Daewoo Drives Off the Beaten Path," *Business Week,* June 28, 1993.
39. *Daewoo Group Facts* (1994).
40. *News from Daewoo,* September 1, 1994.
41. Ibid., October 1, 1994.
42. Ibid., November 1, 1994.
43. Interview with Chang Byung-Ju, Executive Managing Director, and Lee Jung-Seung, Assistant Manager, Daewoo Group, November 15, 1995.
44. Interview with Yong Nam, managing director, November 17, 1994.
45. Ibid.
46. Ibid.
47. "Goldstar Is Burning Bright," *Business Week,* September 26, 1994.
48. Ibid.
49. Ibid.
50. Ibid.
51. Ibid.
52. Ibid.
53. *The 1993–94 Business Korea Yearbook,* 503.
54. Interview with Park Je Hyuk (vice president), Lee Hong Hyung (executive counselor), Daechang Lee (research fellow), Kim Jun Ho (manager), November 14, 1994.
55. *The 1993–94 Business Korea Yearbook,* III-47–48.
56. Harry Lie, personal communication, May 1989.
57. Interview with Kim Duck-Hwan (president), Joon Jae Lee (manager), Duk Keun Cha (coordination team leader), Dong Joon-Youk (manager), November 16, 1994.
58. *The 1993–94 Business Korea Yearbook,* III-50–51.
59. Interview with Paul H. Chung, Executive Managing Director, November 17, 1994.
60. *The 1993–94 Business Korea Yearbook,* III-22–23.
61. Interview with Sung Tae Ro (president), Young Sang Lee (general manager), Kang Jin Lee (manager), November 16, 1994.
62. In April 1990, Samsung settled out of court with Advanced Micron Devices over patents on programmable logic devices. Also, in 1987, the International Trade Commission ruled that Samsung had violated Texas Instruments' DRAM practices.

Chapter 7

1. "South Korea Plans Major Push into High Technology Fields," *Los Angeles Times,* December 11, 1989.

2. Amsden, *Asia's Next Giant.*

3. Joint ventures involve ownership by both venture partners; strategic alliances involve any form of partnership between two firms with preconceived objectives.

4. S. T. Park, T. Y. Lee, Y. Y. Cho, and D. H. Kim, *Policy Guidelines to Reduce the Technology Gap between Korea and Japan in the Electronics Industry* (Seoul: KIET 1993).

5. Ed Parsley, "Drive for Recovery," *Far Eastern Economic Review,* May 26, 1993.

6. Linsu Kim, *Imitation to Innovation: The Dynamics of Korea's Technological Learning* (Boston: Harvard Business School Press, forthcoming).

7. Technological capabilities can be separated into three broad areas: production, investment, and innovation. The first capability is for operating productive facilities, the second is for expanding capacity and establishing new productive facilities, and the third is for developing technologies. Further details are available in L. E. Westphal, L. Kim, and C. J. Dahlman, "Reflections on the Republic of Korea's Acquisition of Technological Capability," in *International Technology Transfer: Concepts, Measures, and Companies,* ed. N. Rosenberg and C. Frischtak (New York: Praeger, 1985). The original source of the characterization is Y. Hayami and V. W. Ruttan, *Agricultural Development: An International Perspective* (Baltimore: Johns Hopkins University Press, 1971).

8. Benjamin Gomes-Casseres and Seung-Joo Lee, *Korea's Technology Strategy* (Boston: Harvard Business School Press, 1989).

9. Ibid.

10. Readers may want to refer to the following sources for information on Korea's technology acquisition during the 1960s and 1970s: Amsden, *Asia's Next Giant,* and Westphal, Kim, and Dahlman, "Korea's Acquisition of Technological Capability."

11. Gomes-Casseres and Lee, *Korea's Technology Strategy.*

12. Ibid.

13. Park, Lee, Cho, and Kim, *Policy Guidelines.*

14. Technology imports were slowed down in 1992 and 1993 owing to economy-wide recession.

15. Ministry of Science and Technology, *Science and Technology Improvement Policy* (Seoul, 1991).

16. "More Technologies Introduced from the U.S. than Japan," *Business Korea,* January 1995.

17. A selection model is presented in F. J. Contractor, "Technology Acquisition Choices for Newly Industrializing Countries," *International Executive,* September–October 1993.

18. The dependence rate on foreign technology = technology import/(research and development + technology import). See Park, Lee, Cho, and Kim, *Policy Guidelines.*

19. Gomes-Casseres and Lee, *Korea's Technology Strategy.*

20. N. Nohria and R. Eccles, *Networks and Organizations* (Boston: Harvard Business School Press, 1992).

21. In 1993, Samsung was granted the permission by the government to enter the commercial auto market.

22. C. E. Lee and M. K. Chung, "Hyundai Auto's International Network Strategy" (paper presented at the symposium on International Network Strategy to Enhance Korea's Global Competitiveness, sponsored by Korea, Chamber of Commerce and Korea Business Association, Seoul, Korea, November 4, 1994).

23. Ford did not allow Hyundai to use Ford's global marketing network or to export Hyundai's parts and cars to where Ford was already operating. Ford also tried to limit Hyundai's operations to the domestic market and allowed Hyundai only one technology, diesel engine, while Hyundai was expecting gasoline engine technology as well.

24. "Automakers' Sales Up, But Profits Lag Behind," *Business Korea*, April 24, 1995.

25. H. K. Lee and Y. J. Lee, *Strategic Alliances between Korean and American Corporations* (Seoul: KIET, 1994).

26. Parsley, "Drive for Recovery."

27. Ibid.

28. Ibid.

29. "How Europe Has Failed" (*Economist* 4, no. 3 [November 24, 1984]: 93–98) analyzes the erosion of Europe's positions in high technology, as evidenced by declining market shares and trade deficits.

30. See Thomas R. Howell, Brent L. Bartlett, and Warren Davis, *Creating Advantage: Semiconductors and Government Policy in the 1990s* (Cupertino, Calif.: SIA Dewey Ballantine, 1992), 353–355.

31. Ibid., 152.

32. "Samsung Electronics Forges Tie-up with Japan's NEC Corp," *Business Korea*, March 1994.

33. Lucky-Goldstar, *Lucky-Goldstar* (Seoul, 1994).

34. Kim Linsu, *Imitation to Innovation*.

35. Further details on the mode of technology acquisition are available in Contractor and Lorange, eds., *Cooperative Strategies in International Business*.

36. Wayne Sandholtz, Michael Borrus, John Zysman, Ken Conca, Jay Stowsky, Steven Vogel, and Steve Webber, *The Highest Stakes: Economic Foundations of the Next Security System* (Oxford: Oxford University Press, 1992).

37. Gomes-Casseres and Lee, *Korea's Technology Strategy*; Parsley, "Drive for Recovery."

38. Contractor, "Technology Acquisition Choices for Newly Industrializing Countries."

39. "Strategic Alliances," *Wall Street Journal*, April 20, 1995.

40. Korea Foreign Trade Association (KFTA), *Current Status and Utilization of Strategic Alliances* (Seoul, 1993).

41. Chun Sang Kyun, "Conglomerates Step Up R&D and Facility Investments," *Business Korea*, February 1994.
42. Ungsuh Park (speech given to the University of Oregon MBA Class, Eugene, Oregon, May 22, 1995).
43. Kraar, "Korea's Tigers Keep Roaring."
44. *1994 Hyundai* (Seoul: Hyundai Group, 1994).
45. *Daewoo Around the World.*
46. "Daewoo Group's Establishment of 650 Foreign Business Centers," *Han'gul Kyongje Sinmun* (Korea Economic Daily) November 15, 1994.
47. For recent activities, see Michael Schuman, "A Survival Strategy for Korean Firms," *Asian Wall Street Journal*, May 9, 1996.
48. "Daewoo Drives Off the Beaten Path," *Business Week*, June 28, 1993.
49. Steve Glain, "Korea's Daewoo Places Bet on Selling to Third World," *Asian Wall Street Journal*, October 12, 1993.
50. Ed Parsley and Terrence Clernan, "Reforms Boost Capital Flows," *Far Eastern Economic Review*, May 26, 1994.
51. Gomes-Casseres and Lee, *Korea's Technology Strategy.*
52. Park, Lee, Cho, and Kim, *Policy Guidelines*, 149–153.
53. Holstein and Nakarmi, "Korea: Headed for High Tech's Top Tier."
54. Parskey and Clernan, "Reforms Boost Capital Flows."
55. "Samsung Electronics Knows No Boundaries," *Business Korea*, February 1995.
56. Ibid.
57. Hyundai acquired the division for more than $300 million.
58. "Samsung Electronics Knows No Boundaries."
59. According to the new law, Korean corporations must register and get permission from the government to transfer any element of technologies (except foreign construction projects) for which they have ownership the value of which exceeds $30,000 (raised to $100,000 in 1990). Accordingly, our discussion focuses on technology exports after 1978.
60. Alice Amsden and Linsu Kim, *Korea's Technology Exports and Acquisition of Technological Capability* (Washington, D.C.: Productivity Division of the World Bank, 1982).
61. "China Prefers South Korean Technology," *Business Korea*, June 1994.
62. Ibid.
63. "Double-Density Video CD Jointly Produced by Goldstar, SKC," *Business Korea*, November 1994.
64. KFTA, *Current Status and Utilization of Strategic Alliances.*
65. Ibid.; Y. S. Hong, *Strategic Alliances and Globalization of Technology Innovation* (Seoul: KIET, 1994).
66. Orion Electric Co. is a subsidiary of the Daewoo Group.
67. KFTA, *Current Status and Utilization of Strategic Alliances.*
68. This know-how was exported to Smith Klein of Britain and a Japanese firm for $26 million.

69. For further details, see Park, Lee, Cho, and Kim, *Policy Guidelines.*

70. For an excellent case study of Hanki, see Yoon Suck Yoon, "Absorption, Assimilation, and Diffusion of Imported Technology," *Seoul Journal of Business* 1, no. 1 (1996): 143–154.

71. "South Korea Plans Major Push into High Technology Fields."

Chapter 8

1. Cho Dong-Sung, "A New Paradigm of International Competitiveness" (paper presented at the 13th Annual International Conference of Strategic Management Society, Chicago, September 15, 1993).

2. Joe Hawke, "Asia's Miracles Are No Miracles," *San Jose Mercury,* June 11, 1995.

3. Kyuhan Bae, *Automobile Workers in Korea* (Seoul: Seoul National University Press, 1987); Kyuhan Bae and William Form, "Payment Strategy in South Korea's Advanced Economic Sector," *American Sociological Review,* February 1986, 120–131.

4. Rebecca Wright, "Guide to Investing and Managing in South Korea" (working paper, College of Business, Virginia Polytechnic Institute and State University, Blacksburg, Va., 1988).

5. Kyong-Dong Kim, "Cultural Aspects of Higher Productivity," in *Toward Higher Productivity: Experiences of the Republic of Korea,* ed. D. K. Kim (Tokyo: Asian Productivity Association, 1985).

6. Sunkyong Chairman Chey Jong-Hyon, personal communication, 1988.

7. Kim Woo-Chung, cited in Boye deMente, *Korean Etiquette and Business Ethics* (Lincolnwood, Ill.: NTC Business Books, 1983), 35.

8. Song-Hyon Jang, *The Key to Successful Business in Korea* (Seoul: Yong Ahn, 1988).

9. Louis Kraar, "Daewoo's Daring Drive into Europe," *Fortune,* May 13, 1996, 148.

10. Victor Vroom and Philip Yetton, *Leadership and Decision-Making* (Pittsburgh: University of Pittsburgh Press, 1973).

11. Barry Wilkinson, *Labour and Industry in the Asia-Pacific: Lessons from the Newly-Industrializing Countries* (Berlin: deGruyter, 1994).

12. Kae Chung and Harry Lie, "Labor-Management Relations in Korea," in *Korean Managerial Dynamics,* ed. Kae Chung and H. C. Lee (New York: Praeger, 1989).

13. Ibid. See also Young-bum Park and Michael Byungnam Lee, "Economic Development, Globalization, and Practices in Industrial Relations and Human Resource Management in Korea," in *Employment Relations in the Growing Asian Economies,* ed. A. Verma, T. Kochan, and R. Landsburg (London: Routledge, 1995), 27–61.

14. Robert Kearney, *The Warrior Worker: The Challenge of the Korean Way of Working* (New York: Henry Holt, 1991).

15. Chung and Lie, "Labor-Management Relations in Korea."

16. J. J. Choi, "Interest Conflict and Political Control in South Korea: A Study

of Labor Unions in Manufacturing Industries: 1961–1980," Ph.D. diss., University of Chicago, 1983, 282.

17. Chung and Lie, "Labor-Management Relations in Korea."

18. Kyuhan Bae, *Automobile Workers in Korea* (Seoul: Seoul National University Press, 1987).

19. Mark Clifford, "Inoffensive Spring," *Far Eastern Economic Review*, May 23, 1991, 28–31.

20. Kim Chi-sun, "Korea's Labor Legislation: Past and Present," *Korea Focus* 3, no. 3 (May–June 1995): 78–84. See also Michael Byungnam Lee, "Korea," in *Industrial Relations Around the World*, ed. M. Rothman, D. Briscoe, and R. Nacamulli (Berlin: deGruyter, 1993), 245–269.

21. Chung and Lie, "Labor-Management Relations in Korea."

22. Steers, Shin, and Ungson, *The Chaebol.*

23. Ibid.

24. Clifford, "Inoffensive Spring."

25. Ibid. See also Michael Byungnam Lee and Yinsog Rhee, "Bonuses, Unions, and Labor Productivity in South Korea," *Journal of Labor Research* 17 (1996): 219–238.

26. Barry Wilkinson, *Labor and Industry in the Asia-Pacific: Lessons from the Newly Industrialized Countries* (Berlin: deGruyter, 1994). See also Park and Lee, "Economic Development, Globalization, and Practices."

27. *Change Begins with Me: Samsung's New Management* (Seoul: Samsung Group, 1994), 39.

28. "Improved Efficiency and Enhanced Corporate Image," *Business Korea*, November 1994, 24–25.

29. Kraar, "Korea Goes for Quality," 45–47.

30. Ibid.

31. *Change Begins with Me*, 77.

32. Kraar, "Korea's Tigers Keep Roaring," 52–56.

33. Hanwha Group, *Hanwha: 1994.*

34. Kim Seung Youn, "Chairman's Address on the 42d Anniversary of Hanwha Group" (Hanwha Group, October 10, 1994, 2).

35. Sunkyong Group, *Supex Pursuit* (1994), 7.

36. Kraar, "Korea Goes for Quality," 47.

37. Ibid.

38. Ibid.

39. *The 1993–94 Business Korea Yearbook*, IV-39–40.

40. Interview with Jae Chul Kim (chairman), Soon-Ku Kim (executive director), Kook Jin Lee (team leader), and Dong Bin Oh (president), November 18, 1994.

41. Ibid.

42. *The 1993–94 Business Korea Yearbook*, IV-41–42.

43. Ibid.

Chapter 9

1. Harry Oshima, "Human Resources in East Asia's Secular Growth," *Economic Development and Cultural Change* 38 (suppl.; 1988): S103–122; Kearney, *The Warrior Worker*.
2. C. S. Chang, "Human Resource Management in Korea," in *Korean Managerial Dynamics*.
3. Ibid., S111.
4. Clifford, *Troubled Tiger*.
5. Ibid.
6. Sam Jameson, "Soldiers to Help Ease Labor Pinch in South Korea," *Los Angeles Times*, July 8, 1991, D1.
7. Shim Jae-yun, "Foreign Workers to Get Free Legal Aid," *Korea Times*, November 13, 1994, 3. See also *Hankuk Ilbo*, September 16, 1995.
8. John Lie, "Is Korean Management Just Like Japanese Management?" *Management International Review* 30, no. 2 (1990): 113–118.
9. Lester Thurow, *Head-to-Head: The Coming Economic Battle among Japan, Europe, and America* (London: Nicholas Brealey, 1993).
10. Nam-hong Cho, "Human Resource Management in Korean Enterprises" (paper presented at the 10th International Industrial Relations Association World Congress, Washington, D.C., 1995).
11. This section is based on earlier research reported in Marianne Koch, Sanghoon Nam, and Richard M. Steers, "Human Resource Management in South Korea," in *Human Resource Management on the Pacific Rim*, ed. Larry Moore and Devereaux Jennings (Berlin: deGruyter, 1995), 217–242. See also Park and Lee, "Economic Development, Globalization, and Practices."
12. Lee Tae-gyu, "Revolution in Recruiting New Employees" *Korea Focus* 3, no. 1 (January–February 1995): 81–85.
13. Lee Yoo-Lim, "More Companies Rely on Employee Interviews," *Business Korea*, November 1994, 22–23.
14. Steers, Shin, and Ungson, *The Chaebol*.
15. Chan Sup Chang and Nahn Joo Chang, *The Korean Management System* (Westport, Conn.: Quorum Books, 1994), 162–164.
16. Office of the Chairman for Planning and Management, Sunkyong Group, "Outline of Human Resource Management System," 1987.
17. deMente, *Korean Etiquette and Business Ethics*.
18. Choong Soon Kim, *The Culture of Korean Industry: An Ethnography of the Poongsan Corporation* (Tucson: University of Arizona Press, 1992), 93.
19. "Education and Training Department," Daewoo Corporation, 1991.
20. "Samsung Revamps Personnel Management," *Korea Times*, October 18, 1995, 4.
21. "Wage Hikes Are Causing Problems in South Korea," *Korea Times*, July 5, 1995, 5.

22. Korean Ministry of Labor, National Statistics Office, 1995.

23. "Daewoo Warns on Labor Costs," *International Herald Tribune*, November 16, 1994, 19.

24. Steers, Shin, and Ungson, *The Chaebol*; Chung and Lee, *Korean Managerial Dynamics*, ch. 7; Michael Byungnam Lee, Vida Scarpello, and B. Wayne Rochmore, "Strategic Compensation in South Korea's Publicly Traded Firms," *International Journal of Human Resource Management* 6 (1995): 686–701.

25. S. K. Kim, "Labor and Employment," in *Doing Business in Korea*, ed. A. Whitehill (London: Croom, Helm, 1987), 39–56.

26. Cho Hyoung and Chang Pil-wha, *Gender Division of Labor in Korea* (Seoul: Korean Women's Institute, Ewha Women's University Press, 1994).

27. "Planting the Seed of Feminism," *Business Korea*, January 1990, 19.

28. Lee Yoo-Lim, "More Companies Rely on Employee Interviews," 22–23.

29. Chang and Chang, *The Korean Management System*; Park and Lee, "Economic Development, Globalization, and Practices."

30. Choong Soon Kim, *The Culture of Korean Industry.*

31. Nam-hong Cho, "Human Resource Management in Korean Enterprises."

32. Koch, Nam, and Steers, "Human Resource Management in South Korea."

33. L. F. Moore and S. Robinson, "Human Resource Management Present and Past: Highlights from a Western Canadian Survey of Practitioner Perceptions," in *Proceedings of the Administrative Sciences Association of Canada*, ed. A. Petit and A. V. Subbarou (Montreal: Personnel and Human Resources Division, McGill University, 1989), 23–34.

34. Sanghoon Nam, "Culture, Control, and Commitment in International Joint Ventures," *International Journal of Human Resource Management* 6 (1995): 553–567.

35. Kearney, *The Warrior Worker.*

36. Chung and Lee, *Korean Managerial Dynamics*, ch. 8; Park and Lee, "Economic Development, Globalization, and Practices."

Chapter 10

1. "Toward the Globalization of the Republic of Korea and Asia" (address by President Kim Young Sam at the 7th Annual Corporate Conference of the Asia Society, May 9, 1996).

2. John Naisbitt, *Megatrends Asia* (New York: Simon & Schuster, 1996).

3. Krugman, "The Myth of Asia's Miracle," 62–78.

4. Ibid., 71.

5. Ibid., 68.

6. Ibid., 77.

7. Urban C. Lerner, "Is the Vaunted 'Asian Miracle' Really Just an Illusion?" *Wall Street Journal*, October 20, 1995. Not surprisingly, Krugman's thesis has been hotly debated in Asia. Critics assert that growth accounting is an inadequate tool for assessing Asia's prospects; other criticisms center on measurement

issues. Our own view of this debate, presented in this chapter, focuses on the trajectory of technological development.

8. Vincent Brandt, "Korea," in *Ideology and National Competitiveness: An Analysis of Nine Countries,* ed. George C. Lodge and Ezra F. Vogel, 207–239 (Boston, Mass.: Harvard Business School, 1987).

9. Ibid., 208.

10. Harvard Professor Tu Wei-ming, world authority on Confucianism, notes that "Confucianism is not simply the advocacy of obedience to government, but also the accountability of government." Cited in Naisbitt, *Megatrends Asia,* 61.

11. Korea's Fair Trade Commission announced that measures have been adopted to phase out debt-payment guarantees among group subsidiaries over the next five years. See Park, "New Industrial Policy Faces Stiff Opposition from Firms," 9.

12. Min Chen, *Asian Management Systems: Chinese, Japanese and Korean Styles of Business* (New York: Routledge, 1995): 213–227.

13. See Chalmers Johnson, ed., *The Industrial Policy Debate* (San Francisco: Institute for Contemporary Studies, 1984).

14. George C. Lodge, "Ideology and Country Analysis," in *Ideology and National Competitiveness,* 6–7.

15. Amsden, *Asia's Next Giant.*

16. Alice Amsden (lecture to University of Oregon and Portland State University MBA Classes, Portland, Oregon, June 3, 1995).

17. See *Korea Business,* 26.

18. Ibid.

19. See Hak K. Pyo, "The Transition in the Political Economy of South Korean Development: Issues and Perspectives," in *The Southeast Asian Economic Miracle,* 1–14, ed. Young C. Kim (New Brunswick, N.J.: Transaction Publishers, 1995).

20. Schuman, "A Survival Strategy."

21. *San Jose Mercury News,* May 25, 1995.

22. James C. Abegglen, *Sea Change: Pacific Asia as the New World Industrial Center* (New York: Free Press, 1994), 2–4.

23. This expansion is not limited to Southeast Asia but applies to the entire world. See Schuman, "A Survival Strategy."

24. Francis Fukuyama, *Trust: The Social Virtues and the Creation of Prosperity* (New York: Free Press, 1995).

25. From Kenichi Ohmae, *The End of the Nation State* (New York: Free Press, 1995), 82–83.

26. Ibid.

27. Abegglen, *Sea Change,* 86.

28. Ibid., 66.

29. Ibid., 82.

30. Ibid., 131.

31. Rhee Song Ni (speech to the University of Oregon MBA Class, May 15, 1995).
32. Fukuyama, *Trust.*
33. Ibid., 88–89, 130.
34. Dieter Ernst, *What Are the Limits to the Korean Model? The Korean Electronics under Pressure* (Berkeley: University of California Press, 1994).
35. Ibid., 5.
36. Ibid., 7–8.
37. Il SaKong, "The East Asian Economies," *Business Korea* 12, no. 10 (September 1995): 31–32.
38. A good discussion of chaos theory is found in W. Brian Arthur, "Positive Feedback in the Economy," *Scientific American*, February 1990, 92–144.
39. J. A. Schumpeter, *Capitalism, Socialism, and Democracy* (New York: Harper & Row, 1942).
40. Ungsuh Park, personal communication, May 1994.
41. A good discussion of increasing returns to scale is found in Arthur, "Positive Feedback in the Economy," 92–144.
42. Ungsuh Park, personal communication, May 1994.
43. Contractor, "Technology Acquisition Choices for Newly Industrializing Countries."
44. Since 1992 many American and Japanese corporations have participated in technological alliances with Korean corporations in the computer industry, including Motorola, Hewlett Packard, Toshiba, GI, Array, and HMS. The CATV industry has also benefited from technological alliances, such as between Samsung and Matsushita, Goldstar and Texaco, and Daewoo and Sony. For further details, see Y. S. Hong, *Strategic Alliances and Globalization of Technology Innovation;* KFTA, *Current Status and Utilization of Strategic Alliances.*
45. U.S. Ambassador James Laney (speech to the Asia Society in Seoul, Korea, May 12, 1996).
46. Ibid.
47. Jo Yung-Hwan, "After Unification: Korea's Place in World Affairs" (speech given at the Sixth International Conference on Asia-Pacific Affairs, Korea, and the Future of Northeast Asia, Portland, Oregon, May 4–5, 1995).
48. Laney (speech to the Asia Society).
49. Jo Yung-Hwan, "After Unification."
50. *Korea in the Twenty-first Century*, 72.
51. Ibid., 172–173.
52. Ohmae, *End of a Nation State.*
53. Speech given at the 7th Annual Corporate Conference of the Asia Society, May 9, 1996.

Index

About the Authors

Gerardo R. Ungson is the Victor P. Morris Professor of Management in the Charles H. Lundquist College of Business at the University of Oregon, where he specializes in the areas of global strategy, strategic alliances, and organization theory. He has been a visiting professor at the Amos Tuck School of Business, Dartmouth College; the University of California, Berkeley; Nijenrode University, The Netherlands; and the International University of Japan. He has served on the editorial board of *Academy of Management Review* and *Journal of High Technology Management Research*. Among Professor Ungson's publications are three books, including *The Chaebol: Korea's New Industrial Might* (with Richard M. Steers and Yoo Keun Shin), and articles in *Administrative Science Quarterly, Academy of Management Journal, Academy of Management Review*, and the *Journal of Management*.

    Richard M. Steers is the Kazumitsu Shiomi Professor of Management in the Charles H. Lundquist College of Business at the University of Oregon, where he teaches courses in organizational behavior and global management. He also serves as the university's vice provost for international affairs. He has been a visiting professor at the University of California, Irvine, Nijenrode University, The Netherlands; University of Cape Town, South Africa; and Oxford University, United Kingdom. Professor Steers is a past president of the Academy of Management and a fellow of the Academy of Management, the Society of Industrial and Organizational Psychology, and the American Psychological Society. The author of nineteen books on management, he has served on the editorial boards of *Administrative Science Quarterly, Academy of Management Journal, Academy of Management Review, Journal of International Management, Journal of Management Inquiry,*

Journal of Business Research, Asia-Pacific Journal of Human Resources, and *Asia-Pacific Journal of Management.*

Seung-Ho Park is an assistant professor of management in the School of Management at the University of Texas at Dallas, where he teaches courses on business strategy and international management. He previously taught in the Graduate School of Management at Rutgers University. His research interests include global strategy, the management of strategic alliances, and the competitiveness of Asian multinational firms. Professor Park currently serves on the editorial board of the *Academy of Management Journal.* His publications include articles in *Management Science, Academy of Management Journal,* and *Strategic Management Journal.*